FOOD STUDIES

FOOD STUDIES

An Introduction
to Research Methods

Jeff Miller and Jonathan Deutsch

BLOOMSBURY

LONDON • NEW DELHI • NEW YORK • SYDNEY

Bloomsbury Academic

An imprint of Bloomsbury Publishing Plc

50 Bedford Square
London
WC1B 3DP
UK

1385 Broadway
New York
NY 10018
USA

www.bloomsbury.com

Bloomsbury is a registered trade mark of Bloomsbury Publishing Plc

First published in 2009 by Berg
Reprinted by Bloomsbury Academic 2013, 2014

© Jeff Miller and Jonathan Deutsch 2009

British Library Cataloguing-in-Publication Data
A catalogue record for this book is available from the British Library.

ISBN: HB: 978-1-8452-0680-2
PB: 978-1-8452-0681-9

Library of Congress Cataloging-in-Publication Data
A catalog record for this book is available from the Library of Congress.

Typeset by Apex CoVantage, LLC, Madison, WI, USA
Printed and bound in Great Britain

For my wife, who is my cheerleader, my partner, my best friend.
For my parents, who are my inspirations for service and teaching.
For my students, who keep me wanting to go to work everyday.
—JEFF MILLER

For my students.
—JON DEUTSCH

CONTENTS

PART ONE

PART ONE

1 FOOD STUDIES

WHAT IS FOOD STUDIES?

Before we discuss what food studies is, let us consider what it is not. Food studies is not really the study of food. There are many fields that study food itself—its production (agricultural sciences, meat and poultry science, aquaculture); its chemical, physical, and biological properties (food science, biochemistry); its physiology when consumed (nutrition); and its preparation (culinary arts). And while offshoots of these fields—such as cultural and community nutrition, agro-economics, and food marketing—come into play in food studies, they are their own distinct fields of study.

Food studies, then, is not the study of food itself but rather the study of the relationships between food and the human experience. These relationships are examined from a variety of perspectives and from a range of places in the food system, from production to consumption, or from farm to fork.

The term *food studies* tends to mean two different things in the field:

1. A collective of people studying food and people from a variety of humanities and social science perspectives. The Association for the Study of Food and Society, for example, is a food studies organization comprised of food historians, food anthropologists, sociologists of food, nutritionists, interdisciplinary food scholars, and others who gather to discuss their work. Similarly, the journal *Gastronomica*, which publishes an eclectic range of scholarly and literary writing as well as art that explores food and people, would be considered a food studies journal. In this way, food studies is *multidisciplinary.*

2. The *interdisciplinary* field of study of food and culture investigates people's relationships with food from a range of humanities and social science perspectives, often times in combination. For example, Krishnendu Ray's (2008) work on ethnic restaurants, which incorporates theory and methods from sociology, business, and history, is practicing interdisciplinary food studies. Often food studies scholars have training in one particular discipline but incorporate theories and methods from other disciplines to take an interdisciplinary approach. Other scholars may be trained in the field of food studies but not in any predominant discipline.

FOOD STUDIES IS AS DIVERSE AS FOOD ITSELF

Defining *food studies* as the study of people's relationships with food, food studies research runs a broad gamut of topics, home disciplines, theoretical orientations, and research methodologies. As such, it is at once vibrantly rich and challenging to clearly demarcate. Here, for example, are four abstracts of food studies research articles from some leading food studies journals showing diverse topical, theoretical, and methodological approaches to food studies:

> In this article I present and explore the school cafeteria childhood memories of four Mexicano (Mexican-origin) adults as illustrations of the importance of the school cafeteria as a complex public eating space for ethnic minority students. For students from non-dominant groups, the school lunchroom is more than just a place to eat lunch, it is a place where assimilative food pressures and peer relationships collide, forcing children to negotiate a home-school cultural divide through food and eating choices. The stories and memories of the adults considered here reflect the various ways they as Mexicano children balanced the social and class dynamics of the school lunch program and the potentially disparate food norms and dietary lessons of the school institution, those of their school peers, and those they knew from their own homes and communities. In addition, their stories had nutritional implications as well—specifically how school food served as a daily "American food" contact point for them as children, and how the school lunch catalyzed changes in their childhood food habits and those of their families. Personal accounts like those presented here display the significance and complexity of the American school cafeteria as a problematic "public" eating space for Mexicano children and a need for nutritionists, educators, and food service professionals to consider this setting in discussions of multicultural schooling and dietary acculturation. (Salazar, 2007, p. 153)

The one document in the history of American cuisine that is probably cited more frequently than any other is the so-called "1834 Delmonico menu" that situates an early Delmonico restaurant at 494 Pearl Street in Manhattan. Allegedly printed in 1834, this bill of fare is often touted as the first restaurant menu printed in America. It has been mentioned in a variety of other contexts, too: in histories of Delmonico's restaurant and of that quintessential "American" food, the hamburger, in discussions about the semantics of menu language, and as an illustration of early menu design. The prices it quotes have been used to illustrate historical food costs and inflation, and it has even been co-opted to tout restaurants aspiring to the standards set long ago by the famed restaurateur Lorenzo Delmonico.

Our investigation suggests the so-called "1834 Delmonico menu" was never issued by the celebrated Delmonico family. Rather, it was a handbill for a "cheap dining hall" called "Small Delmonico's," at 494 Pearl Street, in New York City, owned and operated during the late 1880's by an Italian immigrant named Barnabo. (Steinberg and Prost, 2008, p. 40)

The article forms part of broader research that interrogates the prevalence of food in the media and the paradigm shifts generated and perpetuated by new forms of media such as food television and the internet. This work departs from previous food research by concentrating not on what is communicated about food, but how it is communicated. The analysis is guided in part by Guy Debord's *The Society of the Spectacle* (1967), which offers a Marxist economic analysis of an increasingly image-dominated culture. With a primary focus on celebrity chefs, this paper argues two points. First, that celebrity chefs, like Hollywood stars, are overwhelmingly media products, implying an arbitrary relationship between food and celebrity. Second, that the real product of food media is not the celebrity chef, but the consumer. Food media creates a base of consumers whose appetites are literally and figuratively kept wanting; this is the new business of food. (Hansen, 2008, p. 49)

The role of group and individual variables in the purchasing of ethnical food products was tested through an extended theory of planned behavior (TPB) model. A total of 100 Indian female immigrants, living in Rome, Italy, were administered a self-reported questionnaire measuring the classical TPB variables (attitudes, subjective norms, perceived behavioral control, behavioral intentions and self-reported behaviors) plus 3 additional variables: identification with the Indian ethnic group, perceived norms of the Indian ethnic group, and past behavior. Results confirmed that the new variables introduced are distinct from the original TPB components. As expected, variables at both the individual and group level play a role in predicting purchasing of ethnical foods products. Hierarchical multiple regressions showed that past behavior, ethnical identification, and perceived group norms explain an additional proportion of variance in intentions and self-reported behaviors, independently of attitudes, subjective norms and perceived control. A significant 2-way interaction between ethnical identification and perceived group norms was also detected: as predicted, the highest levels of ethnical food purchasing behavior were reported by high ethnical identifiers with stronger ethnical group norms, while the lowest levels were reported by low ethnical identifiers with weaker ethnical group norms. Theoretical and practical implications of results are discussed. (Carrus, Nenci, and Caddeo, 2009, p. 65)

The abstracts listed each represent the major broad methodological baskets of food studies discussed in this volume—studying people through observation and interview (ethnographic methods); studying the past through documents, artifacts, and oral histories (history and narrative); studying culture, communication, and cultural artifacts like art and literature (cultural/media studies); and studying people through experiments, quasi-experiments, or surveys (quantitative methods). Salazar's paper, from the journal *Food and Foodways,* uses an interview method. This method is common among anthropologists and sociologists and is used extensively in food studies. Steinberg and Prost do food history using documents in their paper published in *Gastronomica.* Hansen, in her *Food, Culture and Society* piece, applies a theoretical framework to analyze popular culture and mass media. And Carrus et al. surveyed the eating habits of a group of people in their *Appetite* article. We consider all four to be food studies—they examine the relationships between food and the human experience, but in very different ways, using very different approaches, among different people, from different cultures, in different countries. They consider food consumers (Indian immigrants living in Rome), food acculturation (adults' food memories of childhood), food businesses (Delmonico's restaurant), and food entertainers (celebrity chefs/television hosts). The authors themselves, as well as their methods and theories, come from a wide range of disciplines and fields of study including anthropology, sociology, social psychology, cultural studies, media studies, history, business, and literature. Such diversity makes food studies compelling and opportunities numerous—there is a research project in what we ate for lunch today, another in what they are eating at the international space station, and still more in what our ancestors farmed, preserved, cooked, and ate.

WHY FOOD STUDIES?

The need for food is our primary biological drive. Without it, without enough of it, or with the wrong food, we die. Food's importance to our bodies makes it important elsewhere. The world's largest industry, the food business is estimated to be a $3–4 trillion endeavor, representing 10 percent of global Gross Domestic Product and employing tens of millions of workers. Beyond its material importance, food has tremendous cultural and symbolic import from the Christian Eucharist, to pork taboo in Islam, to the widely recognized symbol of the American hamburger throughout the world. Food habits—how we produce, procure, prepare, and consume food—represent powerful systems of symbols whose associations are closely held, in their own way, by nearly everyone. Looking at people's relationships with food can speak volumes about the people—their beliefs, their passions, their background knowledge and assumptions, and their personalities—all elements whose explorations can be strengthened by good research.

Given its importance, one would think that food studies would have a prominent place in the academy, in mass media, and even in primary and secondary education. However, while it's beginning to gain that prominence with more books on food subjects, television shows, educational initiatives, and conference panels, food studies is relatively new to the table. University food studies programs are few, and until the last couple of decades, even food studies classes as part of a larger program were relatively rare. Belasco (2005, 6–8) details many factors that might contribute to food studies' under-representation in the academy, among them: the dualistic tradition in Western philosophy that prizes the mind over the body, the association of food with the domain of women by men, and the efforts of industry to "obscure and mystify the links between the farm and the dinner table" (Belasco, 2008, p. 4). To this list we add another: food is fun (Rozin, 1999). Research can be tedious, isolating, and frustrating, even if you're interested in the topic. Our colleagues who study challenging and emotionally trying topics such as prison reform, literacy, or climate change may have a certain fascination for those of us who spend our days cooking, eating, thinking, and writing about a topic as fun as food—and a certain amount of corresponding resentment.

There is now a large and rapidly expanding body of literature intentionally or accidentally considered food studies, which is written from a diverse array of disciplinary and interdisciplinary perspectives. These works span the spectrum of philosophies and methodologies in the humanities and social sciences. They include histories from biological, cultural, geographic, and world systems perspectives. Other works look at contemporary food issues using philosophical, geographical, nutritional, political, economic, literary, or folkloristic methods. What all of these works have in common, despite their diverse range of approaches, is food at the forefront of their well-researched anthropology, history, sociology, geography, philosophy, or literary criticism, rather than as a tangential aspect to a larger issue, as is often done in all of these fields.

FOOD AS METHODOLOGICAL TOOL

Food is not only an important topic worthy of study but can itself be used as a means to gain insight to two other issues. Hauck-Lawson (2004) in her work on the *food voice* has shown that food choices—what one eats or, as importantly, chooses not to eat—can communicate aspects of a person's identity or emotion in a way that words alone often cannot. Following Carole Counihan's work on food-centered life histories (see interview) and Hauck-Lawson's work, Abarca (2007) developed a research technique centered around food, *charlas culinarias* (culinary chats) where kitchen-based conversations with women about food and cooking open up evocative conversations about life that might have been difficult to elicit in a traditional (non-food-focused) interview. Deutsch (2004) used a similar technique in talking with normally taciturn men about food and masculinity. By doing much of the interviewing during routine cooking, a conversational rhythm was established where the men's thoughts were volunteered rather than drawn out.

Food can tell the stories of migration, assimilation or resistance, changes over time, and personal and group identity. In short, many facets of the human experience can be accessed through what is eaten, avoided, no longer or more often eaten, and, of course, what is produced and prepared and how it is done.

Perhaps most obviously, food choices—what a person or group decides to produce, prepare, and consume—can represent a conscious affirmation and expression of personal, group, ethnic, or national identity. Beyond who we are, food is often politicized in the form of food protests, philosophies of eating, and socially conscious food choices to additionally express how we feel and what we want. And food can work in tandem with the spoken and written voices in order to enact a holistic representation of identity, politics, and human experience (Hauck-Lawson and Deutsch, 2008, pp. xiv–xv).

FOOD STUDIES RESEARCH METHODS

A central question we faced in writing this book is are there distinctive food studies research methods, and, if so, what are they? Is this a book that describes research methods with food examples, or is this a book that explores how food can enhance research methods, or is this a book that details methods particularly useful in food studies? The answer is a resounding yes to all. Some examples may clarify:

- **Research methods with food studies examples.** As an interdisciplinary field, food studies employs a variety of methods from diverse disciplines. In many cases, a particular method applied to food is little different than the same method applied to another topic. The fundamental principles of experimental design, for example, are the same whether the experiment is designed to test tensile strength of car doors or human responses to "hot" foods as measured in Scoville units. Our aim here is to present a variety of methods that may be helpful in food studies.
- **Using food to enhance methods.** As mentioned above, there are instances where methods are not only usefully applied to food studies, but where studying food in

particular can enhance traditional methods. In the Abarca (2007) example above, interview is a method widely used across topics, but the *charlas culinarias* (culinary chat) is an enhancement of the more traditional interview. One would be challenged to do a *charla culinaria* on the topic of military strategy or fashion design, though one could certainly do interview.

■ **Methods unique to food studies.** Food studies employs some methods that are particularly useful for food scholars. For example, data collection methods like dietary recall, which come from nutrition sciences, are helpful in learning what people eat. Food science methods such as designs for sensory testing may be useful in studying taste preferences. We highlight these methods within the broader method types.

In this book we invite you to *do* food studies. We begin with some common features of any methods book, though with a food studies spin—an overview of the research process, the importance of ethics and institutional approvals, and the literature review. Later we deal with large baskets of research method types commonly found in food studies: historical methods, ethnography and narrative, quantitative methods, and using physical objects. We have chosen these methods not because they represent the entirety of the field but because together they represent the sort of work currently being done, as presented at food studies conferences and in peer-reviewed journals in the field. We try to balance the "how to" part of research methods with examples from food studies and interactive exercises to help you along in your own research. Chapter 3 deals with ethical issues in food studies, including the use of human subjects, and Chapter 9 introduces a variety of technology tools that may be helpful in your research. Coupled with a good theoretical basis in food studies (in addition to this text, we recommend Warren Belasco's *Food: The Key Concepts*), a reader who follows us through this book will be able to begin doing research in the field of food studies.

This book is written with two main types of readers in mind:

■ Students in introductory food studies courses learning to do research.
■ Students or scholars with research training in other fields who are entering food studies.

The usual caveats apply—food studies is as diverse as the academy in general. We try to maintain a broad generalist approach for the novice food researcher. A student specializing in a specific field such as archaeology, community nutrition, or classics would of course be served by using methods books from those fields as well. Indeed, volumes have been devoted to detailing each of the methods—interview, survey, experiment, participant observation—mentioned in this slim book.

Interdisciplinary and Multidisciplinary Food Studies

The Association for the Study of Food and Society (ASFS), an academic association of food studies scholars includes membership from a wide range of disciplines. Issues of interest to ASFS scholars include:

Food Policy	Eating Behaviors
Food Habits	Marketplace Ethics
Food Programs	Applied Nutrition
Dietary Change	Food Production
Malnutrition/Hunger	Nutritional Epidemiology
Nutrition Education	Food Distribution
Agricultural Issues	

The organization has grown to serve as an interdisciplinary forum for those interested in food and society. Members of ASFS represent a diversity of disciplines, including:

Agriculture	Economics
Folklore	Performance Studies
American Studies	Epidemiology
Food Management	Political Science
Anthropology	Ethics
Food Science	Psychology
Behavioral Sciences	Family Sciences
Geography	Public Health
Culinary Arts	Film Studies
History	Literature
Dietetics	Sociology
Nutrition	

Source: Association for the Study of Food and Society home page, http://food-culture.org/.
Reprinted with permission from the Association for the Study of Food and Society

2 WHAT IS RESEARCH?

Before examining the various research methods, it is necessary to understand what research is and what research is not. In this chapter we will look at various definitions of research, various approaches to research, and how to design and report your research. Choosing a research topic and writing effective research questions are important aspects of the research process, and how these areas are informed in relation to your methodology is a key component of this chapter. This chapter also covers the various modes for conducting your research. It must be designed in a way that you are able to answer your research questions, so we will talk about research design here, too. Finally, while your research may be interesting whether or not it is disseminated to the world at large, it is more useful if it is, so we cover formats for reporting research in this chapter as well.

Before you spend hours and hours reviewing the literature, writing a research proposal, and designing instruments for the collection of data, it is very important to have a firm conception of what research is, and possibly even more importantly, what research is not. There are likely as many definitions of research as there are researchers. *Webster's Third New International Dictionary* defines research as a "careful or diligent search, a studious inquiry or examination . . . the collecting of information about a particular subject." The term *research* comes from the French *rechercher*, to go about seeking, so *Webster's* definition is good as far as it goes, but research in academia is much more than mere reportage. Research properly done requires an analytical component—an interpretation of the data presented, not just the data itself. The data itself may be extremely interesting, but without some explanation to give it context, it is merely a collection of numbers or words. For commercial research, this may be adequate. In academic research, as opposed to research in the social and commercial arenas, we take the next step and evaluate what we have found so we can interpret, analyze, and report it to the world.

Throughout our school lives prior to coming to college (and maybe even during our quest for a baccalaureate), we are told that our fact-finding excursions into articles, books, encyclopedias, and online material are research. In the academic sense, they are not research, but merely the first step in the research process. Information discovery is a good skill to have. If you have had good teachers, these excursions have you likely skilled at locating information and its sources. In the "research" process as secondary students we gathered a number of facts and then presented them in a written or oral presentation to our teachers and/or classmates. If we were reporting on Spanish cuisine, we would talk about the various regions of Spain, what kind of foodstuffs are common in the country, and what dishes are prominent in the cuisine. We might have mentioned the influence of the Moors on the cuisine of Spain and regional variations in the cuisine. But likely it went no further. Usually the recitation of facts sufficed and little attempt was made at analysis and interpretation. When we talk about research in food studies, these would have been good first steps in an attempt to understand something deeper about food in Spain, but they are only the first steps in the research process, the accumulation of a factual basis. When we talk about research in the formal academic sense, we are talking about something that is more of a process than a product, a never-ending journey rather than a destination. This is not to say that we don't stop at some point and report on what we have found, but our report is something that can be used as a foundation for further research and is a part of a much greater whole.

As we said earlier, research has numerous definitions. Burns (2000, p. 3) says that research is a "systematic investigation to find answers to a problem." Payton (1979, p. 4) defines research as a "process of looking for a specific answer to a specific question in an organized, objective, reliable way." In *Practical Research: Planning and Design,* Leedy expands upon this definition by going beyond the idea that research only provides answers to problems, saying that research is performed to "increase our understanding of the phenomenon with which we are concerned or interested" (p. 3). Creswell (2005) explains research as series of three simple steps that exemplify the three core elements of research process. The first step is to pose a question. The second step is to collect data to answer the question. The third step is to present the answer to the question based on the collected data. The first two steps in Creswell's method are germane to almost every type of research. In food studies, we might be able to argue that even when we have done high-quality research we may not have answered the question in the empirical sense of "this happens because of, and therefore"—that is, a causal relationship. But that is fine, sometimes just by knowing about a phenomenon we add to the knowledge base. While this traditional definition of research still is quite applicable in many forms and arenas of research, the last fifty years or so have seen what we accept as research and the ways that we obtain the knowledge used in the research report expand greatly. Traditional empirical research is still the status quo in many fields, but researchers in food studies are utilizing a wider range of methods to enhance knowledge in this new field. Many postmodernists would argue that in the social sciences especially there are no one-size-fits-all answers, that there are as many answers to a problem as there are perspectives. Given all the new approaches to research that have been proposed in the past half century, it may serve us to enhance our definition of what we call research and talk about the ways we collect and analyze information as a means to increase our understanding of a topic, in addition to the quest for finding answers to a problem.

Research should be thought of as an investigation. In most cases this investigation will be based on the notions of others who have come before you in the area that you intend to research. A research teacher that one of the authors of this text had as a graduate student went so far as to claim that there were no more original research ideas, that all research being done today is an offshoot of some ground that has already been tilled. She defined the research process as "searching and re-searching, hence the name research." There may be few new fields to till, but even new areas of knowledge need to be explored with a careful understanding of people who have worked in relevant areas before you. As Isaac Newton said, "If I have seen further it is by standing on ye shoulders of Giants."

While your research should be based on a solid foundation of those who have made investigations before you, it should make some attempt at originality. Ideally you will gain some new insights into the topic you are studying, but an improvement in the existing knowledge is a desirable accomplishment especially for the novice researcher. Sometimes research will have immediately applicable practical uses; other times it will be more foundational and informational in nature—such is the nature of research. The key to being a successful researcher in any arena is to collect and analyze your data in a systematic manner.

WHY DO WE RESEARCH?

The creation and maintenance of the intellectual infrastructure of food studies is the overarching goal of research in the discipline. This happens in a number of ways. At the highest level, we perform research to develop theory in our discipline. *Theory* is a term that is often misunderstood. In general society, it means an uneducated guess, speculation, an opinion, a possibility, or even just a hunch. In this formulation, when we say something is "just a theory," we mean that it might be true or it might not be true, and we often imply that the speaker lacks credibility. But in research, a theory refers to a way of explaining behaviors or phenomena that, having been extensively researched, is generally accepted by the research community in question. One of the best illustrations of the misuse of the term *theory* is shown in the battles between those who believe in the evolution of the human species and those who believe in a creationist or intelligent design model and their disagreement over how this issue should (or should not be) presented in schools. Arguments before school boards or other organizations nearly always include the statement that evolution is "just a theory," as if its theoretical basis were lacking in empirical evidence and credibility in the scientific community. Barnum (1990, p. 1) defines theory as "a statement that

purports to account for or characterize some phenomenon." In food studies, we use theory as an explanation of relationships between phenomena and the "mechanisms or structures presumed to underlie such relationships" (Marx, 1976, p. 237).

Theories are susceptible to change as more information is gathered about a topic, and researchers tinker with a theory to make it more concise, more workable, or more encompassing. This reworking of theory usually doesn't change the fundamentals of theory; it only makes it more useful or more understandable. Theories can be superseded as more information is gathered, but this doesn't mean that proceeding from a theoretical basis is undesirable. Theories can be comprehensive explanations of the way something works or they can provide comprehensive frameworks for describing a social phenomenon; in food studies they give structure to the ways in which we observe and interpret phenomena. Theories represent the current forefront of thinking in a field and until they are superseded, they are excellent lenses for looking at phenomena, so you will want to pay attention to the most current theories in food studies and other related disciplines as you make decisions about the research process. Developing a theory can be a very difficult undertaking, but it can provide a very useful vocabulary and set of precepts for scholars when carried out successfully.

Another reason for performing research is to increase the knowledge of a topic in your field. Since food studies is a young field, there are many topics that are not fully understood in food studies and beg for greater investigation, from the meanings of authenticity in food, to what makes comfort food comforting, to the origins of many of our food habits.

Research is also conducted in order to improve practice in a discipline. This means that sometimes research is performed for practical reasons. Sometimes we want to find out what will improve the efficacy of delivery or some similar goal. A good example of this is research that was recently done in conjunction with the food stamp program at the U.S. Department of Agriculture (Winn et al., 2008). Researchers conducted a study where a lesson on cooking ground meat to the correct internal temperature of 165ºF was stressed. Two groups were studied. Both groups were showed how to use the thermometer to check the internal temperature of cooked ground beef patties. One group (the experimental group) was given instant-read meat thermometers to take home after the lesson. The second group (the control group) was given the same lesson, but members were not given instant-read thermometers to use at home. In the study's follow-up survey, the group that was given the thermometers to take home was more likely to use a thermometer to check the internal temperature of ground beef patties than the group that was not provided the instrument to take home. The implication is that if you provided the participants with a thermometer, they were more likely to follow safe ground beef preparation procedures at home. In this way, research was used to inform practice in the area of food safety.

We can also use research to inform people outside of our discipline about important issues related to the study of food. Policymakers frequently rely on research to inform themselves about issues they themselves don't have the time, resources, or inclination to investigate. Beyond the official sphere, food studies research can also be used to inform the general public about critical issues. For example, the Center for Science in the Public Interest used previously published research on the impact of various food production practices on the environment in order to develop its "Eating Green Calculator," which accepts inputs on the dietary intake of consumers and calculates their impact on the environment (http://www.cspinet.org/EatingGreen/calculator.html).

Purposes of Food Research: Examples

Generating Theory

"Cooking Up Change in Haute Cuisine: Ferran Adrià as an Institutional Entrepreneur," by Silviya Svejenova, Carmelo Mazza, and Marcel Planellas (2007)

Based on a longitudinal, inductive study of a critical case from a cultural sector, this article explores how institutional entrepreneurs initiate change. Our explanation points to four mechanisms: creativity that generates continuous flow of new ideas; theorization that takes stock of these ideas; reputation within and outside the field that endorses ideas as worthy of attention, and dissemination that brings ideas to the public domain. As novel ideas challenge received practices in the field, paradoxes of logics and identity emerge and provide potential for change. The study contributes to institutional theory by examining a preliminary, understudied stage of institutional change that provides a potential for change. Further, it shows how institutional entrepreneurs engage in the theorization and dissemination of their work. Finally, it reveals how reputation plays a critical role in the dissemination of new ideas and thus in the shaping up of the paradoxes and the potential for change.

Increasing Knowledge

"Food and Politics: Nazi Agrarian Politics in the Occupied Territories of the Soviet Union," by Gerhard Gesine (2009)

This article explores the connection between food politics and genocide in the occupied eastern territories. The examination focuses on Herbert Backe, the "second man" in the agricultural administration during the period

---

of Nazi rule. Backe was in charge of food rationing during the war, and was involved in the planning of the economic exploitation of the Soviet Union after the invasion. Under Backe's directive, food policy turned into "starvation policy" for people in the occupied lands of the Soviet Union. The author uses a range of archival sources, including rarely used personal letters and diaries of Backe and his wife, to understand Backe's role and motivations.

Improving Practice

"Consumer Trust in Food Safety—A Multidisciplinary Approach and Empirical Evidence from Taiwan," by Mei-Fang Chen (2008)

Food scandals that happened in recent years have increased consumers' risk perceptions of foods and decreased their trust in food safety. A better understanding of the consumer trust in food safety can improve the effectiveness of public policy and allow the development of the best practice in risk communication. This study proposes a research framework from a psychometric approach to investigate the relationships between the consumer's trust in food safety and the antecedents of risk perceptions of foods based on a reflexive modernization perspective and a cultural theory perspective in the hope of benefiting the future empirical study. The empirical results from a structural equation modeling analysis of Taiwan as a case in point reveal that this research framework based on a multidisciplinary perspective can be a valuable tool for a growing understanding of consumer trust in food safety. The antecedents in the psychometric research framework comprised reflexive modernization factors and cultural theory factors have all been supported in this study except the consumer's perception of pessimism toward food. Moreover, the empirical results of repeated measures analysis of variance give more detailed information to grasp empirical implications and to provide some suggestions to the actors and institutions involved in the food supply chain in Taiwan.

Informing Policy

"Household Behaviour and Attitudes with Respect to Recycling Food Waste: Experiences from Focus Groups," by Karen Refsgaard and Kristin Magnussen (2009)

It is a challenge to reduce the ever-increasing flow of waste. In Norway the systems for recycling of organic waste, paper, glass, metals, etc. differ between municipalities, both with regard to organizational and to technological structures. Our hypothesis is that people's attitudes and behaviour may differ with different systems of waste management. People's behaviour and attitudes regarding (organic) waste recycling were investigated in two municipalities with differing technical and organisational systems. Data came from interviews with municipal employees, questionnaires, focus groups and multi-criteria mapping. People seem to be better informed and more positive about organic waste recycling in one of the municipalities (MH, which has recycling of organic waste) than in the other (MS, which has no such recycling). The two municipalities had similar sets of important criteria for waste management (price, environmental friendliness, easy solutions, information). Many participants stated that they had learned from the group process, though only a few reported changed preferences. The institutional context seems to be important for people's behaviour and attitudes towards waste management. This implies that people's recycling behaviour does not only depend on technical and organisational aspects, but also on institutions. These are important messages for policy makers. On an individual basis, the different systems in the two municipalities seem to affect people's stated attitudes. These differences diminish when they are in a common setting where process and dialogue stimulate new thoughts and encourage people to act more altruistically.

THE RESEARCH PARADIGMS

Inside the big tent we label research, we tend to divide research methodologies into qualitative and quantitative paradigms. There are vivid, and sometimes virulent, debates in the research community about which paradigm is superior, in what settings, and for what topics of research. These debates are philosophical in nature, and the scope of that debate is beyond the ken of this book.[1] What we want to talk about in this section of the book are the two paradigms and what they mean to researchers. Participants in what some have termed the "qualitative-quantitative wars" often see the two research styles as polar opposites with no overlap, and some go so far as to say that there is really only one legitimate style of research and that the other paradigm either doesn't exist or is the conception of a faulty worldview. At one extreme, Miles and Huberman (1994, p. 40) quote Fred Kerlinger, a noted behavioral researcher, as saying, "There is no such thing as qualitative data. Everything is either 1 or 0." At the other extreme are researchers who make the point that all quantitative data is based on questions that have their grounding in how the researcher selects questions to ask and how they state the questions, thereby making all research qualitative. It may be more useful to you to think of quantitative and qualitative as two places on the research spectrum with commonalities and overlaps. In food studies, nearly all of our research is intended to increase understanding of the human experience as it is represented through food. Quantitative research in food studies uses numerical data to examine and represent that experience. Qualitative research in food studies uses detailed, thick description and analysis of the quality of the experience to represent the human experience of food. Neither approach is necessarily "truer" or more rigorous than the other. One may be better suited to the research question at hand, the skills and epistemology of the researcher, or the pervasive methodology of field.

At the risk of being overly reductionist, we will start by trying to define differences in the paradigms by saying that quantitative research is based in numbers and that qualitative research is based in words and language. We know some of your professors will be howling as they read that simplistic statement, but bear with us as we attempt to put some flesh on these bones. If we think of a research as a spectrum and holistic in nature, then strict differentials like these are overly simplistic. Neither paradigm is a monolithic or absolute. Both contain variations and inconsistencies and contrasting philosophical approaches within them. Nevertheless, quantitative and qualitative are distinctions that many, many people do make and they serve as excellent places to discuss the differences and similarities in approach and method. Qualitative and quantitative research approaches are distinguished by different views of human behavior, assumptions about the nature of reality, and the researcher's opinion regarding the ability of these concepts to be measured. These factors make up worldviews that are sometimes labeled positivist (for quantitative approaches) and constructivist or interpretivist (for qualitative approaches) (Guba and Lincoln, 1998). Positivism in its most basic sense is a worldview that we can only truly (positively) know only that which we can observe *and* measure. For positivists, this means that concepts like emotion and belief are unknowable in the sense that we can't objectively measure these concepts through numeric quantification. Constructivists or interpretivists object to this narrowly constructed view of what we are able to claim to have knowledge of due to the lack of tools to objectively measure it. These epistemologies have led to two arch and oppositional paradigms in research, ones that the participants in the "quantitative-qualitative wars" mentioned previously argue so vociferously about.[2] For the sake of ease of use and general familiarity, we will use the terms *qualitative* and *quantitative* as we discuss research styles and methods in this text. The choice of a paradigm to work in is often based in an individual's worldview, the dominance of one paradigm or the other in the researcher's chosen field of endeavor, and the assumptions that a researcher makes as a basis for choosing a topic and conducting the research in it. Often the research question you ask will drive your choice of paradigm to work in, including the decision to use a mixed-methods approach.

As we said earlier, views of human behavior drive people's perceptions about which paradigm to work in. Quantitative researchers frequently feel that cognition and behavior are highly predictable and explainable behaviors. Quantitative research is deterministic (Seale, 1999) in the sense that quantitative researchers tend to feel that there are probabilistic causes for behavior and that these causes are detectable, able to be put into discrete categories, and then measured. Quantitative research often tries to detect cause-and-effect relationships that will enable the researchers to make probabilistic predictions and generalizations about human behavior. Quantitative researchers feel that there is an objective reality that can be categorized and measured and that "rational observers who look at the same phenomenon will basically agree on its existence and its characteristics" (Johnson and Christensen, 2008, p. 36). In quantitative research, method is considered the most important characteristic of the research. On the other hand, qualitative researchers often view human behavior as fluid, dynamic, and highly situational over time and place. In qualitative approaches, individuals and groups are said to create individualistic realities based on the social constructions of the individual or group and the lenses through which they view the world at large (Berger, 1966). These constructions then influence what they see as normal and abnormal and thus inform how they act, think, feel, and believe. Qualitative researchers expect behavior to be highly situational and tightly bound to the context of that situation. Qualitative research results often are not generalizable to populations other than one being studied for the research; they attempt to explain the phenomenon at hand.

Examples of Quantitative, Qualitative, and Mixed-Methods Food Studies

Quantitative

"A National Study of the Association between Neighbourhood Access to Fast-Food Outlets and the Diet and Weight of Local Residents," by Jamie Pearce, Rosemary Hiscock, Tony Blakely, and Karen Witten (2009)

Differential locational access to fast-food retailing between neighbourhoods of varying socioeconomic status has been suggested as a contextual explanation for the social distribution of diet-related mortality and morbidity. This New Zealand study examines whether neighbourhood access to fast-food outlets is associated with individual diet-related health outcomes. Travel distances to the closest fast-food outlet (multinational and locally operated) were calculated for all neighbourhoods and appended to a national health survey. Residents in neighbourhoods with the furthest access to a multinational fast-food outlet were more likely to eat the recommended intake of vegetables but also be overweight. There was no association with fruit consumption. Access to locally operated fast-food outlets was not associated with the consumption of the recommended fruit and vegetables or being overweight. Better neighbourhood access to fast-food retailing is unlikely to be a key contextual driver for inequalities in diet-related health outcomes in New Zealand.

Qualitative

"The social and environmental factors underlying maternal malnutrition in rural Bangladesh: Implications for reproductive health and nutrition programs," by K. Shannon, Z. Mahmud, A. Asfia, and M. Ali (2008)

Levels of low birth weight (LBW) and maternal malnutrition in rural Bangladesh are among the highest in the world. We surveyed dietary practices among pregnant mothers in a rural area served by a reproductive health and nutrition program. In total, 30 semi-structured interviews and five focus group discussions were carried out, supplemented by participant observations. Despite high levels of awareness of nutritional dietary requirements, half the women reported unchanged or reduced food intake during pregnancy. Dietary taboos and food aversions were widely practiced. Women consistently received the last and smallest food shares during mealtimes. The findings highlight the need to address traditional dietary taboos and preferences, and actively target key household decisionmakers, namely, husbands and mothers-in-law, in nutrition behavior change communication.

Mixed Methods

"In Search of the Concerned Consumer: UK Public Perceptions of Food, Farming and Buying Local," by Charlotte Weatherell, Angela Tregear, and Johanne Allinson (2003).

In developed countries, upstream operators in the agro-food chain are being encouraged to become more market oriented as well as to engage in more localised, alternative food systems. Yet there is a lack of empirical information regarding consumer perceptions of local foods, which limits the extent to which alternative systems can be effectively theorised and developed. This paper reports on a qualitative and quantitative study of consumer perceptions of food and farming, which has the particular aim of examining the links between consumers' priorities when choosing food, their perceptions of farming and food provisioning issues, and their interest in locally produced products. The results raise some important issues regarding the nature of consumer choice for local foods, as well as offering insights into the existence of a distinctive set of "concerned consumers." Implications are given for policy support of localised food systems and for the future development of conceptual work in this area.

Another important distinction between the two paradigms is based on the approach the researcher takes to data collection methodology and analysis. Quantitative research uses what might be described as a narrowly angled focus because the quantitative researcher tends to focus on a very few factors (or even just one) at a time. The quantitative approach often begins with a hypothesis or theory that the researcher is trying to confirm or disconfirm (McMillan and Schumacher, 1997). The instruments or methods that the researcher uses will be formal and will be tested prior to the research at hand in order to later make claims regarding generalizability and validity. Quantitative methods are very useful if the population to be studied is large. If you want to find out about 10,000 people, it is unlikely that you will have the time to sit down with each and every one of them, even if you could assemble a team of researchers and a budget large enough to accomplish the aims of your scheme.

Researchers in the quantitative paradigm go to great lengths to ensure that methods and instruments used in their research are as neutral and free of bias as possible and that the researchers' influence over response is eliminated as far as is possible. The researcher using a quantitative approach will attempt to take himself or herself out of the research process as much as possible to negate what is often referred to as the researcher effect—that is, how the researcher's presence has an effect on how the subject responds to the stimulus or condition (Hitchcock and Hughes, 1989). Often the mere presence of the researcher can have an affect on the way a question is answered or a behavior is performed. An approach that is based in hypotheses and numerical data that can be analyzed with statistical methods is usually described as deductive in nature (Polit and Beck, 2004).

Qualitative research uses what might be thought of as a widely angled focus. While some qualitative research begins with a hypothesis, it is not as critical a starting place as it is in quantitative research. In many instances, qualitative research only offers a hypothesis at the end of the research process and sometimes no hypothesis is offered at all; it very much depends on the goals and methodology of the study. Most qualitative research, if seeking answers in the traditional sense, is seeking answers to larger, broader, and more general questions than is the case in quantitative research. Qualitative researchers may want to study the behavior or phenomenon of interest in a more natural or holistic setting than the clinical setting of the laboratory or experiment. They are concerned that behaviors exhibited in the "real world" are subject to uncontrollable factors (uncontrolled variables) that are not present in a more controlled setting and want to understand how all of these factors interact to create the behavior or phenomenon. This usually requires the researcher to interact with the research participant, something the quantitative researcher is trying to avoid. In place of the artificial imposition of condition or the use of a standardized instrument of measure, the researcher then becomes the data collection instrument. The researcher using qualitative methods wants to understand behaviors or phenomena from the participant's point of view, a condition sometimes referred to as an empathetic understanding (Jones, 1997). To gain this perspective the researcher needs to interact with research subjects and be able to make interpretations of what is being seen and heard. In qualitative inquiry, data is rarely collected in the form of numbers, but in the form of words and thoughts and expressions. While this data is coded in some fashion, the resulting coded data is analyzed to gain a larger sense of the phenomenon in question rather than a strict cause-and-affect interpretation.

STRENGTHS AND WEAKNESSES OF THE PARADIGMS

Both qualitative and quantitative approaches are needed in food studies research because no single approach can answer every research question that is posed. Neither approach is less rigorous than the other; the choice of paradigm depends on the research question you are asking. Quantitative approaches are useful when you want to do comparisons between groups or explore the relationships between variables. If you are trying to determine differences in food consumption patterns between groups, then a numerical approach can be quite useful, and you can use the statistics generated from correlational statistical analysis to make some supported observations about difference. Qualitative approaches tend to be more useful when you are doing exploratory research about beliefs, behaviors, and phenomena about which little are known. Oftentimes a qualitative report on a topic will lead to more specific research in a quantitative vein and in this way the two approaches are frequently complementary. For example, observation of behavior in a local restaurant (qualitative), may prompt some analysis using data that you can collect from the participants or the restaurant customer (demographics; sales).

Quantitative measures will give the researcher a great deal of precision and control. Carefully controlled experimental research allows us to stake some claim to cause and effect (Charles and Mertler, 2002). This allows us to make claims for validity and generalizability. This also allows our research to be replicated by others, a quality that is desirable in many types of scientific research. If we are attempting to prove or disprove a specific hypothesis, a quantitative approach will likely be the most useful.

If we are attempting to learn about the meaning of the behavior or practices of a group or individual we will likely use some type of qualitative methodology. Gaining insight on another person's perspective or a cultural practice requires that a researcher use some type of qualitative method like observation, participation, or interview. The data we get from these types of methods do not as easily lend themselves to quantification and statistical analysis, but the data that are produced (when the work is done thoroughly and reflectively) reflect the perspectives of the participants as opposed to that of the researcher.

The time that it takes to do research thoroughly and effectively is always a major consideration of any project. The time that it takes to plan, execute, and analyze the results of research always surprises the neophyte researcher. Neither research paradigm offers a true advantage when it comes to issues of time. Quantitative research methods tend to be more time-intensive in the planning and execution phases than in the analysis phase. Good quantitative research needs to have all controls in place before the research can commence. If you are using a questionnaire as your data collection instrument, then it needs to be tested for reliability and validity before being offered to participants. This usually means a pilot test before the actual administration to the population (Clark-Carter, 2004). Once the research is under way there must be constant monitoring to make sure all controls are being observed and that the intervention (or other control) is being administered in a consistent manner. On the plus side, once the data has been collected, the use of computer programs for statistical analysis makes this part relatively easy (though interpretation of the results will take more time). Also, quantitative research reports tend to be shorter and more concise than do qualitative reports. Qualitative research tends to have less expenditure of time on the front end and more on the back end. Since the qualitative reporter is more likely to use open-ended questions for survey and observation work, and since there needs to be much less in the way of clinical controls (though permissions can be a thorny issue), it is generally quicker to get to the data collection phase. Because of the open-ended and helical nature of observations used in qualitative research, fieldwork can often take much longer than lab work. If a gatekeeper for the project is not already identified or on board, this will add to the time the researcher needs to get into the field. In qualitative research, observations may need to be performed numerous times over longer periods than in quantitative work. Qualitative research frequently relies on an inductive process that may require a researcher to return to the field to get answers to the questions and new areas of interest that arise in the coding and analysis of data (Goetz, Preissle, and LeCompte, 1984). Since data are rarely delivered in tidy, precoded packages as is frequently the case in quantitative research, the researcher can spend copious amounts of time in the various levels of coding and analysis. Qualitative research reports tend to be longer than quantitative research reports. Because the researcher has to explain many of the analytical structures and devices and then support them with examples from the data, research reports from qualitative projects can be as much as twice as long as those from quantitative projects.

DIMENSIONS OF RESEARCH

Regardless of the paradigm you work in, there are some ways of thinking about, describing, and approaching the research you intend to do. One of the most common distinctions made when classifying research is whether it is theoretical or applied (Gall, Gall, and Borg, 2005, Hart 2007). Sometimes the phrase used to describe this dichotomy is basic versus applied. Basic or theoretical research can be thought of as research for research's sake. While building theory is hardly inconsequential, (indeed it is one of the hardest and most painstaking types of research) the results of this type of research generally don't have immediate application as a solution to a problem or as a way improve the daily practice of a profession. This kind of research generally is intended to "add to our fundamental understanding of the world" (Adler and Clark, 2003, p. 15). The opposite of basic research is applied research. Applied research is frequently thought of as practical research. The result of the research is intended to be useful immediately in the world to solve a problem or improve practice in a profession. For example, a study of visual representations of food and perceived satiety might be an example of basic research. Using these findings to design and test consumer satiety of a restaurant item with various plate presentations would be a similar topic applied. These are useful and convenient distinctions in the qualitative and quantitative paradigms but don't cover all avenues of research in either.

When research is conducted in an area that has received scant or no attention by other researchers and for which little or no theory has been developed, we term the research *exploratory* (Adler and Clark, 2003). From a problem-solving point of view, this type of research is often conducted to give definition to the problems, players, and perceptions in a situation. Exploratory research doesn't usually happen in a clinical laboratory setting. The exploratory researcher will spend a good deal of time combing literature sources for elements that relate to the topic at hand as well as performing some fieldwork in the form of talking to affected players, perhaps forming focus groups, conducting in-depth interviews with key informants, or writing a case study that is somehow illustrative of the larger problem. Exploratory research can be useful when deciding how to proceed with basic or applied research in a relatively uncultivated area. Exploratory research can help when making decisions about writing research questions, designing data collection methods, selecting populations or samples, and determining data analysis methods. For example, if you want to study the relationship between certain traits of chefs (knife skills, education, location) and career success, you might need to first perform some exploratory research such as interview, focus groups, a pilot survey, or participant observation to better frame the questions in the full study—to even know the traits you might consider.

The next step beyond exploratory research is descriptive research. Descriptive research is intended to gather information about a specific phenomenon or issue without influencing the subject or issue in any way (Adler and Clark, 2003). Descriptive studies are often used as a precursor to studies where a variable is manipulated in order to study cause and effect, though they are useful ways of gathering data in their own right. If you were working for a large food manufacturer and wanted to know how many people were buying your product and for what they were using it, you could send out a questionnaire or conduct a survey to see what percentage of a population was buying the product and ask how they were using it. You wouldn't be trying to influence any behaviors or establish why they were engaging in the behavior; you would just be trying to learn what percentage of the people actually did it. This could be very useful in future marketing efforts or attempts to expand the brand. A lot of research that people categorize as demographic falls into the descriptive category.

Explanatory research is performed in an attempt to explain why a behavior or situation occurs. Explanatory research builds on exploratory and descriptive research and uses theory to explain why certain events occur (Adler and Clark, 2003). A good deal of the research you see in academic journals is explanatory. Explanatory research usually builds on existing theory and increases its richness by providing real-life examples of the theory in practice. In some instances explanatory research will have the effect of refuting theory if the behavior predicted in the theory is not borne out in the practical applications of it in the explanatory research.

Very much in the explanatory vein is evaluation research. Evaluation research is conducted to obtain information and make judgments about the effectiveness of a program or other evaluative object (Johnson and Christensen, 2008). An evaluation object could be a person, a program, a product, or a process. Evaluative research is aimed at proving the worth, value, or efficacy of the evaluation object. Let's say you were working with a local social service agency and you wanted to try to give local food benefit recipients tokens (or some other method of payment) that they could use at the local farmers' market in order to increase the fresh vegetable and fruit intake of the participants. Whoever is funding the project will likely want to know if what you are doing is actually causing people to consume more fresh fruits and vegetables. In order to assess the efficacy of the program, at some point you would perform an evaluative research project (an evaluation) of the success of the project. There are two types of evaluative research that are commonly performed, formative and summative (Gall, Gall, and Borg, 2005). Initially you would likely perform a formative evaluation. Formative evaluations are performed to examine the mechanics of a program or process and suggest improvements for the future. Sometimes formative evaluations are conducted prior to establishing the project in order to look at similar types of programs and then use the information gathered to design the program they wish to implement. Once a program is established and under way, it needs to be evaluated regularly to ensure it continues to function in an effective manner. At some point, legislators or other programmatic officials will have to decide if a program is to be continued. At this point a summative evaluation will generally be performed and the results will inform the decision that is ultimately made. Summative evaluations are very important in the public arena. With so many competing priorities, legislators and administrators constantly have to make decisions about which programs to keep and which to cancel. The future of our farmer's market program would, in part, depend on the information presented in the summative evaluation presented to the overseeing administrator or agency.

Exploratory, descriptive, and explanatory research methods have long been parts of the traditional basic research canon. More recently a method known as critical theory research has joined them in this category of research. Critical theory research or critical research or orientational research as it is variously known "focuses on collecting information to help a researcher advance a specific ideological or political position or orientation that he or she believes will improve some part of our society" (Johnson and Christensen, 2008, p. 13). Critical research is based on criticism of a perceived shortcoming in society. The term *orientational research* is gaining favor as the topics in this area of research expand beyond the economic and into areas such as gender, race, and sexual orientation. Critical topics in food studies research could involve the persistence of hunger on the planet, food deserts in urban areas, and so on. Older than critical research, but somewhat related to it, is action research. Action research is very practical form of research aimed at problem solving (Charles and Mertler, 2002). While no research is ever the definitive word on a topic, this is especially true of action research. Action research is dynamic and is very iterative in nature. Action research is most effective when the construction of the language of the problem and the elements of the research methodology are created in conjunction with the population who is to be the focus of the action research. In this sense, action research is very participatory in nature. This participation by actors in the situation creates local solutions to local problems, solutions that tend to be the most effective.

CHOOSING THE RESEARCH TOPIC

While many of you reading this book will have some topic in mind to research, others of you will not, and many of those of you who do have a topic in mind likely have not reduced your idea into a manageable research area or question. This should not be a cause of concern; most of the researchers you admire or want to emulate were likely in this state of unease at some point in their career. As you get comfortable with research as a professional practice, your problem will be choosing specific topics to investigate (you can't investigate everything that sounds interesting) and then narrowing these topics down to give you a manageable research agenda (you don't have the time or resources to investigate everything that is interesting about a topic).

Hilton (1998) offers some excellent advice for choosing topics for your research. The first thing to consider is the personal interest factor. You need to make sure that what you are going to research is something that you will enjoy reading immense amounts of background material about and that you will remain motivated to study at length as the research process continues. Research is, and should be, fun. Choosing a research topic outside your areas of true interest is a guaranteed prescription for agony. We assume that you have chosen food studies research because of a genuine interest in food and its relationship with society. But even within food studies there are likely areas that will bore you to tears and others that you could happily read about for months or years. Find those areas and research will be a pleasurable activity, not a chore. Hilton's second consideration for choosing a research topic is sources and assistance. Some experienced researchers are happy to sail off into exploratory research where the source material is minimal. As neophyte researchers this may not be the best choice for you. Having grounding in the materials produced by those who have gone before you in an area gives you a frame for doing your own research, even if yours goes beyond anything that has been produced before. In addition, most of you will be working with a major professor or advisor at your side. If that person understands your topic or can at least help you interpret and evaluate the material that you uncover in your research, you will be that much better off. Assistance may also take the form of time and money. If your research has grounding in areas of wide interest, there may be resources of others' time and money that you can tap into to aid your efforts. Hilton's third research consideration is that you should choose a topic that will allow you an opportunity to do in-depth research. As we have noted earlier research is more than the collection of information and collating it into a review. Research needs to bring something new to the table. This may seem at odds with our injunction to avoid exploratory research as a research newbie, but given the parameters of research, this still allows you to explore known topics and make a unique contribution with your research report.

FINDING TOPICS: SOURCES OF RESEARCH QUESTIONS

Questions that are suitable for research are all around us. Sources range from the academic to the popular, from the mundane to the esoteric, from the political to the personal. Food is a regular topic in the mass media. The so-called Gray Ladies of Journalism, the *Times of London* and the *New York Times,* along with nearly every other metropolitan daily, have regular food sections every week. Major newsmagazines like *Time* and the *Economist* regularly provide in-depth coverage of food topics, from the hottest trends to political issues like hunger. The Food Network, what many of us call Food TV, is available in virtually every English-speaking country on the planet. Regular reading and watching of these sources raises many interesting questions for food studies research. Even the media itself can provide research inspiration, as is evidenced by the research presented at conferences like the Association for the Study of Food and Society. Food media allows us to vicariously participate in food preparation and tourism, but many of us travel ourselves, and travel to places outside our home area is so common today as to be nearly un-noteworthy as a phenomenon. But travel can give us many interesting ideas for food studies research. Some may argue that the cultural phenomenon known as McDonaldization (Ritzer, 1996) is flattening food culture, but a visit to a street market in most cultures will prove there is still vigor in local foodways. In many instances we don't even need to travel to get ideas about food in cultures outside our own. Researchers in large urban areas may have access to a large number of food products, sources, customs, practices, and ideas. Some of us may even already be in a situation where interesting food-related topics are crying out to be researched. In the "you are there" scenario you are already involved in the group or process and your problems related to access are greatly reduced. (In this instance you will have a need for extra rigor in your analysis as you will have many preconceptions and biases related to the topic, but with proper consideration and reflexivity, these should not be insurmountable problems.) Outside the media, but still in the public sphere are topical areas such as economics and politics. Even if you disdain politics as a process, you likely have a well-entrenched set of political beliefs and these beliefs might be a good starting point for research in the orientationalist or action vein, because food is a topic of interest and significance in the world at large. Research questions involving food are of interest to the general public, the academic community, and to those in positions to affect public policy.

Sometimes your choice of food studies research topic will come from plain intellectual curiosity: you will be reading and have a question about a topic the writer brings up. This is an excellent jumping-off point for research. One thing you might notice while you are reading is that there is a gap in the literature you are reading. Many research projects begin as an attempt to fill a gap in the literature. For example, Bentley's *Eating for Victory: Food Rationing and the Politics of Domesticity* was conceived and written as a way to fill a gap in the literature of food, rationing, and women's role on the home front in the United States during World War II. As you are reading you may realize that there is a lack of knowledge about certain areas in the literature; perhaps there are parts of the phenomenon that are not understood. For example, you may be inspired by a study of food culture in San Francisco's Chinatown to consider a newer Chinatown, such as that in Flushing, Queens, New York. Related to supplementing what is currently known about a topic and filling gaps in existing literature is the idea that a new point of view is needed. For example, there may be a wealth of research done on food imagery in blues music, but a background in both cooking and early twentieth-century African American history may provide insight that was missing in previous work on the topic.

THE RESEARCH PROPOSAL

If you are a student in a graduate program and using this text as part of a class, seminar, or research program, it is likely that your school will require that you submit a formal research proposal before you are allowed to proceed with your research plan. Most graduate committees want to read and approve your comprehensive written research proposal before you will be allowed to proceed with your research. Best and Kahn (1998) tell us that the research proposal serves three primary functions. First, the research proposal provides a blueprint for action for the process that is to come. Second, it allows the advisor and other committee members to critique elements of the proposed research such as the research questions, the research methodology, and the research analysis process/tools. In addition, once the research proposal is approved, it can be used by the advisor as a tool to provide assistance to the researcher during the research process by allowing them to direct the student to relevant literature and helping with procedural and technical issues. Third, the research proposal provides a "basis for evaluation of the project" (p. 36). Evaluation of research should be based on whether the student has accomplished what they intended to do. Having the research proposal in hand can keep the student headed in the right direction, and it gives the faculty member a guide to ultimately evaluating the project.

While the research proposal serves as a road map for the journey ahead, it is not a document cast in concrete. Many things can change between the creation of the proposal and the ultimate execution of the plan, especially when working in the qualitative paradigm. You may not have access to all of the material, people, or situations that you had hoped to include. Your research questions may get modified or changed altogether as you work in the field and results begin to come in. A well-crafted research proposal will likely stand up to all these changes. Some of the details may change, but the superstructure should remain fundamentally the same.

In most instances, the research proposal will mimic the finished report in structure. Many of you will use a standardized approach to writing your finished research report, be it a small research paper or a thesis or dissertation. In the United States, a five-chapter format is a standard approach to research, and variations of it are widely used depending on the final media in question. The five-chapters in this approach are as follows:

Introduction—What will you study and why?

The review of the literature—What has been done on this topic so far?

Methodology—How will you answer your research question?

A typical research proposal will end here or may suggest some anticipated findings and again underscore the importance of this work. The actual research presentation, whether a thesis, journal article or research report, will likely add:

Results—What did you find?

Discussion—What do your findings mean? Who cares?

There are many variations on this model and some researchers are discarding it all together. But most theses and dissertations and academic journals follow some variation on this format. Hence, most research proposals follow it as well.

The introduction section of the research proposal will state what the problem to be studied is. This can be worded as a question or a statement, but should be one of the first things the reviewer reads. Next comes the significance of the problem, any definitional material that is relevant (key terms, for example), any limitations (or delimitations) to the research, assumptions the researcher is making, and the research question(s)—plainly stated and direct. If you are working in an empirical vein, this is where the hypothesis will be included.

The next section will be a review of the relevant literature. This is the literature that you read that got you as far as writing this proposal. In most instances you will continue to read during the course of research, and your final literature review, especially for a thesis or dissertation, will likely be considerably longer. The literature review should show the reviewer you have considered previous research in the area and illustrate the range of that research as well as what methods are likely to work best for your study.

The third section or topic in the research proposal is usually the methods section. You don't need to go into philosophical discussion about the merits of a quantitative or qualitative approach. Move directly into a discussion about the method of research that you have chosen and why it is the most appropriate for the research questions you have chosen to investigate. You should talk about what specific data collection method you have decided to use. For food studies research this could be questionnaires, interviews, observation, participant observation, document or artifact analysis, or many others. Tell the reviewer why this method is the best for eliciting the data you feel you need to answer the question. In the methods section you should discuss your population or sample if you are going to be working with human subjects. Why did you choose the women's auxiliary of Holy Family Catholic Church of Fort Collins, Colorado, for your sample? How are you going to gather data from this group? Are you going to observe or participate in the production of meals for Lent, or will you interview the members in a face-to-face setting, or will you mail questionnaires to members whose addresses you can obtain? You will also need to address the way in which you will analyze the data once you get it. Will you code it by hand? Use a computer for statistical analysis? Whether you have decided to use a standard research instrument (a standardized questionnaire like the ASA24 for dietary food recall studies) or have designed one specifically for this project, the discussion of the instrument should occur here. Oftentimes the use of a certain method or instrument will have the effect of making the decision about how to proceed with the analysis for you, but this discussion should be included here nonetheless.

Once you get past the methods section, your proposal will be unfinished, because you don't know what your results are going to be and you won't be able to discuss them until you do. In the section that follows the methods section you may want to discuss what you think the outcomes are going to be, especially if you are using the scientific method and have a hypothesis you are trying to prove or disprove. This section may also be a good place to discuss issues germane to the conduct of the research such as time lines, costs, concerns, and so on. You will finish up the research proposal by submitting a bibliography of all the sources you have used to create the proposal. Like the literature review, this will likely be much less complete than in the finished research report. There is no standard length for a research proposal. This is not the place to stretch out and be wordy, however. The best research proposals are succinct and pithy documents.

The remaining chapters explore the review of literature, the research process, and research methods in greater detail.

3 THE RESPONSIBLE CONDUCT OF RESEARCH AND THE PROTECTION OF HUMAN SUBJECTS*

All of the hard work you perform in the course of your research is for naught if you perform research that violates the law or basic codes of ethics. For example, it may be perfectly sound research design to learn the effects of starvation by withholding food from a research subject, but it clearly violates basic ethical standards.

This chapter briefly considers two important ethical issues—financial conflicts of interest and academic honesty—and then considers in depth one particularly important, complex, and highly regulated issue—the protection of human subjects.

FINANCIAL CONFLICTS OF INTEREST

To be sure, research can be an expensive endeavor. Some studies take the full-time attention of multiple researchers, in multiple countries, over a number of years. They may require expensive equipment and rooms or even entire buildings devoted to them. Even a relatively low-cost study such as a doctoral dissertation based on statistical analysis from previously published data has significant costs associated with it—the time to do the research (or the opportunity cost of not doing something more lucrative), computers, research assistance, consulting on statistics or writing, software, conference travel, and printing, to name a few.

* The section on human subjects was written by Jane Calhoun, *Senior Research Officer, Committee on the Use of Human Subjects,* Harvard University, Cambridge, MA. We are indebted to her for her involvement and are grateful for the contribution she has made by clearly outlining the responsibilities of the academic researcher.

Sources of funding vary. Some studies are funded by the researcher him- or herself. Others are self-funded but rely heavily on in kind institutional support such as library services, internet access, computers, copiers and so on. Still other projects, and especially large research projects, may be fully or partially funded by academic institutions, private foundations, government agencies, or private entities.

It is important in doing research that the researcher maintain *academic freedom.* The American Association of University Professors provides the following definition of academic freedom:

> **Academic Freedom:** This is the essential characteristic of an institution of higher education. It encompasses the right of faculty to full freedom in research and in the publication of results, freedom in the classroom in discussing their subject, and the right of faculty to be free from institutional censorship or discipline when they speak or write as citizens. (AAUP Informal glossary)

To preserve academic freedom it becomes critical to learn about the funding source of academic research—both the literature you read and your own work—in order to learn what are the goals of the funding agency. Many funding sources are relatively benign. For example, if a university awards a graduate research grant or a course release to a professor in order to allow time and support for research, this funding has relatively few "strings attached." It is typically awarded on the basis of the promise and rigor of the research rather than the expected findings or outcome of the study.

The same cannot be said of every funding source, however. Imagine that an organic food company wanted to fund research into the nutritional and sensory properties of organic produce compared to conventional produce. As a researcher, you may find that the organic produce is healthier and more delicious—but you could also find the opposite, that conventional produce is superior in these areas. Would the organic food company be happy to fund your study either way or would they expect your findings to support their mission? Further, would they let you carry out your research with academic freedom, or would they attempt to interfere or direct the outcome?

When academic freedom is compromised by funding, politics, or other outside influences, the ethics of the research comes into question and it may represent a *conflict of interest.* That is, the reliability of the research may conflict with the stated or implied goals of the outside influence.

The field of food studies is particularly fraught from a funding perspective because the social and cultural aspects of food is a poor field of study, especially when compared to hard sciences. The scarcity of funding makes dollars from a wide range of sources that could support our work appealing. At the same time, the food industry is the world's largest, and much of the research funding to be had comes at the hand of major companies who have vested interests and could potentially provide such a conflict by funding your research.

ACADEMIC HONESTY

The next ethical consideration is the honesty of the research. That is, is the research your own? When you draw on the work of other scholars do you clearly indicate which ideas and words are theirs and not your own? Were your data collected in the way you describe they were?

Most colleges have an academic honesty policy that describes in detail the expectations for your work. One particularly egregious type of academic dishonesty is plagiarism—taking the words or ideas of others and representing them as your own. Here is an excerpt of the plagiarism definitions from the School of Professional Studies of the City University of New York:

> Plagiarism is the act of presenting another person's ideas, research or writings as you own. The following are some examples of plagiarism, but by no means is it an exhaustive list:
>
> - Copying another person's actual words without the use of quotation marks and footnotes attributing the words to their source.
> - Presenting another person's ideas or theories in your own words without acknowledging the source.
> - Using information that is not common knowledge without acknowledging the source.
> - Failing to acknowledge collaborators....
> - Submitting downloaded term papers or parts of term papers, paraphrasing or copying information from the internet without citing the source, and "cutting & pasting" from various sources without proper attribution. (*CUNY Policy on Academic Integrity*, 2004, p. 1)

Many examples of plagiarism are egregious and it is easy to avoid them. Buying a research paper from someone else and putting your name on top is clearly unethical, wrong, and plagiaristic. Others, though, are more insidious and potentially done unintentionally. Perhaps you've read somewhere that sheep tail fat is the most highly prized fat among nomadic tribes in present-day Jordan but you can't remember the exact source. Is it acceptable to use this fact in your writing? Because the fact is not common knowledge and the idea came from someone else, until you find the source (much easier than it used to be, thanks to the Internet), you should not use it in your writing without attribution. But you can see how this type of plagiarism is more easily done.

Apart from plagiarism, another form of academic dishonesty is cheating. This could take a variety of forms. For example, some scholars have been accused of massaging data—whether words or numbers—to show more dramatic results or results that meet some sort of ideological standard. For example, if you are a passionate animal rights activist undertaking a study showing the stress responses of pigs in the slaughterhouse, you might record biometric data such as brain activity. But if your findings show that the pigs are not as significantly stressed as you thought they would be, is there a temptation to round the numbers up?

To prevent accusations of both plagiarism and cheating it is imperative that you maintain accurate records of your research. You can prevent misattributing a quotation by maintaining good records of your literature searches. Interview tapes and transcripts should be stored, locked, so that you can examine any discrepancy should the need arise. And multiple researchers can be used in quantitative studies to take measurements. Double-blind studies also help maintain the integrity of the data.

THE PROTECTION OF HUMAN SUBJECTS IN RESEARCH
WHY REVIEW?

The well-being of those who participate in research as subjects ultimately resides with those conducting the research, so why involve others in scrutinizing a project? The answer lies in relationship.

> At least three parties have legitimate interests in any research venture involving human subjects: the investigator who initiates it, the society that provides the conditions for it, and the subjects who participate in it. Ultimately, if the study is important, their interests do not conflict, but in the short range they can and often do. Sad experience has demonstrated that able and conscientious scholars sometimes fail to give proper weight to considerations that are salient to the interests of either the public or the subjects. To leave all the decisions solely in the hands of one of the parties involved is not wise....
>
> No one has illusions that the committee system—or any other set of institutionalized procedures—is a substitute for ethically alert scientists who are sensitive to the well-being of their subjects. That is the *sine qua non* of meaningful protection and no system relieves the investigator of the *primary*

responsibility for securing subjects' rights and welfare. The committees serve only to remind all concerned of the network of interdependence that exists and to interpose a disinterested judgment where necessary. (*The Intelligent Scholar's Guide [ISG]*, 2008, p. 2)

WHAT IS AN IRB?

An institutional review board (IRB) is an ethics committee devoted to the review and approval of research projects using human subjects, prior to the involvement of the human subjects. The task of an IRB is to serve as a stand-in for the society that provides the conditions for the research and for the human subjects who will participate. The primary duty of the members of an IRB is protect the rights and welfare of research participants. To do so, an IRB needs members familiar with research activities commonly carried on in its institution; the professional competence necessary to review specific research activities; and knowledge of community attitudes, the institution's commitments and regulations, applicable law, and standards of professional conduct and practice. When needed expertise is not available from among an IRB's membership, it may seek advice from external experts.

In the United States IRBs rely primarily on the Belmont Report (1979) and the federal Code of Regulations (45 CFR 46) as their model, whether or not they review federally funded projects. However, it is important to remember that IRBs may, and often do, develop policies in addition to those in the federal regulations, and that there is wide variation across institutions in the procedures by which policy is implemented. It is therefore advisable to check your own institution's policies and procedures when planning a research project. The federal regulations specify that an IRB must have at least five members with varying backgrounds, including at least one member who *is* a scientist, one who *is not* a scientist, and one who is not otherwise affiliated with the institution. More recently, it has also become customary to have at least one community member rather than relying solely on the diversity of other committee members, and their expertise and experience, to represent community attitudes.

IRBs are granted broad powers by the federal regulations:

■ "An IRB shall review and have authority to approve, require modifications in (to secure approval), or disapprove all research activities covered by this policy." (45 CFR 46.109(a))
■ "Research covered by this policy that has been approved by an IRB may be subject to further appropriate review and approval or disapproval by officials of the institution. However, those officials may not approve the research if it has not been approved by an IRB." (45 CFR 46.112)

■ "An IRB shall have authority to suspend or terminate approval of research that is not being conducted in accordance with the IRB's requirements or that has been associated with unexpected serious harm to subjects." (45 CFR 46.113)

HISTORY

The modern era in human subjects protection in the United States began in the 1970s with passage of the National Research Act of 1974, authorizing the Department of Health, Education and Welfare (now Department of Health and Human Services) to issue regulations on the use of human subjects in federally funded research. This was prompted in particular by re-examination of the Tuskegee study of "Untreated syphilis in the Negro male" (Jones, 1981), sponsored by the Public Health Service, which continued from the 1930s through the early 1970s. Over the course of forty years, a sample of African American men with syphilis received many very valuable, and therefore coercive, inducements to participate in a study of the natural course of syphilis in which most of them were neither informed of, nor did they receive, available treatments of the time. Publicity and controversy over a number of ethically complex and/or troubling studies from the previous two decades also contributed to the law's passage.

The law created the National Commission for the Protection of Human Subjects of Biomedical and Behavioral Research. One of the charges to the commission was to identify the basic ethical principles that should underlie the conduct of biomedical and behavioral research involving human subjects and to develop guidelines to assure that such research is conducted in accordance with those principles. The Belmont Report (named after the Smithsonian's conference center where the commission met) was published in 1979.

As the commission acknowledged, "These principles cannot always be applied so as to resolve beyond dispute particular ethical problems. The objective is to provide an analytical framework that will guide the resolution of ethical problems arising from research involving human subjects" (National Commission for the Protection of Human Subjects, 1979).

The three principles set forth in the Belmont Report are respect for persons, beneficence, and justice. These principles are applied in human subjects research through the mechanisms of informed consent, assessment of risks and benefits, and equitable selection of subjects.

Following the acceptance of the Belmont Report, rules and regulations for the protection of human subjects in federally funded research were revised in the Code of Federal Regulations (CFR) at 45 CFR 46. The regulations are also known as "The Common Rule" because seventeen federal agencies have accepted them.

WHAT IS "RESEARCH" AND WHAT IS A "HUMAN SUBJECT"?

Research is a "systematic investigation, including research development, testing and evaluation, designed to develop or contribute to generalizable knowledge" (45 CFR 46.102(d)). A research investigator may be faculty, student, or staff. The intent of the project need not be to generate results for publication. Research may involve *direct* interactions, such as obtaining data by taking medical histories or other interview procedures, or administering psychological tests, or drawing blood samples or collecting saliva samples, or conducting other diagnostic procedures. Research may also involve *indirect* interactions, such as the analysis of specimens or data already obtained from people (either by the current investigator or by others).

A *human subject* means a "living individual *about whom* [italics added] an investigator (whether professional or student) conducting research obtains (1) Data through intervention or interaction with the individual, or (2) Identifiable private information" (45 CFR 46.102(f)).

("About whom" can be a confusing concept. For instance, if you are interviewing Inuits about the use of whale blubber as a foodstuff, you may be collecting data only "about" whale blubber, not about the humans you are talking to. On the other hand, if you interview Inuits about how they themselves use whale blubber, you may well collect information about individual people, that is, "about whom.")

Intervention includes both physical procedures by which data are gathered (for example, venipuncture, EEG recordings, etc.) and manipulations of the subject or the subject's environment that are performed for research purposes. *Interaction* includes communication or interpersonal contact between investigator and subject. *Private information* includes information about behavior that occurs in a context in which an individual can reasonably expect that no observation or recording is taking place. Private information also includes information that has been provided for specific purposes by an individual, and which the individual can reasonably expect will not be made public (for example, a school or medical record or a loan application). Private information must be *individually identifiable* (i.e., the identity of the subject is or may readily be ascertained by the investigator or associated with the information) in order for obtaining the information to constitute research involving human subjects.

WHAT DOES AN IRB NEED TO KNOW ABOUT PROPOSED RESEARCH?

A good starting place for researchers seeking an answer to this question is to consider their projects from the point of view of a potential subject. What is the purpose of the research? What is the objective and the plan to reach that objective? Who are the subjects? How are they being recruited? Is it through an institution (i.e., my school, health care facility, employer) that should be consulted? Might I feel under pressure to participate? What will I actually do, and what will be done to me, during the study? Might I be injured, uncomfortable, embarrassed, stressed, or offended by what is expected of me as a subject? Might there be long-term consequences? Could I be endangered or compromised if confidentiality were breached? "The possible considerations are myriad, but not so difficult to perceive in a particular case if one assumes the subject's perspective" (*ISG,* 2008, pp. 3–4).

These questions are usually posed in far more detail and in more technical language on most IRB application forms, but the questions on forms are generally posed in the same sequence as those above, and it may be helpful to keep in mind the simpler version of the questions as you proceed through the application process. It is also important to remember that IRBs must follow rules when they review and approve research. These rules are spelled out in the federal regulations (45 CFR 46.110) and specify that the IRB consider each of the questions mentioned above.

CORNERSTONES OF ETHICAL RESEARCH WITH HUMAN SUBJECTS

As indicated in the discussion of the history of IRB review, the three principles set forth in the Belmont Report are respect for persons, beneficence, and justice, and these principles are applied in human subjects research through informed consent, assessment of risks and benefits, and equitable selection of subjects.

INFORMED CONSENT

While the *process* of consent that occurs between the investigator and the prospective participant is the more important issue, consent forms seem to receive a disproportionate amount of attention in many IRB reviews, perhaps because it is relatively simple to make a judgment as to whether a consent form, which is a written document, contains the information needed for a cautious and thoughtful person to make an educated decision about whether or not s/he wishes to participate. In the simplest terms, *informed consent* means that the investigator has shared enough information about the study with a prospective subject that the subject knows what the experience and effects of being in the study will be like and, with that knowledge, agrees to participate. "The *consent form* is simply a written confirmation of the agreement between investigator and the subject concerning the content and terms of the proposed activity" (*ISG,* 2008, p. 4). The federal regulations at 45 CFR 46 prescribe specific guidelines for the informed consent process. Many IRBs provide a template that guides the investigator in "filling in the blanks" with the information specifically prescribed for the consent process in the federal regulations.

However, it is important to know that although in some cases consent must be written, in others, an oral exchange is sufficient, and even preferred, should the presence of a written document that links the subject to a study increase risk of harm to the subject. The application to the IRB must include a script of what the investigator will say, or an information sheet, when oral consent is to be used. An information sheet typically looks like a consent form, minus the signature statement and the place for a subject's signature. Information sheets are particularly useful when participation includes several steps, or interviews or surveys over time, because they enable the prospective participant to more easily and quickly comprehend what is being asked of him or her, and they provide a reference for subjects if participation takes place over an extended period of time. Use of a script or information sheet is not "consent lite," however, and the script or information sheet needs to include the elements of consent, just as a form does.

One requirement of the federal regulations too often honored in the breach prescribes that information be given in language understandable to the subject. When subjects for a study will be college students and the investigator is him- or herself a college student, information about the study is often presented in language understandable to the subject. However, the language used to explain a study and to obtain consent for participation may be understandable to the investigator and IRB reviewers—but not to the intended subjects. The *American Heritage Dictionary* defines *readable* as "1. Easily read; legible. 2. Pleasurable or interesting to read" (*American Heritage Dictionary*, 1985). What follows are suggestions to keep in mind, primarily drawn from *All about readability* (Stephens, 2000), both as investigators speak to subjects, and in preparing written materials for them. For the sake of brevity, some suggestions are presented in question form, and refer to written materials, but apply equally to spoken language:

Is the content presented in logical order? Is it free of gender, class and cultural biases? Is the language simple, direct, succinct, and familiar? ("You come to our laboratory for about two hours. You will eat the lunch you bring with you, and then have your height and weight measured and complete questionnaires about your educational and medical history and your eating habits. You will then complete simple computerized tasks about perception, attention, and memory.") Are needless words omitted? Are sentence structures simple? Are sentences and paragraphs short? Are signal words (now, then, but, later, next) used to facilitate the flow of the narrative? Would the use of numbering, bullet points, and paragraph headings help the reader distinguish the steps being described ("In this study you will be asked to do the following: 1...2...3...," etc.) or the content areas being covered ("Purpose of the Study," "What You Will Do," "Confidentiality," etc.)? Is there sufficient white space on written documents? (Adequate margins and spaces between paragraphs make them easier to read.) The suggestions presented here are hardly exhaustive, but hopefully serve as a reminder to keep one's audience in mind when presenting information.

In some cases informed consent may be *waived* altogether by an IRB, or the board can approve a consent procedure that alters, or does not include all of, the elements of informed consent. However, in such instances the board must make and document the following findings: (1) that the risk is no more than minimal, (2) that the waiver will not adversely affect the rights and welfare of the subject, (3) that the research could not practicably be carried out without the waiver or alteration, and (4) if possible, that subjects will be provided with additional pertinent information after participation.

Some projects could not be carried out if subjects had to give consent in advance. Other projects require that subjects be unaware of the exact nature of what is being studied if valid results are to be obtained. In a study of the effects of stress on health awareness and food consumption, for instance, it would not be possible to obtain valid results if subjects knew in advance that the effect of stress on their food choice was being measured. In still other experiments, particularly some research in social psychology, fully explaining the purpose of a study to subjects in advance may bias subjects' actions or responses. For instance, in a study of how the sequence of restaurant server actions affects dessert sales, customers' reactions to the two experimental manipulations could not be observed and measured without bias if they knew that they and their server were part of an experiment.

In each of these examples, the IRB either waived the consent requirement or approved procedures that altered some of the elements of consent. Although some information can be withheld in the consent process, risks must always be explained up front.

ASSESSMENT OF RISK VS. BENEFITS

The principle of beneficence is the basis of *risk/benefit assessment,* in which investigators, institutions, and IRBs all seek to ensure that any risks of harm are minimized and are reasonable in relation to anticipated benefits, if any, to subjects, and the importance of the knowledge that may reasonably be expected to result. We most often think of *physical risks,* such as might happen if subjects were asked to eat food without first determining whether potential subjects have allergies to the foods being used, or asking inexperienced subjects to drink a lot of alcohol. However, there are risks of other kinds harm that also can be quite serious. As Gallant noted, giving subjects false feedback about their mental health, attractiveness, or intelligence, or putting them into a stressful situation, or misleading them into behaving in a way that they may later regret may pose *psychological or emotional risks* to subjects. In such cases, IRBs want to know if the deception or stress is necessary, or if there is some way to get the same information without deception or stress. The study of behaviors or conditions considered stigmatizing in many groups may present *social risks.* For instance, people who cross-dress, use alcohol, use birth control, obtain abortions, attend AA or other self-help groups, or are HIV-positive may be up front about their behavior or membership, but others may want to keep such information about themselves private. If identifiable information, or even the fact of subjects' participation in a study of sensitive social issues, is inadvertently disclosed outside of the research context, relationships, employment, and reputation may all be damaged. Investigators therefore need to be very careful about how they recruit subjects and protect information about individuals' participation in the research as well as their data. "A fourth type of risk is *legal,* such as asking subjects about illicit drug use or other crimes they may have committed, without taking proper precautions to ensure that their responses are kept confidential, or, preferably, anonymous" (Gallant, 1996, pp. 17–19).

SELECTION OF SUBJECTS

The equitable *selection of subjects* is the application of the principle of justice. Simply put, it is not fair to ask one group of people to take all the risks and bear all of the inconvenience of research participation, only to have the benefits of the research go to others. It is not fair to use a group of people simply because they are handy or inexpensive to enroll, like prisoners, schoolchildren, college sophomore psychology students, residents of poor communities or countries, if they will bear the risks and inconvenience but will not benefit from participation, or if the benefits of the research itself will result in drugs, for instance, that the subjects or their countries will not be able to afford. For this reason, the Common Rule includes special rules to follow when subjects are prisoners, children, or pregnant women. In addition, IRBs are instructed to consider including in their membership one or more individuals who are knowledgeable about and experienced in working with these subjects and to be particularly cognizant of the special problems of research involving vulnerable populations.

Research about cardiac disease is an example where it turned out that some of the benefits of research devolved only to the class of individuals that participated— white men. As Davis (2006) explains, in 1994, in recognition of the need to balance the interest in fairly distributing the benefits of research with the interest in protecting the vulnerable, the National Institutes of Health required that women and minorities be included as subjects as well, unless there is a clear and compelling rationale and that inclusion is inappropriate with respect to the health of the subjects or the purpose of the research.

TYPES OF REVIEW
"EXEMPT"

"Many educational, behavioral, and social science studies [are 'research' and involve 'human subjects' as defined in the regulations, but] present little or no risk to the participants. Likewise, research involving existing data, medical records, and pathologic specimens usually has little, if any, associated risk, particularly if subject identifiers are removed from the data or specimens" (Prentiss & Oki, 2006, p. 93). Federal guidance states that an investigator should not have the authority to make an independent determination that research involving human subjects is exempt (*Exempt Research*, 1995). The Common Rule does not specify who may decide whether a project is exempt from the review requirement, but institutions have policies indicating who does have the authority to do so, so the prudent investigator will check his or her local institution's requirements.

In addition, institutions may have policies that require review of some projects that are exempt from the regulatory review requirement, a common one being student research that may not meet the federal definition of research. Although projects may be exempt from the review requirement, this does not relieve the investigator of responsibility for the welfare of subjects and their rights.

The exempt categories are as follows:

(1) Research conducted in established or commonly accepted educational settings, involving normal educational practices, such as
   (i) research on regular and special education instructional strategies, or
   (ii) research on the effectiveness of or the comparison among instructional techniques, curricula, or classroom management methods.
(2) Research involving the use of educational tests (cognitive, diagnostic, aptitude, achievement), survey procedures, interview procedures or observation of public behavior, unless:
   (i) information obtained is recorded in such a manner that human subjects can be identified, directly or through identifiers linked to the subjects; and
   (ii) any disclosure of the human subjects' responses outside the research could reasonably place the subjects at risk of criminal or civil liability or be damaging to the subjects' financial standing, employability, or reputation.
(3) Research involving the use of educational tests (cognitive, diagnostic, aptitude, achievement), survey procedures, interview procedures, or observation of public behavior that is not exempt under paragraph (b)(2) of this section, if:
   (i) the human subjects are elected or appointed public officials or candidates for public office; or

(ii) federal statute(s) require(s) without exception that the confidentiality of the personally identifiable information will be maintained throughout the research and thereafter.

(4) Research involving the collection or study of existing data, documents, records, pathological specimens, or diagnostic specimens, if these sources are publicly available or if the information is recorded by the investigator in such a manner that subjects cannot be identified, directly or through identifiers linked to the subjects.

(5) Research and demonstration projects which are conducted by or subject to the approval of department or agency heads, and which are designed to study, evaluate, or otherwise examine:

(i) Public benefit or service programs;

(ii) procedures for obtaining benefits or services under those programs;

(iii) possible changes in or alternatives to those programs or procedures; or

(iv) possible changes in methods or levels of payment for benefits or services under those programs.

(6) Taste and food quality evaluation and consumer acceptance studies,

(i) if wholesome foods without additives are consumed or

(ii) if a food is consumed that contains a food ingredient at or below the level and for a use found to be safe, or agricultural chemical or environmental contaminant at or below the level found to be safe, by the Food and Drug Administration or approved by the Environmental Protection Agency or the Food Safety and Inspection Service of the U.S. Department of Agriculture. (45 CFR 46.101(b))

Thus, many projects in food research may be exempt from the review, either under exemption 2 or 6. Once a study has been determined to be exempt from the review requirement, there is no requirement in the federal regulations for further IRB action, *unless* changes are made to the project after the determination is made. If an investigator wants to make changes once the project has been determined to be exempt from the review requirement, he or she *must* check with the appropriate authority at the institution to see whether further review may be required. Because exempt projects that last over a period of years may "morph" without the investigator realizing that what seem like small and logical alterations or "next steps" in the research will change the risk/benefit ratio for subjects, some IRBs require that a determination of exemption be made annually for projects lasting longer than a year.

Example: A project in which a faculty member studying how married couples made financial decisions interviewed spouses separately, promising both parties confidentiality and taking notes without identifiers, was determined to be exempt. When the researcher began teaching a research methods course he realized that he could obtain a larger sample and provide good practice for his students if they interviewed couples as well. He did not recognize that interviews conducted by students who had never done research interviews before might present risks not present when the interviewer was an experienced researcher and did not check with the IRB before he made this change to his research protocol. One of the students, anxious that he might fail to note important information, asked if he might tape record his interviews. Once again, the researcher changed his protocol without consulting the IRB. When a subject called the researchers to ask if he might have the tape recording of his wife's interview because she had just died of a heart attack and he wanted the tape of her voice as a memento, the researcher called the IRB very quickly! (D. R. Gallant, personal communication 2008).

"EXPEDITED"

An expedited review is an administrative one, conducted by the chair of an IRB or other members designated by the chair. These must be experienced reviewers who are voting members of the IRB. Only research that presents minimal risk of harm to the subjects may be reviewed by the expedited procedure. The research must also use procedures included in a list of categories appended to the federal regulations (Categories of Research, 1998). With these conditions met, the reviewer may exercise all of the authorities of the IRB except that he or she may not disapprove the research. It is important to realize that an expedited review is not "review lite," and all of the conditions for approval must be met before a project may be approved by this type of review.

The categories from the list appended to the federal regulations that are most commonly relevant to food research include:

(2) Collection of blood samples by finger stick, heel stick, ear stick, or venipuncture as follows:
   (a) from healthy, nonpregnant adults who weigh at least 110 pounds. For these subjects, the amounts drawn may not exceed 550 ml in an 8 week period and collection may not occur more frequently than 2 times per week; or
   (b) from other adults and children, considering the age, weight, and health of the subjects, the collection procedure, the amount of blood to be collected, and the frequency with which it will be collected. For these subjects, the amount drawn may not exceed the lesser of 50 ml or 3 ml per kg in an 8 week period and collection may not occur more frequently than 2 times per week.

(4) Collection of data through noninvasive procedures (not involving general anesthesia or sedation) routinely employed in clinical practice, excluding procedures involving x-rays or microwaves. Where medical devices are employed, they must be cleared/approved for marketing....

Examples: (a) physical sensors that are applied either to the surface of the body or at a distance and do not involve input of significant amounts of energy into the subject or an invasion of the subject's privacy; (b) weighing or testing sensory acuity; (c) magnetic resonance imaging; (d) electrocardiography, electroencephalography, thermography, detection of naturally occurring radioactivity, electroretinography, ultrasound, diagnostic infrared imaging, doppler blood flow, and echocardiography; (e) moderate exercise, muscular strength testing, body composition assessment, and flexibility testing where appropriate given the age, weight, and health of the individual.

(5) Research involving materials (data, documents, records, or specimens) that have been collected, or will be collected solely for nonresearch purposes (such as medical treatment or diagnosis). (NOTE: Some research in this category may be exempt from the HHS regulations for the protection of human subjects. 45 CFR 46.101(b)(4). This listing refers only to research that is not exempt.)

(6) Collection of data from voice, video, digital, or image recordings made for research purposes.

(7) Research on individual or group characteristics or behavior (including, but not limited to, research on perception, cognition, motivation, identity, language, communication, cultural beliefs or practices, and social behavior) or research employing survey, interview, oral history, focus group, program evaluation, human factors evaluation, or quality assurance methodologies. (NOTE: Some research in this category may be exempt from the HHS regulations for the protection of human subjects. 45 CFR 46.101(b)(2) and (b)(3) This listing refers only to research that is not exempt or (Categories of Research, 1998).

"FULL COMMITTEE"

IRBs have differing policies regarding which projects must be reviewed at a convened meeting, but all require that the full board review studies presenting risk that is judged to be more than minimal. IRBs also differ widely in how often they meet and how often the investigator is invited, or required, to attend when his or her project is being reviewed. The inexperienced investigator is well advised to check the local submission guidelines and deadlines for application at the outset of planning a project in order to minimize the risk of delay due to IRB review requirements.

An agenda and all of the materials related to each application to be considered at a given meeting must be sent to the members well in advance of the meeting so that members have a chance to review those materials and prepare their questions and suggestions. Typically, one member will present a brief description of the study, indicating questions, concerns, and suggestions for revisions. A general discussion follows, in which other members voice any questions, concerns, or revisions that the initial presenter did not address. General discussion and a vote follow. Most boards try to operate by consensus whenever possible, but the regulations require that a vote be recorded, as well as a summary of the discussion of any controverted issues and their resolution, and the basis for requiring changes in or disapproving research. After the meeting, the IRB communicates its decision to the investigator. If the IRB decides to disapprove a research activity, it must include in its written notification a statement of the reasons for its decision and give the investigator an opportunity to respond in person or in writing.

If the board approves a study contingent upon changes being made, the research cannot proceed until those changes have been made and the revised protocol has been reviewed and approved by the board. According to the regulations, such changes to the protocol must be reviewed at a convened meeting. However, if the board has written policies and procedures for minor changes that can be approved by expedited review, it may be able to have the primary reviewer or a staff member approve the changes. For example, specific changes that can be easily verified, for example, "Discrepancies in the application, recruitment poster, and consent form regarding the amount of time participation requires and the amount to be paid should be corrected," or "Debriefing form should be written at a 6th to 8th grade reading level," may be covered by such a policy and will not have to be returned to a meeting for approval. More complicated changes requiring new input by the investigator will likely have to be reviewed by the full board at another meeting, for example, "The protocol should be revised to explain how and when compensation is awarded," or "The protocol should be revised to explain what will be done should a participant express or exhibit distress related to participation."

INVESTIGATOR RESPONSIBILITIES FOR THE PROTECTION OF HUMAN SUBJECTS

Once a project has been reviewed and approved by an IRB, or determined to be exempt, the investigator continues to be responsible for the protection of the subjects in his or her study and continues to be obligated to the IRB in the following ways:

- Obtaining informed consent in keeping with the plan reviewed and approved by the IRB.
- Obtaining approval from the IRB for any changes to the previously approved research plan *before* implementation, except when the changes are necessary to

eliminate apparent immediate hazards to subjects. Minor changes can, and often are, quickly approved by expedited review. Some IRBs have specific forms for requesting amendments. Others will accept e-mail requests for simple amendments but may ask for a revised protocol to review if there are many changes, and if the changes will significantly alter the subjects' experience or change the risk/benefit assessment.

■ Obtaining continuing review from the IRB on time. Many IRBs now have software that can send out automatic reminders to investigators as the approval expiration date nears, however it is the investigator's responsibility to make sure that human subjects aren't participating and their identifiable data are not being used without current IRB approval.

■ Promptly reporting to the IRB any unanticipated problems that involve risk to subjects or others. Examples include any breaches of confidentiality, loss of identifiable data, new risks that were not mentioned in the application when the study was reviewed and approved, and reports in the literature or other findings that indicate an unexpected change to the risk or potential benefits of the study. For example, one researcher paying clients at a senior citizens' center to participate in a brief experiment had multiple subjects write their names, addresses, and social security numbers on a payment record instead of providing individual forms. One alert participant reported the practice to the senior center staff and the local police! Another investigator discovered that a programming error had enabled subsequent subjects to view data entered by a previous subject.

■ Promptly reporting to the IRB any research-related harm. Minor, transitory harms that are expected and have been mentioned in the consent process and the protocol that the IRB approved, such as reddened skin as a result of having monitoring electrodes applied, do not need to be reported. But if, for instance, subjects have allergic reactions, or a breach of confidentiality results in harm to a subject's relationships, these should be immediately reported.

SUMMARY

No one has claimed that research ethics and IRB review make research easier or quicker, but they certainly contribute to better research, the well-being of people who volunteer to be research subjects, and to societal trust in and support of scientific research. Awareness of conflicts of interest, financial and otherwise, careful and honest record keeping, and accurate attribution of sources all add value to the final research report, which in the long run benefits society and the individual researcher. Anyone who has been involved in an investigation of allegations of research misconduct can testify to the unpleasantness and cost (in time, money, anxiety) for all involved.

Experienced and capable researchers with the best of intentions and genuine concern for the well-being of their human subjects may miss considerations relevant to the interests of the subjects. Although in the midst of getting a project under way, IRB review may, to the researcher, seem like (and be!) yet another hoop to jump through, it is well to keep in mind that, at its best, it is also the process of obtaining thoughtful feedback from concerned and experienced individuals who believe in and are dedicated to research.

4 REVIEWING THE LITERATURE OF FOOD

The literature review—"a redundant chore or necessary step? An ordeal to be endured or a fulfilling learning experience?"

Adams and Schvanaveldt (1985)

Most research studies begin with a review of the existing literature on a topic. The term *literature review* can be used to refer to both the actual section of the document where the review appears and to the process that is used to obtain the information that goes into this section of the document. Fink (1998) defines the literature review as a "systematic, explicit, and reproducible method for identifying, evaluating, and interpreting the existing body of recorded work produced by researchers, scholars and practitioners" (p. 3). According to Mills, Gay, and Airasian (2006), the literature review is a critical step that "involves the systematic identification, location, and analysis of documents containing information related to the research problem" (p. 39). Some of the most common sources of material for a review of the literature come from scholarly (refereed) journals, books, conference proceedings, and bibliographies. The basic purpose of the literature review is to find out as much of significance as possible on your topic before you begin to do your own research. By performing a thorough literature review you will become familiar with what has already been accomplished in the area that you wish to find out more about, familiarize your readers with the most current state of knowledge in the field, and set the stage for the contribution you hope to make.

Research of all types is based on what is already known about the world. All research has, as its basis, a footing on what other researchers have already contributed. To omit the step of surveying existing research on a topic makes for poor work to follow and is a false economy of time. (There is discussion in the research world about when is the most appropriate time to do the review of literature; we will address this later in this unit). The review of literature allows you to develop a working knowledge of your topic and gives you an idea about the nature and scope of the activity that has already been done in the area in which you wish to work. The literature review should illuminate the seminal ideas in your area of interest, give you an idea of the current trends in research and practice, and brief you on areas of controversy within your topic. Perhaps most importantly, a good review of the literature will allow you to see any areas that have been neglected by previous researchers. Those gaps in the published knowledge on a topic represent opportunities for new research, perhaps by you. Adams and Schvanaveldt (1985) make the point that the "literature review is a key tool in telling [us] what is new, important, believable and useful" (p. 50). Reviewing the literature will also allow the researcher to define terms, refine her or his topic, make sensible decisions about methodology, and serve as a reference when it comes to analyze the data that has been collected for the project.

The literature review is not the place to create new theory, nor a place for the author to posit new ideas, but a place to sum up what is already known about a certain topic. It can be argued that there is a place for new interpretations of extant research in the literature review, but in most iterations, the literature review is about showing what the current state of affairs is in the area the researcher is interested in expanding. That being said, it is certainly legitimate, even desirable in some instances, to indicate your reaction to the work of others included in your review of literature, especially if the positions of established researchers contradict the tenor of research you intend to carry out or the hypotheses you wish to prove or disprove. A well-written literature review will provide a justification for further incursions into your topic. In addition, a good review of the literature will both summarize and synthesize the best and most current scholarship in an area of research. If you have done a good job of this step in the research process, your final research product should be "well conceived, integrative and justifiable" (Adams and Schvanaveldt, 1985, p. 74).

Some scholars conceptualize the literature review as "a conversation with the literature" (van den Hoonaard and van den Hoonaard, 2008, 187). This is a useful metaphor as it justifies the types and amounts of literature that should be included. If you find yourself on a tangent or not in keeping with a conversational flow, you may need to rein in the writing. Ely, Downing, and Anzul (1997) suggest this conversational approach as a way to both understand what the literature is saying and respond to the question of how it relates to your study.

DO I REALLY HAVE TO READ *ALL* THIS JUNK—CAN'T I JUST GO OUT AND DO MY RESEARCH?

The answer, unfortunately, is yes; you do have to read all this junk. Until you have an idea of what researchers before you have discovered, you are really in no position to do your own research. With most topics there will be so much material that you will feel overwhelmed. This is a perfectly normal experience that all researchers face, sometimes for every project throughout their careers. One of the things that novice researchers feel most overwhelmed about is the sheer volume of the material that is out there. There is a plethora of material out there to read, and since the advent of the Internet, it seems to grow exponentially with every passing day. What is unfortunate is that the chaff is disproportionate to the amount of grain, but you will develop a discerning eye for what will be relevant to your topic and what will not, how to recognize the research that is gold and that which is lead.

In addition to the topical material you will need to read, another consideration is the reading you may need to do on the methods you will use in your research. One of the key components of research literature, though not always included in the literature review section of a research report, is the method or methodology section. Those of you writing a dissertation or thesis will have an entire chapter devoted to methodology and though you may cover the literature of methodology in that section rather than in the review of literature, you will need to do the research on the topic. So as you do your reading for your literature review, keep your eyes open for material that will help you with the methodology as well as the topical foundations. In addition, by reading in methodology as well as topic, you will become better able to evaluate the research reports you do read while preparing the literature review. By having an extended familiarity with the methods used in the research you are citing, you will be able to better justify what you are proposing to do in your own research.

There is no substitution for doing a great deal of preliminary reading, but that does not mean that it cannot be done in an efficient manner. By developing a discerning eye for the literature and keeping in mind the idea of relevance to what you propose to do, you should be able to keep the task of reviewing the literature manageable. The material in this chapter should help you use your time as efficiently as possible when conducting the literature review.

WHAT IS THE LITERATURE?

Broadly speaking, the literature is everything in written and oral form that is available and useful to your project. Needless to say, for most topics this would be an overwhelming, if not crushing, amount of literature to review. Don't panic. In the pages that follow, we will share some techniques for winnowing the amount of literature that you will have to read and consider in order to get your project done. The literature review is important because the literature is the primary domain of material that has been created specifically for the transmission of ideas, theory, and knowledge in an area of study.

RECORDING WHAT YOU FIND DURING THE LITERATURE SEARCH

How you want to record what you find is a matter of personal preference. Electronic databases or files are the most time efficient way to approach storage, but various older technologies like photocopies of everything or note cards or some other variant of pen and paper work just fine. You can make the electronic equivalent of index cards for all your references with your word processor and record all the details you deem pertinent about each source on the "card." If you are intimidated by computers, or just don't care for them, index cards are practical, cheap, and widely available. They have the distinct disadvantage of not being easily backed up with the click of a button, but they are easy to rummage through to find bits of information you are looking for and are easy to sort when you are in the initial stages of organizing your information. Some researchers use composition books or loose-leaf binders to record and store data. A popular way to collect data is to make a photocopy or printout of every article or book chapter you intend to use as a reference, making sure that at least one of the pages contains a complete bibliographic citation. This method has the advantage of being exceedingly complete, but involves an extreme amount of paper, tends to be expensive and resource-intensive, and may entail tedious searches through mounds of paper if a highly detailed organizational system doesn't accompany it. There are endless variations on paper methods and, as you will see later, there are some hybrid methods that have great efficacy, even in this digital age. If you decide on a paper method, especially note cards with your own comments on them, you may want to make a second set of materials that are kept separate from the originals in case of some catastrophe.

If you decide on an electronic format for your research materials, you will do well to break them down into the smallest units possible and store each unit in its own folder. At some point, you may want to collapse many smaller units into fewer larger ones, but sorting through huge computer files to find what you want to reference can be quite tedious. Keeping hierarchies of folders will help you locate information efficiently. For example, you might keep a folder of articles related to your method choice and subfolders related to studies that employ the method you want to use and another with commentary on problems or limitations of the method. Always use multiple forms of backup if you are using your computer as your storage area for your notes and writing. For example, as we wrote this book, we constantly backed up to a mainframe server and our individual personal computers and kept a copy on a flash drive as well. If one of the methods had failed, we would not have had to re-create the project from scratch. You may not have access to a server for storage, but try to constantly back up to at least two places while you do your research; be what is known in Britain as a "belt and braces" kind of person. Increasingly, commercially available software such as Endnote and RefWorks can help to manage your literature. Microsoft Word 2007 now has a "References" tab and can maintain a database of sources you use in your writing.

WHAT TO KEEP

When you are making notes for your literature review there are a number of details that all researchers agree are critical. Every time you read a piece of literature and decide that you are keeping it for reference use, you should record the critical information about it. The biggest favor you can do for yourself is to do this as you go along. This kind of information can be very hard to go back and re-create, especially if you are searching in databases in your school's library. We can't emphasize enough the need to document your resources as you continue the research process. What is accessible to you one day is often gone the next. When using online resources, save or print your desired article immediately, noting the source of it somewhere in the file. This process will not only save you many hours of backtracking when it comes time to write up the research, but you will be doing much of the tedious detail work as you go along rather than facing hours of it at once when it comes time to turn out the finished product. One of the authors of this book, early on in the research process for his dissertation, found a quote that stayed in his mind the entire time he was researching and writing, but when it came time to use it in the finished document, he had only the quote on a scrap of paper and no way to find its source. While no one quote makes or breaks a document, the lack of a particularly useful piece of data will be very frustrating to you as an author. When you find a piece of useful information, record the following about it:

- The author(s)
- Title of the book, journal article, monograph, or Web page
- Date of publication
- Publisher and place of publication
- If it is a chapter in an edited volume, the editor of the book and the author of the chapter as well as the page numbers
- If it is a journal article, the title of the journal, the volume and issue numbers, and the page numbers
- If it is a monograph, the author, the publisher, and any other publishing details that would make it easy to find if another researcher needs to confirm your information
- If it is a Web site, as much titular information as would help another researcher locate the information on the Web page and the date you accessed the page
- For specific quotes, you need to record the page number where the quote occurs. (Blaxter, Hughes, and Tight, 2001)

THE BIBLIOGRAPHY IN THE REVIEW OF LITERATURE

One of the critical components of a literature review is the bibliographical piece. As you work on research articles, research proposals, theses, and dissertations, your bibliography will be a critical component of your credibility in the academic world. Students are frequently worried that being a brilliant original thinker is the most important impression they have to convey to their advisor or teacher. This is simply untrue. Most faculty members know it is unlikely that your research will consist of all original insights and discoveries. What they, and future readers of your research, will want to know is from what influences did your ideas originate, in what theoretical base are they anchored, and what are you contributing to the knowledge base. All of your writing needs to be carefully annotated in the sense of having sound bibliographical foundations.

As a practical matter, find out early in the process what citation style is going to be required for your finished work (paper, journal article, dissertation, etc.) and keep your citations in that format from the beginning. This will save you the step of reformatting your resources when you get to the end of the research process. There are many good bibliographic software programs available that will make this task even simpler. One of the most important purchases you can make at the beginning of your research career is a good piece of bibliographic software. A quick browse of the Internet at this writing shows at least a dozen different acceptable ones ranging in price from very cheap to moderately expensive. Many schools have access to a preferred brand already available through their computing services or information technology department, and if you are writing and storing your writing on a school server, you can use it free of charge. This is often a good strategy if you haven't already learned to use a different system as there is frequently free tutorial help and other support available to help you learn the system. The better versions of this software automatically format your citations in your preferred format, such as APA or MLA, and will also import them directly from your database and store them in a designated file already formatted and in alphabetical order, saving you hours of very nit-picky work when it comes time to turn out your document.

TYPES OF LITERATURE

We said earlier that the literature is everything in written and oral form that is available and useful to your project. There are three basic types of literature you will come across when doing your research; primary literature, secondary literature, and tertiary literature (Anslem Library, n.d.). A primary source of literature is literature that has been created firsthand from data collected by the researcher. Firsthand, or primary, literature encompasses a wide range of material. In a historical study, primary literature might be the agricultural records of foodstuffs maintained by a governmental agency or a diary kept by a farm wife or a journal article that describes the results of an experiment conducted by the authors of a nutritional study. These are considered primary sources because they are firsthand descriptors of data recorded by the people who performed the research or actually lived the experience they are describing. A secondary source is any type of material that was written by someone who was not an observer of the action or a party to the research. Some types of secondary research, such as abstracts in databases, are very useful in locating primary sources. Secondary sources can be useful in filling holes in your knowledge of a topic, but primary sources are generally considered the gold standard of reference in research. Tertiary sources of information are sources that are compilations of other sources. Sometimes they can be useful in giving the researcher a quick definition of a term or to point the way to a useful primary or secondary source, but they are generally unacceptable as sources of material upon which your research will be based.

There is another type of literature that deserves mention as it is gold for any researcher—the review article or bibliographic essay. Such a piece is a (usually) peer-reviewed summary of published research on a topic. So if you're writing about articles linking chocolate to health outcomes, a review article or bibliographic essay on that topic will list and discuss the major studies that have linked chocolate and health. Such an article, like "Food Studies: A Multidisciplinary Guide to the Literature" (Deutsch and Miller, 2007) provides a useful—and legitimate—shortcut in the literature review.

EVALUATION OF SOURCES IN THE LITERATURE REVIEW

Quality of source material in the literature review is critical. As noted earlier in this section, there is much chaff to be sorted from the wheat. There are a number of criteria by which you should evaluate the material you are going to include in your review of the literature. What follows is a list of considerations when thinking about the quality of the material you are using as a foundation for your own research:

■ Who is the author? Is the person writing the article a known expert in the field? What is their institutional affiliation and academic background? If you are reading the diary of a seventeenth-century chef, the affiliation question may be moot, but if you are reading an article from a nutrition journal, this is a legitimate question to ask. Some organizations and journal titles adopt names that hide their true purpose of advancing a specific social or political agenda. Research into the background or goals of an institution may save embarrassment later in the process.

- Substantiation—who are your source's sources? Does the article cite major sources on the topic and include citations up to the time the piece is written? In short, did the author of the piece you are citing do a diligent literature review?

- Journals—refereed or not? Refereed journals are periodicals that subject material to a process known as "peer review" before they accept it for publication. People who have knowledge in the field are asked to review a submission for its suitability for inclusion in the journal, hence the concept of "peer review." This process generally ensures a minimum level of scholarship and an adherence to accepted standards of research and behavior of the discipline in material that is published in the journal. Most scholarly refereed journals exist to report primary research in the discipline they represent. They tend to be excellent resources for your literature review. Refereed journals in food studies include *Food, Culture and Society* and *Food & Foodways*, both excellent sources of primary research. Journals are different than magazines, which exist for the purpose of entertaining and informing their readers. There can be material of excellent quality in popular magazines, but special care must be taken when considering when to use it in one's review of literature. There may be instances in food studies research where popular literature would be used as resource material, such as when a researcher looks at the recipes published in *Bon Appetit* magazine and *Gourmet* magazine in the 1970s in order to try to determine how home cooking trends were changing during that period.

- Timeliness—is the material you are reading up-to-date or is it dated? While all good research is based on the research that came before it, the frontiers of research are being expanded all the time. That is why most journals are published multiple times a year. While there are some areas, especially historical research, where you may want to emphasize older material in your literature review, it is generally best to have your review reflect the most recent scholarship in the field.

- Opinion or fact? One of the truisms of research is that researchers are supposed to deal only with facts, not opinions. But it is often hard to determine what is fact and what is opinion. Many postmodernist thinkers will argue that there are no facts, only opinions. While this may be a stretch, it is true that much "factual" writing is colored with unacceptable levels of bias and some is intentionally written to support some agenda. Food research is especially prone to bias as a number of forces with much at stake—food companies, advocacy organizations, farmers and food producers, restaurants and retailers—have an interest in the research produced. As a reader of research, you will have to read with a critical eye in order to make sure your base pool of material is as bias-free as possible. Research that contains terminology designed to strike emotional chords may be suspect in this regard.

HOW BROAD A SCOPE?

The question always arises, how broad or narrow should a review of literature be? In the words of Mills, Gay, and Airasian (2006, p. 40), "bigger does not mean better" when it comes to the scope of the literature review. The literature review usually takes a considerable amount of time and effort to conduct and because of the level of effort it represents, it is tempting to include everything you have found, even items that are only tangentially related. There is also the fear that when the literature review is presented to your professor or published in some format, that it will be pointed out that you have missed something significant, so everything goes in to forestall that possibility. This kitchen-sink strategy is generally not a good idea. If you have already written your research questions or your hypotheses, then use them as a guide to focusing what you are going to include in your review. If you are working on the topic of Caribbean foods you may find something really great in Sidney Mintz's *Sweetness and Power* and want to put it in because Mintz is the seminal food scholar, especially when it comes to the study of food in the Caribbean and your instructor has likely mentioned him in class. Unless the reference is truly on target for your specific topic, the reference is likely better omitted.

Creswell (2005) suggests mapping out the potential literature you will need to look at in advance of conducting the literature review. This exercise, he suggests, will help you to identify the main areas of inquiry, limit your review to what can reasonably be read (after all, a truly comprehensive review is impossible), and help you to avoid reading on tangents that take you away from your main topic. For example, imagine you were developing a research project on the intellectual history of food studies. Even before beginning research we know there are a few baskets of literature that must be included in a literature review:

- Intellectual history methods
- Seminal works in food studies
- The intellectual histories of other fields such as women's studies, cultural studies, and fashion studies
- Food's role in other disciplinary studies such as health and nutrition, anthropology, sociology, history, and the humanities

With these categories as a starting point you can map out your search to be sure you're covering the major areas. At the end of this chapter is a sample literature map in food studies and a template for you to create your own.

Some areas of food studies research have been much more heavily researched than others. For example, themes like identity, authenticity, consumption, agency, and sustainability are food studies staples. When working in one of the more highly researched areas, you will want to try to limit your review to those works with the most direct connection to your topic. On a related note, if you are working in one of the more highly researched areas of food studies, make sure you use the literature review to stake out your own territory. Just because a topic has been researched a good deal doesn't mean there isn't more to do, but you will have to be more strategic in figuring out something novel to research and present.

The worth of a topic is not always proportional to the amount of research that has already been done on it, but when you are investigating an area where little has been done you may have a harder time finding literature with direct bearing on your topic. In this instance you may have to review some literature that is not directly about your topic, but is related to your topic in the sense that it may offer some meaningful ideas about how to study your topic or frame your research questions. If you pick a little-researched topic you will have to be much more creative about how you go about searching for literature and how you relate it to the topic at hand. For example, if you're researching cultural uses of acai berries and aren't finding much in the literature, a good strategy would be to consider other plants and functional foods for the literature review and see what information can be applied to the subject at hand.

HOW LONG SHOULD THE REVIEW OF LITERATURE BE?

There is no exact answer to this question. The ideal literature review is long enough to be effective and succinct enough to be readable. The literature review is the basis of your research and should be proportionate to what you are discovering and reporting as a result of your work. One idea frequently used by beginning researchers is to look at the work of others who have attempted similar research and see what they have considered long enough and then use this as a gauge. This is a crude instrument, but it may be helpful as a guide until your research is fleshed out enough that you can come back and fine-tune your review. If you are using this book as a guide or manual toward writing a thesis or dissertation, you can go online and see what dissertations and theses have been successfully defended recently and see how they have handled the literature review. Databases like ProQuest have the full text of thousands of dissertations available online and some diligent Internet searching will likely turn up other sites as well. If your advisor is young enough or new enough to academia, you can likely find their dissertation online and see what she or he felt was enough. Consider the format of the finished piece. A literature review in a dissertation or scholarly book may require fifty or sixty pages, whereas one in a journal article may need to be kept to within a few manuscript pages.

A good idea to keep in mind is that the review of literature is only the first step in a long research process. Don't give all your energy to doing the literature review only to run out of energy for the rest of the process. With the exception of a comprehensive literature review article on a topic for a journal, the idea of the literature review is to ground your research, not to *be* the research. As with most things, there is a reasonable middle ground between not enough and too much, and you should seek to find it. Some researchers feel a long list of references speaks to their erudition and others feel the need to document every shred of information that may have influenced their thinking about the topic. The best thing you can do is keep the term *relevance* in mind. If you are wondering if a certain document has a place in your literature review, consider its relevance to the research you want to conduct. If it is important, then keep it in. If you are sitting looking at a piece of literature and wondering where it fits or how to spin or tweak it so it fits someplace in your review, then it likely can be omitted without harm to the quality of your review.

FORMS THE LITERATURE REVIEW CAN TAKE

Literature reviews can take various forms and be hybrids of these various forms. Some literature reviews are primarily descriptive in nature, others are summative in nature, and yet others delve into critical evaluations of the literature in question. Descriptive literature reviews are helpful when you find very few items in journals and books and other resources that are directly relevant to your topic. Often when a researcher is breaking new ground in research, for example studying a community, group, or phenomenon that has never or only lightly been written about previously, there will be little literature that bears directly on her/his topic. In this instance, the literature review needs to focus on topics and information that illuminate the process the researcher is intending to use rather than on all previous research in the area. What are needed are examples of ways this type of topic has already been approached and how you, the researcher, intend to model (or not model) your research in this mold. You can be accepting of previous styles or reject them as inadequate to your needs, but a thorough review of the literature will reinforce either argument you intend to make (Student Learning Support, n.d.).

Undergraduate and graduate student researchers commonly use summative literature reviews. This type of literature review covers a wide array of literature, categorizes it, and then offers a summation of the literature according to the categorization scheme the researcher has devised. A well-executed summative review will cover a large number of sources and viewpoints depending on the topic chosen. This type of literature review should take the reader through the material somewhat briskly without omitting any key points. When skillfully presented, this style of literature review can be an extremely interesting read, even to the layperson, as it covers the important points put forth in the literature without spending too much time in the minutia of the topic (Paltridge and Starfield, 2007).

The most intensive style of literature review is the critical evaluative style. In this type of literature review, the reviewer must not only gather, categorize, and sum up the relative material in the topical area, but she/he must then critique it with an eye toward quality of evidence, convincingness of argument, validity, and so on. When using the critical style the author has to be well versed in the theory and methods employed in the literature she or he is critiquing (Paltridge and Starfield, 2007).

ORGANIZING THE LITERATURE REVIEW

Literature reviews can be written in a few different ways. If you follow Creswell's literature map, the easiest way may be to let each category of the literature map represent a section of the literature review. Some other approaches may be:

- Chronological. Useful for showing how thinking on a topic changed over time or how new findings contributed to the discourse. For example, in a paper exploring the origins and evolution of Nouvelle Cuisine it would be useful to present restaurant reviews and cookbooks on the subject chronologically.
- Trends and/or themes. Often the literature can be grouped thematically. A paper on humane meat production may group literature variously by themes of animal rights and animal welfare, socially responsible marketing, and technical aspects of slaughter.
- Methodologies. Often the *type* of study may be a good organizing system for the literature. For example, a project on the experiences of immigrant restaurant workers may organize the literature by workplace ethnographies, policy papers, interview studies, and labor market/industry research. (Adapted from Anslem Library, n.d.)

ANALYZING, ORGANIZING AND REPORTING THE LITERATURE

Once you have gathered a significant amount of material, you can begin to organize it. This step need not wait until you have all your literature collected; in fact, you will likely find you need to go back and get more literature in certain areas once you have begun to organize and analyze what you have. At this point the outline doesn't need to be highly detailed, but it should cover all the main points you think the review of literature will cover. The following organizational scheme has been adapted from Mills, Gay, and Airasian (2006) for use in a food studies literature review.

ANALYZING THE LITERATURE

Once you have collected some of your literature, you need to think about how you want to arrange it topically within your organizational plan for the review. Get out a piece of paper and brainstorm potential topic headings that will support various areas of the research that you want to perform. Try to think in terms of headings and subheadings if you are good at visualizing these kinds of things in your head. Once you have done that you are ready to begin to sort your references.

An easy way to sort your references is by what we call the pile system. Whether you use physical piles of cards or articles or whether you use virtual piles on your computer, the system works exactly the same. You take each reference you have collected and label it with one of the topical headings (or, in Web 2.0 terms, *tags*) from your brainstorming session. As you go through your literature, you may find that some new topic headings arise, and that is fine: create a new pile for each of those headings. Put your labeled cards, photocopies, or abstracts in the pile that corresponds to the topic heading. If you have done your saving on your computer, then you drag or copy and paste your references into a folder with that topic's heading. Do not despair if there are references that do not fit into one of the piles or if you have a number of piles that have only one item in them. Don't try to force material into piles; initially, assign an item only to the pile that is a natural fit. Once you have gotten all your material distributed, go back to your orphan material and make a decision about each piece of research. Does it fit in one of the bigger piles? Is it more tangential than core? Did it look good in the gathering process, but now it seems superfluous? Or is it unique but important enough to warrant its own mention? Once you have made these decisions, store your remainders of research for another project or put them aside in case you decide later that you do need that piece after all. Don't discard the remainders right away, though you may want to do so after you have delivered the finished piece of research. If you have lots of orphan pieces of research or you have small piles in topical areas that you think are key to creating the foundation for your research, you may want to stop and think about the reason why. Did you use ineffective keywords in your search? Is there something wrong with your topical headings? Did the direction of the literature review change as you began to learn more about the topic? You may need to revisit the literature search and collect some entirely new material.

A common mistake of beginning researchers is to try to shoehorn everything they find in the literature search into the review. If you are doing a comprehensive search you will find many things that are fascinating, but tangential to the task at hand. That is a natural part of the research process. As we said before, part of the review process is to separate the beans from the hulls; by doing so you will be creating a superior product. Your review will be much stronger if you only include the pieces that mostly clearly support your research goals. Oftentimes during the search we find something so beautiful or moving or interesting that we are bound and determined to use it in our review, even though it doesn't really fit in the project we are currently working on. When that occurs, keep it—that is what files are for. As your career as a researcher moves forward, there will likely be a place for it and you will have ready access to it.

ORGANIZATION WITHIN HEADINGS AND SUBHEADINGS

Once you have gotten your piles established, go to them individually and see what the main points of each piece of research are. (This is where doing your own abstracting of each piece of research will come in handy). When multiple references say much the same thing, you can go over them each individually, which reinforces your case nicely, but you don't have to have a separate line or paragraph for each one if you think your review is getting a little wordy. Summarize what is similar in all the references and put that information in the line or paragraph as a summation and then reference all the authors at the end of the passage.

DON'T JUST LIST AND SUMMARIZE, GIVE CONTEXT AND PERSPECTIVE

Your literature review needs to be more than just a recitation of who said what and when. You should make an attempt to succinctly and concisely explain the implications and ramifications of the research you cite if you possibly can. Do not omit research that contradicts what your research is trying to explicate. Try to explain why contradictory studies have a different perspective or result than what you are attempting to put forth.

ORDER YOUR HEADINGS FOR GREATEST EFFECT

The general rule of thumb for organization in the review of literature is to go from the general to the specific, though this is not a hard-and-fast rule by any means. In a historical study, you might want to organize your review chronologically, going from the oldest source material or interpretations to the most current. The beginning of the literature review should be concerned with topical overviews, defining terms and any other type of general material that is pertinent. As you proceed through the review, you should be focusing ever more tightly on the topic at hand. Visualize the literature review as a funnel or inverted pyramid, with the material concentrating from the general to specific. If you are proposing a hypothesis in the next section of your research document, then the material that most strongly supports it should be at the end of the literature review.

CONCLUSION

The literature review needs a conclusion. Don't leave the reader hanging. Always sum up the major points of the review in a way that leaves the reader clear about the foundations that you have chosen to support your research. The length of the conclusion will depend on the length of the review, but if you have solidly laid out your material in the body of the review, a pithy conclusion will serve you best. It's a good idea to use the conclusion of the literature review to set the stage for your research that will follow. For example, "While we have seen that much has been written on the community, environmental, and economic aspects of sustainable agriculture, comparatively little has been written on its consumer acceptance as a component of the marketing concept."

PROBLEMS OF THE LITERATURE REVIEW

Of the many technical issues that can arise while reviewing the literature for your research project, three seem especially common among novice researchers. The first is not finding enough literature directly related to your topic; the second is finding too much literature on your topic; and the third is doing the literature review only to discover that someone has beaten you to the punch and has produced a masterwork on your topic (Blaxter, Hughes, and Tight, 2001). This section will address all three of these issues.

Problem One—there has been nothing written on my topic. Congratulations, you have virgin soil to plow and no one else has realized what a great research topic has been out there just waiting to be discovered. We say this somewhat tongue-in-cheek because originality of this level is rare, even at the most rarified levels of academia. But the field of food studies is young and expanding, and there are new opportunities in the field. Should you have such a topic in mind and are bound and determined to plow the virgin soil, be aware you have some very hard work ahead of you. One of the problems of virgin territory is the lack of support you can expect from your advisor or editor as they are not going to be able to direct you to useful literature and other resources that young researchers often need while working on their research project. Another problem associated with virgin soil is the fact that not only will you have a hard time finding foundational material in the literature, but when you do you will often have to explain why it is relevant to your topic and how you intend to manipulate it in order to make it functional for your purposes.

To give you an example, in a recent thesis project a student was examining the problem of the sales and marketing of healthy foods in sports arenas. As you might imagine, there was little literature on this topic, especially in refereed journals. This was not surprising as most academic journals on sports management are of fairly recent origin and thus far have devoted very little space to the issue of food marketing in sports venues. Nutrition journals tend to have good information on healthy foods, but again, very little on the marketing of it and virtually nothing about sports arenas. When it came to researching the marketing of healthy foods in sports arenas, the student was in fact plowing virgin soil. What we did was refocus our literature search in areas that were similar, but where we could reasonably argue that the points the authors made were relational, because our research was similar in tenor and method, just in slightly different topic area. We wound up looking at how healthy foods were marketed in other market segments and how food marketing was done in sports arenas, and we had to incorporate a certain amount of material from nonrefereed sources because the topic was so new. But by framing our literature review in terms of what had already been written about and what it had in common with related topics, we were able to write a reasonably strong literature review in an area that heretofore had been only very lightly covered in academic journals.

Problem Two—there is too much information about my topic. Where do I start? What do include? What do I exclude? It is perfectly normal to be overwhelmed by the amount of literature that has been published about a given topic. When using a search engine for some preliminary research the problem is rarely that only a few hits are returned, rather the problem is that millions of hits are returned. The question for the researcher then becomes, how do I winnow the literature down to what is relevant and appropriate?

The approach to take here is somewhat philosophical in nature. Keep in mind that this is a project that is only a part of your life and that no matter how much time you can devote to it, you will never cover all the material that is out there that is related to the topic. This being realized, you will have to become more selective about what you include and be more liberal in what you omit. As you begin to do your reading talk with your advisor about what she or he feels are the key issues and what is more tangential. If you are not good at skimming articles to determine if they contain useful material, some practice in this skill will be very useful. Think about putting some more restrictive limits on what you want to report about for your finished product. Limiting what to read and report on is not a bad thing. It is better to do a comprehensive job on a limited topic than a poor one on an extensive topic. Do not feel bad that you must limit what you do; very few of us are Edward Gibbon and can write a comprehensive history of the decline and fall of the Roman Empire. Most of us will do a better job if we find a tightly focused area of research to read about and do research in. A history of the lemon meringue pie in the American South will be much easier to write than a world history of pastry.

Problem Three—someone has beaten me to the punch; what I thought was such a great idea has already been done to death. Given your topic, this may or may not actually be the case. If you honestly can't think of a new spin or take on a topic, then it may indeed be time to move to plan B. For example, there has been very little new work on the baguette since Kaplan's exhaustive history (Kaplan, 1996). But in many cases if you look at your proposed sample, population, site, instrument, or focus area, you may find that what you are proposing does vary enough from what has been done and may add valuable knowledge to the field. If what you propose doesn't vary enough, could your project be modified in such a way that it remains of interest to you and still adds something new to the realm of knowledge?

A DIFFERENT APPROACH TO THE REVIEW OF LITERATURE

There are some who feel that in a purely exploratory qualitative study, the literature review is best performed after some of the initial findings emerge and the direction of the research is beginning to take shape. Sometimes researchers go into the field to investigate a phenomenon and truly have no idea what is happening or why. In these instances, researchers will go out and conduct interviews or do a good deal of observation and then try to work out an explanation of what they have observed. Under these circumstances, some researchers believe, it is better to gather some data, see where the research is headed, and then go back to see if other instances occur in the literature or if theories that are being formed have support in the existing literature. Shank (2002) is an advocate of an approach based in "ignorance" and believes the researcher must set aside any preconceived notions before going out into the field so as to not be prejudiced when observing and interviewing. He says there must be a "fully exploratory approach" to fieldwork and reading in advance of it will induce unnecessary bias into your reporting. Shank feels you should do your fieldwork, see what research questions and/or hypotheses emerge, and then see if it integrates with the prevailing literature. Glaser (1978) agrees, urging researchers to use grounded theory to generate constructs, relationships, and theory. He says this works better if the researcher is "uncontaminated" by theory prior to entering the field. Once theory that is "grounded in the data" is formed, then the researcher can compare it to what already exists to see if it has antecedents in the current literature or if a different process is at work.

This is a controversial idea in the world of research theory. Those who advocate this idea argue that by not being influenced by previous research, the researcher enhances the inductive process that drives the research forward. Those who inveigh against this idea note that the literature review is essential for establishing the background of a problem and that the researcher may spend time covering previously plowed ground if they haven't read in the literature before commencing research.

They also argue that reviewing the extant literature will generally improve the inductive reasoning process by providing structure for the processing of ideas and analysis. Strauss and Corbin (1998) also feel knowledge of the literature will let you ask questions you might not have thought of while doing research and that reading about the area, situation, or population you wish to interact with will inform your research in a positive way.

If this approach intrigues you, a compromise we have found effective for qualitative research is to focus the initial literature review on the topic but not the theory. That is, if you're going into the field to research foie gras production it would be useful to have reviewed the literature on foie gras—its history, its market, its production methods, its controversies and so on—before entering the field. After all, there's a difference between open-mindedness and ignorance. Then, once you've gathered some data and reached some preliminary findings, return to the literature in a broader way. Perhaps there has been similar work in other areas that would have altered your work if you had read it prior to conducting your research but now can inform your findings.

CONCLUSION

The literature review is a critical step in nearly every type of academic research. Time spent reviewing the literature is never time ill spent.

To Abstract or Not Abstract, That Is the Question

Some researchers like to write abstracts of the material they are using as a basis for the research they intend to perform. Abstracts are summaries of important data points in the researcher's own words. There are various rationales for creating your own abstracts but the two primary ones are (1) when you can summarize material in your own words, you are more likely to understand it; and (2) abstracts in various tertiary sources can be flawed or incomplete. If you decide to write abstracts of your source material, here are some strategies that will make the process more effective.

1. Start your abstract with all the pertinent bibliographic information.
2. Summarize in your own words all the main points the author is trying to make.
3. Make notes about your thoughts on the article and where it fits in your research plan.
4. Make notes of any quotes you think you will want to use later.
5. Classify the note card (physical card or e-card) so you can organize it with others to be used in that section of the literature review. (Adapted from Mills, Gay, and Airasian, 2006, pp. 51–53)

Primary, Secondary, and Tertiary Sources in Food Studies

Primary Sources

- Autobiographies
- Diaries
- Travel narratives
- Interviews
- Works of art with food subjects
- Food receipts
- Original recipes
- Letters with food descriptions and/or observations
- Legislation (legal codes) on food topics

Secondary Sources

- Biographies
- Books written on food topics using primary sources
- Criticism of food literature
- Reviews of food history
- Analyses of food topics in journals
- Food essays
- Cookbooks

Tertiary Sources

- Encyclopedias
- Food bibliographies and similar review articles
- Dictionaries

Evaluating Resources on the Internet

The Internet is both a blessing and a curse for today's researcher. Never before has a tool offered so much access to information, and never before has a tool offered so much access to misinformation. One of the real challenges for the researcher is to make sure they are getting the best of what the Internet has to offer without getting the worst as well.

The thing that has made the Internet such a phenomenal success is the exact thing that makes it problematic for the researcher; that is, the fact that it allows anyone to post their material without review or mediation. While there are some Web sites that are like journals in terms of how rigorously they screen the information they present, there are many, many more that are not mediated in any way and are, in fact, organs of propaganda for various causes. One of your authors not long ago had a paper turned in that cited the satirical newspaper *The Onion* as a source of information; the student had used this source because Google had returned it along with a number of serious resources on the topic. In addition, the prominence of a source in the search hierarchy is not a guarantee of content solidity. Wikipedia is one of the first references returned in many searches on the Internet. Wikipedia makes no claim to being a research Web site and includes a disclaimer on one of their main pages that they are merely a compiler of information and that they expressly *do not* publish any original research. You may wish to use this site as a way to get a quick definition or to direct you to secondary or primary sources, but it is a tertiary resource and should not be cited.

If you are considering using information found on a Web site, be sure to investigate the site thoroughly before including the information you have found on it. Institutional sponsorship can be a good clue to reliability. If you are writing a paper on the eating habits of Hispanics in the United States, a reference from the American Dietetic Association Web site would be generally acceptable, while one from Chowhound or other "foodie" sites would certainly be questionable at best. Consider authorship as well. If there is an author listed, then you can do further researcher on their credentials and level of expertise on a topic. Often Web sites do not attribute authorship of articles and so can be suspect sources of information. If you keep in mind that most Web sites are created to advocate for a cause or to sell a product, then you can use the Internet wisely to guide you to information that may prove useful.

Using Databases

The good news is that research has gotten significantly easier in recent years. The advent of online databases, or metadatabases (which search multiple databases), allow you to search inside journals, newspapers, and books down to a single word or phrase.

Decades ago, to search for the *New York Times* coverage of the hamburger throughout history, you would have had to look an annual indexes for each year and trust that the indexers did not miss any of the references you would have liked to see. Then you would have had to find a hard copy or microfiche version of each reference and make a copy for your research file.

Now you can find all *New York Times* references to the topic with a single click.

The key is good search terms: garbage in, garbage out. Try multiple terms, try filtering overwhelming results, and try multiple databases.

Each library has its own database subscriptions, and because food studies is interdisciplinary, many of them will be useful. Try, for example:

- Agricola
- Academic Search Premier
- Ethnic Newswatch
- Business Source Premier
- PubMed
- Wilson Social Sciences

And there are many, many more.

Many libraries have food subject guides recommending resources that they have that are useful for food research. It is also recommended to have a good relationship with the librarian—this person's help can save you a lot of time and effort.

Literature Maps

Creswell (2009, pp. 33–36) suggests that even before embarking on a literature review, you can map out the literature that you expect to need to put your proposed research into context. A literature map is especially helpful as a guideline since it is easy to be overwhelmed and diverted by a particularly interesting or well-researched aspect of your topic. You cannot allow such a diversion to prevent you from accomplishing your research goals!

Even without entering the library or the library online databases, you can know the major areas you will need to cover in researching your topic. For example, imagine you are researching the incorporation of new food products among Sudanese immigrants in Washington, D.C., through dietary recalls and participant observation. Even before embarking on your literature search you can map out major areas of consideration:

- Sudan and Sudanese immigrants
- Sudanese food
- Sudanese immigration in Washington, D.C.
- Food habits of other immigrant groups
- Dietary recall method
- Participant observation method

And so on.

Through the literature map, you can find sources in each of these areas and when you feel you have a strong handle on the major works in each area that could relate to your study, move on. In writing your literature review, each bullet (point on the map) then becomes a section of one or more paragraphs.

Exercise—Thinking about Your Literature Review

After reading the chapter on the literature review, answer the following questions using your research topic as a guide.

What is your research topic? _____
_____
_____
_____
_____

What literature areas do you expect you'll need to include in your literature review? _____
_____
_____
_____
_____
_____

Which, if any, of the problems described do you imagine encountering in your literature review? How will you handle them? _____
_____
_____
_____
_____

What method will you use to organize your literature? Why? _____
_____
_____
_____
_____

Research a piece of bibliographic reference software. What are its advantages and disadvantages? What is the value in comparison to its cost? _____
_____
_____
_____
_____

Blank Page Template: Create Your Own Literature Map

PART TWO

5 HISTORICAL METHODS IN FOOD STUDIES RESEARCH

A knowledge of history gives us a feeling for the possibility of change.

Peter Smith, 1995

Peter Novick (1988), in his book, *That Noble Dream,* a look at "objectivity" in historical research, relates the story of a politician who says that writing a clear, concise, and objective history is like "trying to nail jelly to a wall" (p. 8). Novick was colorfully making the case that it is a near impossibility to write an objective account of what has happened in the past. To gather and consider every ort or scantling of material and make decisions about what to include and exclude and then put it together into a fluid and cohesive narrative is a formidable task. But when you look at the vast amount of research literature that is based in historical research you see that, indeed, the task can be done.

Historical research is important because it explains how we got to where we are today. Everything we do in everyday life is grounded in things that happened in the past. One of the best ways we have of understanding who we are today is to understand yesterday. History can help us understand the things that are deeply rooted in a culture by examining what human beings have thought, attempted, and accomplished. History is a valuable method in food studies research because it helps us discover how food choices, patterns of commensality, the gendered nature of food, and other important food-related issues are rooted in various cultures. By performing historical food research we can gain a valuable understanding of what, why, how, and where we eat as well as with whom we eat.

History can be a valuable tool for understanding who we are, but it can be dangerously misused as well. Histories are written for myriad reasons, reasons that are often less than scrupulous. Although historical research can be used to pursue a political agenda or to perpetuate old myths, that is an inappropriate use of the technique in the academy. Images of food and issues surrounding food are potent commodities in the political marketplace. While food images, food stories, and folklore surrounding food are some of our most cherished referents, there are many idealized versions of these things held in the popular collective memory that are inaccurate. To perpetuate these mistaken ideals for the sake of a political or personal agenda or even because it is the current status quo does both history and research a disservice. For example, in the current political climate much has been made of the purported disintegration of the nuclear family and the importance of the role of the family meal in stemming this disintegration. The picture of a typical family—Mom, Dad, Sister and Brother—sitting around a table eating a meat-and-two-vegetable meal is firmly burned in the consciousness of many western societies. Politicians regularly trot out this Rockwellesque vision to illustrate what is normal and good. The implication is that this has been the natural and preferred behavior of "regular" people for eons. But the work of Alice Julier and Stephanie Coontz, among many others, has shown the classical imagery of the family sitting around the table to be a creation of relatively modern times, historically speaking. We now know there may be no consistent pattern of this behavior prior to the end of the nineteenth century, especially outside the upper classes, and then mostly in societies that were dealing with a number of social issues they felt were best dealt with by encouraging this particular social model (or by being critical of those who did not practice the model). As a historical researcher in food studies, you will want to avoid using your research to advance such an agenda and concentrate on increasing understanding of a person, event, or phenomenon in your area of research.

One often-cited reason for doing historical research is that it offers some kind of crystal ball for looking into the future. People are fond of quoting Santayana's bon mot about the historically uninformed being doomed to repeat the past, but history is not an accurate predictor of the future. It is, however, a useful indicator of what has been important to societies, cultures, and individuals. Generalizations about future behaviors are very hard to make because exact combinations of circumstances and behaviors rarely recur, planning is rarely perfect, and the best-intended plans often have unforeseen consequences (Best and Kahn, 1998). What history can do for us is offer interesting and useful insights into cultural patterns and practices so that we might better understand them. While a good piece of historical research won't solve today's problems, it may inform the situation enough that current problems can be solved because of knowledge of what has and has not been successful in the past. Historical research can be extremely useful in placing current problems into perspective if you can relate past activities to existing ones. Different historians interpret the past differently, that is to be expected in the world of scholarship, but what all good historians do is weigh the evidence from careful research and make a reasoned case for their interpretation based on what they feel the evidence implies.

As is true of other types of research, there is a spectrum of philosophy in food studies historical research. In historical research, this spectrum runs from the positivist to the historicist (Galgano, Arndt, and Hyser, 2008). Positivists see history as a scientific endeavor, one that can produce a relatively objective and accurate account of what has happened in the past. On the other end of the spectrum, historicists feel that human societies are too complex, with too many variables to pronounce any one viewpoint or narrative as accurate and objective. While certain modalities of research along this spectrum are currently more fashionable than others, it is certainly acceptable to conduct food studies research in any of these veins if you feel they are appropriate to your topic.

The novice food studies scholar working in a historical area needs to remember not to fall into the trap of presentism. Presentism is the practice of using a contemporary lens to view what has happened in the past (Galgano, Arndt, and Hyser, 2008). When looking at historical materials be very careful not to use today's values and perspectives to judge what happened long ago, or even yesterday. Modern society may be coming around to the view that both sexes have a responsibility for collecting, preparing, and serving food, but this has not been the case through most of written history, and to view a historical situation through this lens would have you committing the sin of presentism. However, this warning against presentism is not to say that only situational interpretations from the period in question are correct. In many instances the historian may have the advantage of having more information available for examination and contemplation than someone who was contemporary to the scene might have had and the historian may benefit from having a more neutral eye for a situation than a contemporary may have had.

Related to the issue of presentism is the concept of context. Understanding the historical context of the person, group, or phenomenon that you are studying is very important to creating useful historical text. When examining the evidence of food history you always need to keep in mind what influences were shaping the people and events you are investigating. Keep asking yourself what social, cultural, political, religious, economic, and technological influences were in operation during the time period you are considering. These are very important issues to consider when conducting historical research in food studies. Context will play a role in the theoretical element of historical research in food studies (Hiestand, 1986).

When you conduct historical research in food studies, you also need to consider how theory will influence what you read, how you read it, and how it will influence your final report. There are a number of theoretical approaches to historical research including causational, postdeterminist, and postmodernist (Galgano, Arndt, and Hyser, 2008). Many early theoretical bases for historical research were rooted in causation. An example of causation theory is Marxism. Marxism suggests that the elements of a society—cultural, social, political, religious, economic, and technological—are a result of a society's means of productions. In Marxism, these causations lead to determinant outcomes. Causation theories are still seen in historical research, but lately many historians have wandered off the deterministic path of early historical theorists and posited that the best historical research can hope for is to uncover meaning in historical behaviors, a style of research known as postdeterminist. The postdeterminists suggest we accomplish this by use of a highly interpretive and descriptive approach to historical writing, what Clifford Geertz famously referred to as "thick description." Even more recent than the postdeterminists are the postmodernist historians. Postmodernists often claim that modern points of view are so entrenched and acculturated that the past is unknowable in the sense of traditional "objective" historical research and writing and that the best we can offer is an interpretation based on our own set of insights, insights that are tempered by our outlooks and biases. While this postmodern turn in historical research has been the subject of much debate in historical research communities, the postmodern emphasis on using lenses of gender, race, class, and ethnicity to view historical events has, at the very least, enriched our understanding of numerous topics. When reading history, especially from secondary sources, keeping these issues of context and interpretation in mind will make you a more critically effective reader.

There are numerous types of histories that can be read and written. Political, military, religious, economic, social, cultural, and intellectual histories have been the most prominent strains of historical writing in the past and may continue to be so in the future. As in the past, the type of historical writing that is produced today depends on the interests of the researcher, the intended audience, and, in some cases, who is paying for the research. In food studies, social history is one of the most common and widely used approaches. Social history can be defined as "a narrative to describe the everyday lives of people" (Galgano, Arndt, and Hyser, 2008, p. 13). While there continues to be interest in the food habits of the rich and famous, much research in food studies today emphasizes the lives of everyday people. Social history provides valuable perspectives on the lives of those who were often excluded from more traditional histories. In the study of food, much of the older primary historical material we have is focused on the lives of the upper economic strata. This is a result of the material it was considered important to record in the past and what it was considered important to preserve over time. When scribes were at work in the royal courts of old Europe, China, or India, it wasn't considered necessary to consider what the women and men of the hearth and field were eating; therefore, there are many fewer records of their food choices and consumption patterns than exist for the elite. In contrast, today we have copious amounts of information about consumption and preference and the status of food in the world of everyday people, and we are now able to write social histories from many perspectives.

Historical research in food studies can happen at a number of levels. As Best and Kahn (1998) say, historical research can be about "individual(s), idea(s), movements and/or institutions" (p. 77). One of the earliest examples of food studies research, Margaret Mead's studies for the National Research Council's Committee on Food Habits during World War II, occurred at the institutional level. Mead was charged with determining American's food habits so that rationing of foodstuffs during the war would be more successful. Since then, historical research in food studies has continued at the institutional level but has also been expanded to phenomena and activities outside the official realm. At the level of movements, there are researchers like Belasco (2007), who has focused on the way that alternative food movements in the 1960s shaped current food consumption patterns and trends toward more conscious eating. At the individual level, there are studies like Arlene Avakian's *Through the Kitchen Window,* a book that explores the "intimate" relationship that women have with food. While an individual research project (and subsequent report) is focused on one of these areas, researchers consider the influence of the other areas on the topic. While women may have a very personal and intimate relationship with food, this relationship is shaped by external and internal factors ranging from personal relationships to media influences. To not consider all of these influences would be to only get a part of the story.

SOURCES OF DATA FOR THE HISTORIAN

In historical research sources of data are usually classified as either primary or secondary (Storey, 2004). The classification can seem arbitrary at times and different researchers sometimes put things in different categories but a good way to think of the categorization scheme is in terms of distance. Generally the more removed, either in terms of time or distance or social relationships, the more likely the source is to be secondary. Primary sources are generally thought of as analogous to eyewitness accounts; they are firsthand sources of information and are contemporaneous to the event or phenomenon being studied. Secondary sources are those sources that are at least once removed from the action (Gall, Gall, and Borg, 2005; Cohen, Manion, and Morrison, 2000). For example, a transcript of an interview with someone who stood in the breadlines of the Great Depression era would likely be considered a primary document, while Ben Bernanke's *Essays on the Great Depression* would be considered a secondary source. It is nearly universally agreed in the historical profession that the best histories are written from primary sources. This is not to say, however, that secondary sources are not to be used at all. Secondary sources can be extremely useful in giving you a general overview of a topic and as an initial source for locating primary sources. Galgano, Arndt, and Hyser (2008) sum it up nicely by telling us to "think of secondary [sources] as serving as a guide and introduction to a particular topic, but the primary evidence is the actual material from which one can make generalizations and assertions" (p. 6).

HISTORICAL SOURCES IN FOOD STUDIES

Because secondary sources often are our guides to the topic, let's take a look at them first. As we said previously, secondary sources are sources at least one step removed from the activity or phenomenon in question. They are very useful in providing a historical context about the period we are interested in. Encyclopedias, dictionaries, and textbooks are often excellent places to get a generalist background on a topic. In most instances the author has been chosen for known expertise in an area and an editor or other content referee generally vets the material contained within the article or chapter. The material is frequently concise and reliable and may even provide you with a set of references for further reading. Many student writers of history can use this material to begin to develop a hypothesis for their research. (This hypothesis, if developed, is then tested against what is found when examining the primary resources.) Other useful secondary sources include scholarly journal articles, Web sites (if vetted carefully for veracity), monographs and other book-type material, and even material from lectures.

Primary sources of historical research include documents like governmental and corporate records, newspapers contemporary to the phenomenon under investigation, archaeological and scientific evidence, visual images, and oral histories. Even art and literature can be useful primary sources if you think about the manner in which art reflects the time in which it is created. A novel set in India during the British Occupation may reveal a great deal about the relationship between indigenous and colonial food habits, hunger and food insecurity, and how food issues affected people's daily lives.

While primary documents have the benefit of being contemporary, some are more reliable than others. William Storey, in *Writing History,* tells us that Leopold von Ranke, widely considered to be the father of objective, source-based, historical writing, thought government documents to be the "gold standard" of primary sources (p. 18). Every primary source has its problems; in the case of government documents it isn't so much the case of what they record, but what they don't record. There may be excellent records of what kind of food assistance was handed out to white residents in Australia during the Great Depression, but Indigenous Australians were frequently left out of this loop, so what effect this period had on the nutritional health of this particular population would be much harder to gauge because government records of the era may not cover them. In earlier periods, wills are a good source of what kind of food goods people had because these type of goods were often enumerated and left to specific people. But what of the vast majority of people who had so little to leave, or had no money to record a will, that they left no record at all?

VALUABLE HISTORICAL SOURCES IN FOOD STUDIES RESEARCH
PRIMARY SOURCES

■ *Public records/government documents*—There are any number of public records that can be valuable to the food studies researcher. Since their inception, departments of agriculture (USDA in the United States, AFFA in Australia, DEFRA in the United Kingdom) have kept voluminous records about production and subsidies and other policy issues. These records are increasingly available over the Internet, especially current data, and with the ability to travel to an archive, these sources can provide reams of documentation to the food researcher. Other public records of interest may come from various public welfare agencies, census data, and government surveys such as the National Health and Nutrition Examination Survey (NHANES) in the United States.

■ *Business and nongovernmental organizations*—Both business organizations (from small sole proprietorships to large publicly traded corporations) and nongovernmental organizations (NGOs) generate large volumes of records. Business documents not only record the business at hand, but also who worked for the organization, what their roles were, and who their clients were. Charters and constitutions put into word the mission of the group. Bills and receipts give you an idea of the nature and volume of a business. Even catalogs can give you an idea of how an organization is situated in time. A look at the Johnson-Smith novelty catalog from World War II has illustrations of a statue of Hitler with a pincushion for a behind, an excellent comment on wartime sentiments of the Allies. If you wanted to get an idea of the scale and type of food import and export in nineteenth-century Britain, you could examine records of warehouse inventories, shipping manifests, and the like. While not exactly public records, records from NGOs are frequently useful in food studies research as humanitarian projects often have food at their center or at least a food component.

■ *Public communications*—How news is disseminated changes over time, but whatever the method—Internet, newspaper, television, journals, pamphlets, and so on—it is a valuable source of not only the information itself, but of how it was viewed, what prejudices of the era were, what themes dominated period thought, what players dominated the dissemination of information, and who their audience was. The information industry arose hand in hand with the industrial revolution, and as printing became cheaper and more common, the amount of printed public communication snowballed. Food has always been a topic of interest among the general public. If the period you are examining is contemporaneous to or after the beginning of the industrial revolution, there should be quite a bit of public communication for you to scrutinize, depending on how far back you go.

■ *Personal documents*—People have always generated paper. Even prior to the explosion of documentation brought on by the capabilities of the industrial revolution, people kept diaries, wrote letters, made wills, and maintained records of what was grown on their farms and what they sold or traded. Because most societies were largely agricultural prior to the industrial revolution, food is often a topic in these documents. Inventories of households were common in the preindustrial era. Using these inventories can give the researcher a feel for what kinds of culinary tools were available to the householder, what kind of farming equipment was available, and what the owner's standard of living was.

■ *Images*—Images of food go at least as far back as the cave paintings at Lascaux. Most ancient cultures that have left us some kind of visual record chose to record images of food and food production, probably because food was such an important part of daily life. Paintings, engravings, drawings, and sketches can give us valuable clues as to how food was used in earlier times. Later, photography and video added to the stock of visual images we can analyze for clues to food studies topics. From images we can examine food products, food fashions, and other relevant issues of consumption as they relate to food. However, we have to be careful about how literally we take tableaux presented in images. Imagery has always been a rich propaganda source, either intentionally or unintentionally. We need to understand the context in which the image has been created. While there are numerous theories about the depictions of the hunt in the cave paintings of Lascaux and Ardèche, we may never know their true purpose. In modern times, food imagery has had numerous uses socially, culturally, and politically. As a researcher you will have to ask yourself questions such as, when was the image created, who commissioned it, what context was it created in, and what iconography is used to convey a message. We tend to think of photography and video as more "truthful" somehow than painting or drawing, but these media are as easily manipulated as earlier ones. Most of the Great Depression photos in the United States, like those by Dorothea Lange and Walker Evans, were arranged at least to a small degree to capture the emotions the photographer wanted to present to the world.

■ *Artifacts and relics*—Humans have left behind vast amounts of physical material that can be useful in determining what they ate and how they produced and consumed it. Archaeological excavations can tell us both what people ate and how they prepared it in the prehistorical period. Tools like DNA fingerprinting and chemical and microscopic analysis yield evidence of food products, food consumption, and even food systems in the prehistoric period. These tools can also be used in the historical period to ascertain the veracity of written records about the period. Most humans throughout history have left records of their lives in written form, but the artifacts they have left behind can also tell us a great deal about how they lived their lives. In food studies we can examine cooking tools, farming implements, and similar artifacts to add to our understanding of food topics in history.

■ *Literary works*—Works of literature (as opposed to other forms of public communication) can often provide rich clues as to the importance of foodstuffs and manners of consumption. The food memoir and related works are very recent innovations, historically speaking, but literature dating back to the classical period (and beyond) is rich with descriptive material about food and the manner in which it was produced and consumed.

■ *Maps and plans*—Maps are useful because they tell us how land was used and how humans have expanded their reach over time. Plans of towns and buildings can provide valuable clues as to how land and buildings were utilized in society and how they were located in proximity to one another, clues that shed light on relative value in a society.

Evaluating primary sources is generally a matter of asking a number of questions. The first question to ask is, is it genuine? Is the document or artifact authentic? The historian can subject the document or other artifact to various physical tests if needed to establish the bona fides of the item in question. Analysis of language usage, writing style, and other indicators of periodic accuracy can be used to assess the authenticity of documents as well. If the question of authenticity is established in the affirmative, then the historian is still left with the problem of establishing the value of the document. The value of the document lies in how informative it is about the person, event, or phenomenon under investigation. As we have already noted, objectivity is a rare commodity. But given that notion, we assess evidence for relative objectivity and perspective, both of which are important.

As a researcher, you can ask yourself questions that include:

■ Who wrote or used the document or artifact?
■ Is it contemporary to the period in question?
■ If it is authentic, what is the quality of evidence it provides?
■ If a document, who was the intended recipient?
■ Can we determine the conditions under which it was produced?
■ Can the information provided by the artifact or document be corroborated by another, independent source?

Once the researcher has performed tests of veracity to his or her satisfaction, then analysis can proceed.

SECONDARY SOURCES

- *Encyclopedias*—nearly every country and language group in the world has a general knowledge encyclopedia specific to it. In English-speaking countries the most common one is the *Encyclopedia Britannica*. Recently a number of food studies–specific encyclopedias have been published, including the *Oxford Companion to Food*, the *Oxford Encyclopedia of Food and Drink in America*, the *Cambridge World History of Food*, and the *Encyclopedia of Food and Culture*. All are excellent starting places for getting a good grounding in a food topic.

- *Books, monographs, and journal articles*—The recent groundswell of interest in food studies has resulted in numerous excellent titles being published in the last few years. While individual titles are too numerous to mention here, suggestions for starting places include the *Choice* journal article by Deutsch and Miller (2007) and catalogs of various publishers who specialize in food studies such as Berg (United Kingdom). A good catalog search at your research institution, a database search at that same institution, or even quick search with Google or Google Scholar should turn up a plethora of titles in food studies.

ORAL HISTORY IN FOOD STUDIES

Oral history is "the systematic collection of living people's testimony about their own experiences" (Moyer, 1999). Oral history techniques are very useful in food studies historical research because day-to-day perspectives on food and eating have not been considered important historical perspectives until very recently, and oral history is useful in capturing these perspectives. As Boschma, Scaia, Bonifacio, and Roberts (2008) say, oral history is a good way to explore "subjects that have not traditionally been the topics of historical investigation" (p. 79).

In its most basic form, oral history is the practice of interviewing individuals about some topic that the researcher feels has some significance. The oral historian interviews a person and records the interview on magnetic tape, a digital voice-recorder, or in some analogue or digital video format. This idea of capturing the voice (or voice and image) is at the heart of this technique. The captured voice (and image in the case of video recording) is then preserved as an "eye-witness" record of an event, phenomenon, or experience. The practice of oral history is a product of the technological age. Prior to the proliferation of modern audio and video recording devices, the events of the lives of ordinary people usually went uncaptured. This was especially true of women, minorities, children, and other people who were traditionally disenfranchised in society. Oral history is often used in modern feminist histories because researchers see it as a valuable tool in understanding the role and perspective of women in a tradition that has customarily relied on a masculine interpretation

(Gluck and Patai, 1991), a trait that makes it extremely useful in food studies as well. In many situations, oral history is useful in providing multiple perspectives on an event or phenomenon. As a result of the spread of oral history techniques, more and more of these stories are now being preserved for future generations, and for ongoing analysis by researchers.

Oral history begins as a dialogue between two people, the interviewer and the interviewee. This interaction forms the basis of the oral history technique (Yow, 1994). Oral history is not an objective technique, but this is its strength, not a weakness. The in-depth interview that is at the heart of an oral history allows the researcher to not only ask what happened, but why the interviewee thought it happened, and how they felt about what happened, how they reacted to what happened, and how they viewed the outcome of what happened. Yow describes this as an explication of "multiplicities of life experiences in a total life context" (Yow, 1994, p. 24). Researchers will bring their own perspectives to the interview. Everyone arrives in a situation with their own assumptions and influences based on things like gender, class, race, culture, and education. As in any type of qualitative research, the good researcher acknowledges these assumptions and biases and accounts for them in the research design and analysis phases of the research project. Acknowledging these influences while probing into detail and emotion, as well as the "facts" of the situation, makes the oral history a co-creation or construction between the interviewer and the interviewee.

Oral history is one the food studies researcher's best tools for revealing the daily life and intimate detail of ordinary people. The beliefs, motives, emotions, actions, and experiences in the foodways of everyday people have an impact on the course of history. Yet history conducted on a large scale often doesn't take these factors into consideration. Consider, for example, in Deutsch's (2005) study of urban firehouse cooks, the sanitized department history of firehouse cooking, in which its health and nutrition benefits are emphasized, as opposed to the words of current and former firefighters, who cite its antidote to boredom, its teaching of a postretirement skill, and its conviviality. This is where oral history comes into play. Traditional histories are often a record of those in (or wielding) power. Oral history can fill many of the empty nooks and crannies created by these grand narratives, thereby serving as a counter to the hegemonic record (Boschma, Scaia, Bonifacio, and Roberts, 2008).

ORGANIZING HISTORICAL RESEARCH PROJECTS FOR FOOD STUDIES

The purpose of the historical research project in food studies is to describe a person, event, or phenomenon related to a food studies topic, then interpret the situation in terms of one or more of the following: trends, characteristics, attributes, motivations, behaviors, interactions, or significance. This almost always starts with a question that the researcher (or the researcher's supervisor) has about something that has happened in the past. Reading about the topic frequently starts with secondary sources. In food studies we would likely use secondary sources like specialized encyclopedias, food studies research journals like *Food, Culture and Society,* and various monographs to flesh out our understanding of the topic and to help us develop some specific research questions. A common flaw in historical research is trying to answer too broad a research question. Try to narrow your research questions so they may be stated as specifically as possible. To say you are going to write about the Great Famine in China during the Great Leap Forward is to give yourself far too large a task, unless this is to be your life's work. What part of it are you going to investigate? The causes, the effects, the political environment of the times, the psychology of Mao and other leaders in China at the time, the climatological factors involved? This is not to say that the scope of your answers can't be broad ranging, but the questions themselves should have a level of specificity that allows them to be answered in the finished report. You may have several related research questions or some subquestions based on a central question. Your research question may include the frames by which you intend to analyze the data as in the following example from *Food, Culture and Society:* "Using anthropology, ethnohistory, and popular art, this paper explores the many narratives, identities, and authenticities embedded in the cultural biography and cuisine of the luau" (O'Connor, 2008, p. 150). After establishing the hypothesis to be tested or research questions to be answered, the research design needs to be considered. At this stage a research prospectus tends to be useful. In historical research a prospectus should address the historical significance of your problem based on your readings of secondary sources, which primary sources you intend to survey, a work plan and timetable, and an explanation of your theoretical bases and analytical framework. Having an analytical framework will help you determine both the research questions you will ask and the process you will use to analyze your answers. Commonly used analytical frameworks in historical research in food studies include social, cultural, and policy (Buck, 2008). Social frameworks consider the lives of "everyday people" and have a "grass-roots" approach. Because food issues are important in the daily lives of ordinary people, social frameworks are quite useful in food studies research. By comparison, cultural frameworks perform historical interpretation using culture as a lens. Because questions of food and identity are often examined in food studies and both food and identity are often examined at the level of larger cultures, cultural frameworks are frequently used in food studies. Policy frameworks examine the effect of public policy on private lives. Marion Nestle's work on food policy issues in the United States is a classic example of the use of a policy framework in food studies research. Once you have addressed the issues of significance, sources, and frameworks, you can move on to your research.

Historical research in food studies is both demanding and rewarding. Locating and analyzing primary sources, your best source of data, usually involves copious amounts of time and may involve travel to distant repositories where the documents are kept. Unlike many types of empirical research in food and nutrition, historical research is a struggle to fund extramurally. But given these caveats, there is a great deal of personal reward in doing historical research in food studies. While historical precedents are not predictors of future behaviors, they have shaped who we have become today. To be able to understand and explain why food has shaped who we are today is highly rewarding and an interesting way to spend your research career.

5A A CONVERSATION WITH KEN ALBALA

Ken Albala, Professor of History at the University of the Pacific, is the author of nine books including *Eating Right in the Renaissance, The Banquet,* and the award-winning *Beans: A History.* He is also the editor of three food series from Greenwood Press and co-editor of the journal *Food, Culture and Society.*

KA: Well I guess I should explain my background and training. It's as an intellectual cultural historian. My field is the European Renaissance. Which doesn't mean I haven't stolen from other disciplines.

JD: Tell me how you got into food studies.

KA: I was studying at Columbia [University] and told my advisor I really had no idea what I was doing. Some sort of intellectual history topic in the Renaissance. And my advisor said, "Why don't you go over to the New York Academy of Medicine? They have a really nice collection and they're really nice to you. And they have comfy chairs and big tables. And you'll have a pleasant time there. And you can go every day and you won't see anyone else there. It'll be nice and quiet." And I said, "OK, I'll check it out." And it turned out that someone in the 1920s, a nutritionist, had collected—when old books were still affordable—every single dietary tract that was written. Ever. From the late middle ages all the way through the eighteenth century. She collected all of them. So all I really had to do was park myself and read them all. So methodologically, the first thing I had to do was learn all these languages. Most of them were in Latin. A lot were in the vernacular also, like the popular press: Italian and French and Spanish and German and other things, which was a lot of the hard work. For any historian of Europe—and I would imagine most of the world—you have to learn the language first. But the primary documents in that case were nutritional texts. How you should eat healthy, keep yourself in shape, and what foods are good for you depending on the amount of activity you get, things like that. And I think the basic approach is really diving directly into the primary material. Especially with a body of readings that not a lot of people have written about, or they've only written about it thirdhand. And I think when you go directly to the text, medical primary literature, or it could be cookbooks, or it could be texts about food—how to set a table, how to carve properly, how to arrange banquets—in the early modern period there is a vast literature out there of these "how to" books, which tells me that there are people who are wanting to behave like their superiors, or get a job in a kitchen, or serving in a noble household, as a physician or as a chef or as a carver or something, and there's not education for that. They're telling them "how to" basically. Which gives you a lot of direct insight to the readership, the people who are trying to learn these things and what they do know and what they don't know coming to the job. Sometimes they're really, really basic. Basic things. There's one about serving which says things like don't pick your nose when you're serving the table. Things like that. Make sure you're clean. But I think the way to approach it is really just to read as much as you can without any preconceptions and then while you're halfway through or so you make a hypothesis like any research project. And then go back and see if the material really supports your whole project and then you don't have to read every single word that's been built on everything else. That would take you years and years. You can look for the things you're try-ing to prove and hopefully not leave out other important things. You know, it's like any scientific investigation—you can't go completely, ut-terly blind into the whole project or you just have this mass of informa-tion. And you can't make up your mind before you start. You can't say, "I'm gonna prove this," and then look for the source that's never gonna show me what it says. I think the best way to do it is to find a genre or a discipline that has enough critical material in it and then dive in as much as you can and then start to see patterns that emerge, things that are important.

JD: And that will form your argument.

KA: Right, and then I'm going to go back into that material and see, "Was I *really* seeing that in that literature?" and then keep reading. And I'm not going to read the whole thing. I'm going to do as much as I can and hopefully [read] the texts clearly but pulling out the parts that support an argument.

JD: I think that's a challenge for a novice researcher to say enough is enough.

KA: It definitely is. And it depends on the scale of what you're writing. If you start with a 350-page book then that's I think a sane way to approach it. If you start with a more narrow topic, writing about one author, or writing about one type of food or one technique, you can say all right, here's a manageable book or a manageable set of articles to work on. And for history, the approach in history, is, I think, a lot easier than dealing with real people. Because real people don't tell the truth. They don't, you know, they will give you a story that they think you want to hear and things like that. And when you have dead people writing in books what you're really saying is, "This is what this book tells me." It doesn't tell me it's *true*. It doesn't tell me "this is really what was going on in kitchens." It doesn't tell me—if it's a recipe book—"this is what people cooked." You can't make that assumption. What it tells you is that this is what the author wanted to say to the public. And someone wanted to read this. And whether they're actually cooking it is almost beside the point. Let me give you an example that I was just thinking about yesterday. There's a great recipe that starts from the late seventeenth century which is hard to do. It's called One Egg Made as Big as Twenty. You cook it in a bladder. You start by cooking the egg yolk. And mix it with sugar and other things and make it into a little ball. And then you fill this whole bladder with the egg white. And suspend the yolk—already cooked— in the middle of it. And the whole thing is boiled. And then the whole thing cooks solid. And it's garnished inside also, it's not just eggs. It's pistachios and cockscombs and candied orange peel and the whole thing. But it comes out as an egg and it's like two feet high. It's a big egg. And you slice it up and you open it. And this recipe just gets repeated all the way into the eighteenth century. It's in the first cookbooks that are published in the U.S. also. It's in Hannah Glasse. And Williamsburg-era cookbooks. And I don't know whether anyone ever served it. I don't think there's any record of that. To find that out you'd have to look at someone's account in a diary or expense account—a very different kind of literature entirely which I've really never worked with. That told you we spent this amount of money. Or someone saying, "We went to their house and we couldn't believe they served this." You almost never find it. It's really, really rare to find contemporary accounts of it but you do have this idea that for some reason a lot of people were interested in reading about this, thinking, "Maybe someday I can make this egg for twenty and impress my friends." And that's almost more interesting than whether they actually do it.

JD: So is one of the key questions how and why did this recipe develop? And why did it persist?

KA: Right. What were they trying to do with it? What kind of ingredients really excited them? Because that changes over time. It's what's rarest and exotic. And what's interesting. When the recipe starts in the seventeenth century, it's cashews and bone marrow, and sugar is still very interesting to them, candied citron peel, things like that. By the eighteenth century it calms down so there's less garnishing because those things are not really expensive. So that sort of tells you another story. But the fact that they would still have this recipe as a presentation piece for parties. It's sort of the same as if you look at *Gourmet* magazine and wanted to look at turkey recipes and you found that there's a new technique every year, because everyone's bored with turkey so they brine it and they roast it, they smoke it, they do something else with it and who knows if they actually cook those. But the fact that they appear and they get replicated in other cookbooks and you find them in other magazines tells you that people are thinking a lot about doing it. And things go in that fashion. That whole process about how tastes change and why is all very interesting.

JD: Oral history seems like its own genre, very different from the kind of work you do.

KA: It's an entirely different methodology and I think dealing with modern subjects is also odd because they can tell you, "Nope, that's not the way—you got it all wrong." They sometimes make up things. Or reimagine what the past was like.

JD: When you do history it sounds like you start with the archive first or the topic.

KA: Yeah. I would say while that's happening you're reading secondary literature also. So maybe if say you wanted to read about spices, you could find a dozen books about the spice trade, and spices in medieval society, and there's a lot of books about it. I would say read all of them. And they're usually the best places to find where the primary sources are. Unless those authors themselves have taken their research from secondary authors, in which case I would say read them for the hell of it but don't trust what they're saying. And there are some good books that have come out—spices is a good example—that are really popular sources and don't rely on the primary texts. But they're fun and they have good spins on it and you ought to know them anyway. But to prevent yourself from being corrupted by them don't stop with just reading the dozen books about spices. I think you really have to interact with an open mind with the primary stuff. And with spices it's a huge topic so you're not going to cover everything. There's trade documents, and household accounts and cookbooks and dozens of different types of documents to use. I would say the first thing to do is look directly at what people say in the past and then you are always correct because what you're saying is this person said this in the past, this person said this, it's not a matter of interpretation, it's fact. Here it is. You can't say, "Medieval people used a lot of spices because X, Y, and Z," you say, "Here's this author and he clearly says he used these spices on this type of food and for these reasons." And you're starting in a stable footing then. I think if you start with an assumption that medieval people ate spices because of "this" that you got from some secondary source you're probably going to go wrong in the end.

JD: So once you have the facts then you start to shape the argument.

KA: Right. And there are some people who are literally social scientists. History is a weird discipline in that it bridges humanities and social sciences. And there are some people who do counts, even people who work on cookbooks. The whole Annales school in France has been on history being approached scientifically so that you would look for every single cookbook and record the number of instances pepper or cinnamon or whatever appeared, and you'd say, "This percentage of them have this and therefore those people were using cinnamon more often." And that's insane. I think. Statistics can be wrong often. It all depends on how you ask the question. And what you're looking for and how you approach it. But people often assume that because you're putting a number and a percentage there that that means it's true, and I would say exactly the opposite. Look at the example with the cookbook. You can say x number of cookbooks show pepper, which means that these cookbook authors— the ones that survived in print—happened to have thought their audience would want to read about pepper. That's all you can say. Don't say more than your sources will tell you I think is the lesson there.

JD: So when you do food history you don't start with a research question like, "Why is cardamom popular in Swedish desserts?"

KA: Sometimes I do. It depends on the venue. I have done things like that, very recently for almonds. I sort of knew already almonds are everywhere in the medical texts, in the religious literature, in the cookbooks. And then I wanted to say, "Why?" And to do that I really had to read every single place almonds are mentioned to find these consistent patterns. And in this case it was really simple. It was just a food—a dairy substitute for lent, and the authors say that, a very healthy food for recuperation, for healing coughs and stuff like that, the medical authors say that directly, and then something that you could play with in interesting ways. You know cooks are kind of inventive with almonds and things like marzipan and macaroons and things that are invented in this whole period based on the fact that almonds are very malleable ingredients. So I think I could go back to the sources that I knew and say, "Here are three reasons these became popular" and then just give the evidence, line up an argument that supports it. On the other hand there are some times that you'll find an idea and just think it's compelling and really not know a literature at all, and then go back and say, "Let me see if I'm right; if I can prove this." The whole process of forming a hypothesis can start from ground zero, saying, "I'm just going to start reading and see what I find," or it can start halfway between and say, "I want to show that—I don't know—pizzas became important in the U.S. because soldiers were returning from Italy and had tasted pizza there and wanted it back in the U.S." I think that's probably false but a lot of people have said it, and if you wanted to really prove that you'd have to find accounts from servicemen in World War II and say, "Did you eat pizza there? Did you look for it when you came back here?"

JD: What do you think is the difference between doing history in general and doing food history?

KA: There's no difference whatsoever. You could be doing women's history, you could be doing history of industry, machines, intellectual history, I think the basic tools are the same. Having said that, the way that most food historians work is not entirely historical. There are ways of analyzing things sociologically that I would use even though most historians don't. Or I would think things about anthropology only because so much of good food history writing has been done by anthropologists. Sidney Mintz was writing history even though he's an anthropologist. And so the background and the questions that I tend to answer don't necessarily come from history. And in fact there really haven't been that many food historians until recently. There are some here. There are some who fifty years ago wanted to count calories or find out the nutritional status of peasant populations, things like that which would never even occur to me to do in a million years. So there are different kinds of food history is the important thing to mention. And the way I come to it is really through the printed text and the history of ideas. But there are many different ways you could do it. I think the majority of people who do it professionally academically do it that way. Warren [Belasco] does it that way. And I would say Jeff Pilcher does it that way also, just this, "What does the text tell you? Here's the book I'm going to write about it."

JD: Do you distinguish between food history and culinary history?

KA: Yes. Actually I gave a paper on this so I'm going to try and extrapolate. I think culinary history really does have to do with what goes on in the kitchen. Where food history takes in trade and taste and court fashions and ideas and can take in anything that has to deal with food in general. I think culinary history really deals with—not even gastronomy, I think gastronomy is different—gastronomy is the history of what people wanted to eat and restaurants and reviews and fine wines and culinary history I think should literally just be in the kitchen. How are new recipes invented? They can be who's actually doing the cooking or the history of waitstaff or something like that or what a restaurant should be or innovations in taste but I think it should focus on kitchens, professional or home kitchens.

JD: You mentioned recipes, receipts, bills of sale. What other kids of documents are useful for food history?

KA: Menus are great. And account books from households. And restaurants I guess also keep account books. Modern ones certainly. Restaurant reviews are very interesting and gastronomic literature in general that talks about the interesting new recipe or the interesting new restaurant or something like that. There's a whole slew of trade documents also: taxation records, lawsuits. Things that are serious archival hard history: diaries, that are harder to work with because you have to sift through lots of them. But say if I were talking about the spice trade in the New World there's a whole building full of tax documents that could tell me exactly what spices were coming in in what volume and how much the crown got from them. That doesn't interest me at all [laughing]. So you know a number, so what? "A whole lot," is so much easier to say. I guess when you get past the nineteenth/twentieth century, personal narratives are very interesting. What people talked about in their autobiographies or interviews or things like that. I guess there's also what we would call historical re-creation or living history as part of culinary history. Which has a lot to do with figuring out the tools themselves they were using, figuring out how they worked. And cooking the recipes. I know that most historians don't do this. I think it's an integral part of figuring out the importance of a cookbook. Getting the ingredients as close as you can get them, and following the techniques, and producing it because if you want to know why this particular pie that they're making that has 1,800 ingredients, your initial reaction is to look at that and say, "Oh my God that's disgusting or perverse," and that tells you nothing about the past. I think what you should try and do is get as close as you can—and I think you can get pretty close—and then taste it. You know it would be like someone writing music history and never really hearing a Bach cantata. You want to hear it. Or never looking at the actual painting but finding reproductions or descriptions of it. And I think for culinary history, the thing that makes it unique is you can actually cook these things and follow the techniques. None of them are really, really hard. It takes time. The almond project I made a couple of different almond recipes that require you to pound the almonds. It takes about an hour. You have to stand there wailing on them [laughing]. But to make real almond milk it makes a complete difference. I was actually overwhelmed at how the flavor and texture and everything about it was exactly like real milk. Like dairy milk. And it behaved like it—you could make butter out of it, you could make cheese out of it, it was just phenomenal. There's no way on earth I would have known that without just trying it out. And sometimes it's a matter of equipment. There are some pieces of equipment you just can't get hold of. I've actually made them from pottery and cooked with them. Like a pipkin, which is a fifteenth/sixteenth-century clay vessel which is sort of shaped like an hourglass and has three legs and a handle. I've never thought, "Why does it have to be this shape?" The bottom is rounded so the heat actually disperses around the whole exterior. It's unglazed on the outside so you don't have the clay cracking and breaking from the heat. And the interior you cover—you put dough on top so everything stays in. You really don't need much water in it and it stays at a fairly low temperature. You just plop it right on top of coals because the three legs just sort of stand on the coals. And it just cooks gently for hours. Beautiful. And there's no way I would have understood what those recipes were saying or what was going on in the kitchen had I not just started a fire and thrown it in the fireplace.

JD: What advice would you give an aspiring food historian?

KA: I guess the first piece of advice has to do with any research project. You have to be really interested in what you're writing about. You have to like it a lot. Because you will inevitably be sick of it by the end, or tire of it, or not want to do the work. That's true about anything in life I guess— if you love what you're doing it's not work. What I think also is start with the primary sources, trust your instincts, and think of everything as fun. We luck out in that there is no other topic that is fun all the way through. Unless you're working on hunger or famine or something like that most food topics are really a ball. Food and sex—I guess if you picked a bad topic it's your fault—or you're just an uninteresting person.

6 QUANTITATIVE METHODS IN FOOD STUDIES RESEARCH

Quantitative research methods in food studies are the methods that we use when we want to explain, predict, or control phenomena of interest (Gay, Mills, and Airasian, 2006). When we have data that we can express, measure, and analyze using numbers, there are a variety of quantitative research methods that can be useful. In quantitative research, you ask tightly worded and specific questions in order to obtain data that is numerical and that you can then subject to statistical analysis (Creswell, 2005). Most often in food studies this type of research uses data that is collected using instruments that have fixed preset questions (like questionnaires) and whose responses can be quantified with numbers. Once we have gathered this data, we generally subject it to some kind of statistical analysis, after which we see if our hypothesis has been supported or not.

In the broadest sense quantitative research methods are usually chosen because we want to explore the relationships between *variables*. The results of these studies allow us to generate theory, answer research questions or confirm *hypotheses* stated in the study and perhaps even make some statements about *causality*. For example, if we perform research where we give one group a *treatment* such as a nutrition education course or module and do not give another group the treatment, once we have statistically analyzed the outcome data for the two groups, we may be able to make some assumptions about the effectiveness of the training. In the most rigorous form of quantitative research, known as experimental research, we have an *active independent variable* (a variable that we can manipulate) and we assign participants to groups in a random fashion. By random, we mean a subject has an equal chance of being placed either in a group that receives a treatment or in a group that does not. An experimental research design is needed if you want to make any claims about cause and effect or if you want to suggest that your findings would be relevant or applicable in a situation different from the one in which you tested your hypothesis or research question (Gay, Mills, and Airasian, 2006). If we get as many subjects as we need and we have the ability and facility to separate them into randomly composed groups, then we can proceed with an experimental research design and arrive at the strongest set of results.

Food studies research rarely happens under strict laboratory control conditions. If we are working in the field or some other real-life situation, as we frequently do in food studies research, it is very hard to pull together a group of subjects and then randomly assign them to groups for treatment. If you were working with school-aged children in a study of how to increase vegetable consumption, it would be much more likely that you could get two groups of students that were already in groups (like a classroom) and then give one class the curriculum you are hoping will increase their vegetable consumption and not teach the other class this curriculum. In this example, we would be filling one of the conditions of experimental research—manipulating the variable (one class gets the intervention and one class does not)—but we would not have random assignment to groups (classes are already formed prior to the experiment). In this instance, we would be using a quasi-experimental approach (Creswell, 2005). If you use the quasi-experimental approach, you cannot make hard claims to cause and effect, but you can make some suggestions about educational practice based on your outcomes. When you assign participants randomly to groups, you can say that you have accounted for *confounding variables* that might affect the outcome. In this example, maybe the students who didn't get the curriculum (the intervention) have a teacher who already promotes vegetable consumption, or through luck of the draw, the students in the nonintervention class have parents who serve many types of vegetables at home. Factors like these can affect the results of the class who didn't get the intervention. If you had been able to assign students randomly to groups you could have controlled for these variables, but by having the classes already formed, you cannot. In both experimental and quasi-experimental research you have manipulated some type of variable, therefore you could think of these two approaches as intervention research.

If you can neither assign members to groups on a random basis nor manipulate the variable of interest, you can still perform research that explores relationships between variables, but the claims you make for the data are more restricted. If you want to make comparisons between groups, you can use what Gliner and Morgan (1999) call the comparative approach. Comparative studies examine the presumed effect of a nonmanipulated variable (called an *attribute variable*) on a group. The term *attribute variable* is used because this type of research is often used where the subjects already have or do not have the condition (attribute) in question and we want to know how that makes them different in some situation or at some skill. For example, we cannot manipulate the variable of having a baccalaureate degree prior to attending culinary school, but we could use a comparative research design to try and find out how it affects the students' performance in culinary school.

Somewhat related to comparative research is associational research. If we want to find how some degree of a variable affects a process or skill, then we use the associational approach (Gliner and Morgan, 2000). If you wondered how three-year-old children, six-year-old children, and nine-year-old children differed in their attitudes to trying new foods, you would use an associational research method. Children of different ages would be considered different orders of the variable, and we are looking for relationships between different variables and outcomes. Note that in these last two methods there is no intervention or treatment performed by the researcher, the researcher is only comparing outcomes with attribute variables. These two types of research methods are what we will refer to as nonintervention methods.

All four of these approaches (experimental, quasi-experimental, comparative, and associational) study one or more variables that are tested against a *dependent* or *attribute variable* in order to examine causality, compare groups, or find associations between the variables. There is a fifth type of quantitative research that examines only a single variable, descriptive research. Descriptive studies "use only descriptive statistics, such as averages, percentages, histograms, and frequency distributions, that are not tested for statistical significance with inferential statistics" (Gliner and Morgan, 2000, p. 74). Descriptive research, though not able to comment on causality or associations, can be useful in food studies as these types of data can be useful when we are exploring new areas of research, what people's food preferences are, or what people say or how they feel about topics that are important to food studies researchers. If we want to make inferences about cause and effect, we must use an intervention-based research design in the experimental and quasi-experimental categories. If our goal is to compare groups against one another or to see what degree of a variable has what effect on an outcome, we use a nonintervention-based method in the comparative and associational categories. If we want to find out people's feelings about a topic, we would use a descriptive approach.

PICKING SUBJECTS FOR QUANTITATIVE RESEARCH

Earlier we said that one of the important features of experimental methods was the randomization of subject selection. Subject selection is important because in quantitative research, the reaction of the individual to the intervention or condition is what the research is all about. In most instances we cannot test every member of the population we are interested in. Therefore we select a sample of the population and test our theory or intervention on the sample. Good sample selection allows us to generalize the findings to a larger population. Creswell (2005) defines a sample as "a sub-group of the target population that the researcher plans to study for generalizing about the target population" (p. 146). Every member of a sample is referred to as an *element*. If you are able to survey every member of the population in question, the research you perform will be referred to as a *census*, not a survey. The term *survey* implies the use of a sample, not a population.

We get our sample by determining what our *sample frame, sampling unit*, or *target population* is. These are all terms that are used to describe a group of every member of a population of interest (Black, 1999). From that group, we then decide on what our sample size is to be and select our sample. If you were interested in the satisfaction of diners in the dining rooms at Google headquarters in Mountain View, California, your sampling frame would be all Google workers with dining room access at that corporate campus. Because of the size of the population it would be very difficult to survey every member of the population, so you would survey a sample of them. You could choose your sample randomly, or you could make some adjustments to compensate for shift worked, rank of employee, gender, and so on. (How to make these adjustments and why are covered in the coming pages.) While you hope that everyone chosen for the sample will participate, the reality is that most times you will only get some of your sample to participate. You hope that the percentage that chooses to participate is high, and you may have to poke and prod to get a high enough compliance to make your statistical analysis significant. The number of people who respond or participate is expressed as a percentage of those that were requested to participate. This percentage is known as your *response rate* (Adler and Clark, 2003). Most quantitative researchers feel that the higher your response rate, the more claims you can make about your data. There is no magic response rate that makes your data valid. Some statisticians suggest that a response rate of under 70 percent will give you a weak data set to work from, but others will dispute this figure (Keeter, Kohut, Miller, Groves, and Presser, 2000). If you decide to use a quantitative research method, this is an issue that will have to be taken up with the statistician working on your project, and low response rates will need to be addressed in the discussion section of your research report.

Researchers using quantitative methods take one of two approaches to sampling; *probability sampling* and *nonprobability sampling* (Charles and Mertler, 2002). You will also see the terms *systematic sampling* and *nonsystematic sampling* used to refer to the same two categories, though these terms confuse the issue, as systematic sampling is one type of random sampling, not an entire category. The more desirable of the two forms of sampling for quantitative studies, probability and nonprobability, is the probability sample. A probability sample is more representative of the population than a nonprobability sample because it is considered to be an unbiased sample in research terms. If you want to make generalizations about your population from the data that you have collected from your sample, you must use a probability sample

(Clark-Carter, 2004). The other type of sample we could use is a nonprobability (nonsystematic) sample. These kinds of samples are considered less reliable than random samples because they are considered to be biased; that is, they don't truly represent the population as a whole. But there are times and reasons when you may want or need to use a nonprobability sample and these reasons are discussed in the section that follows.

A probability sample is a random sample where every member of the population has an equal chance of being selected to be in the sample. Most of you are likely familiar with the famous Shirley Jackson story, "The Lottery," where names are drawn from the black box to see who will "win" the lottery. In this story all the names of the townspeople are placed in a box and one name is chosen to receive the treatment prescribed in the story. This is a variety of the most basic form of random sampling known as *simple random sampling*. Every townsperson had an equal chance to be selected and the selection was performed randomly. In Jackson's story only one name is chosen, but for research purposes we select a large enough sample that it will represent the population adequately in the research. For example, let's assume we are conducting research in a large culinary program of 700 students. If we decide that 70 students would adequately represent our population of 700, then, from all 700 names, we would draw out 70 names. Today we have moved on from drawing names from a black box, top hat, or fish bowl to using computers to randomly generate samples from the population or using a random number table to make our selections, but the principle is the same regardless of the technology used.

An adaptation of simple random sampling that we sometimes use for convenience is termed *systematic sampling* (Charles and Mertler, 2002). We still determine a sample size that we feel will meet our needs of representation (70, in our example). The researcher selects a random starting place on the list (a total of 700 people, in our example), and then goes down the list selecting every tenth person. This is quicker and simpler than the simple random sampling, but the resulting list is less representative of the population as a whole. The problem with this approach is known as *periodicity*. Periodicity is the potential for there to be patterns in the list that would cause the selected names to be unrepresentative of the population as a whole (Johnson and Christensen, 2008). If you were using a list of students that by some chance had a male's name in every tenth slot, or if the list was ordered by student grade-point average or admission date, your sample would not be representative of all of the students at the culinary school.

Another technique that assures all groups will be proportionately represented in your sample is known as *stratified random sampling* (Charles and Mertler, 2002). In this technique, we would take our culinary school population and first categorize the students according to some attribute like gender. If we wanted our sample to equally give weight to women and men, we would divide the students into women and men, then randomly sample 35 from each of our categories. While this technique would give equal weighting to the opinions of men and women at the school, the sample would not be fully representative of the school where 65 percent of the 700 students were men and 35 percent were women. If we wanted to address the gender imbalance in our sample, we might further refine the sample, using a *proportional stratified sample,* where 65 percent of our sample is selected from males and 35 percent from females. Proportional stratified sampling is a system of obtaining a sample that represents the population in proportion to the desired stratification variable. You could stratify on ethnicity or race or religion or national origin or any number of stratification variables.

If our culinary school was predominately populated by white students and we wondered about attitudinal differences between white students and African American students at the school, we might use a *disproportional stratified sample* in order to get equal numbers of both in our sample so we could compare the groups to each other. Disproportional stratified samples are used when you want to represent various groups in disproportion to their representation in the population.

Another type of sample we could use to survey our culinary students is *cluster random sampling* (Charles and Mertler, 2002). If we decided to randomly select classes to survey as opposed to randomly selecting individuals, this would be an example of cluster random sampling. This type of sampling tends to take less time and energy and resources than simple random sampling techniques, but with a tradeoff in accuracy and generalizability.

MEASURING ITEMS IN QUANTITATIVE RESEARCH

Since most quantitative research is used to explore causality or associations, measurement of these relationships becomes an important part of the research. To measure these things we need to decide on the scale we are going to use to measure them, relate them to each other, or differentiate them from each other. There are five scales of measure commonly used in quantitative research. These five scales are binary, nominal, ordinal, interval, and ratio (Creswell, 2005; Charles and Mertler, 2002; Gliner and Morgan, 1999). Which scale you use will depend on the type of data you are collecting and how you want to use it. Binary and nominal scales are considered unordered scales; that is, they exist only to name things, not give them rank or order. Ordinal, interval, and ratio scales are used when you want to show differences between levels of a variable—either ordered or continuous (Gliner and Morgan, 1999).

Binary coding is a way of labeling items that we are interested in that either have an attribute of interest or do not have the attribute. Binary coding is used when all we are interested in is the presence or absence of the attribute. When the attribute is present we use a 1 to code this presence and when it is absent we use a 0 to code this absence. If we were interested in the presence of MSG in food and were making a list of food items that contained MSG and those that did not, we would code foods that contained MSG 1 and those that did not 0.

The nominal scale, as the name suggests, is about naming things. We use the nominal scale to sort things into categories, to label information, or to classify data into categories. Nominal scales are widely used in survey research, a common type of research that is used with food topics. If we wanted to find out about the demographic characteristics of the people we are surveying for our study, we would use nominal measures. There can be as many categories as you think will be useful for analyzing your data once it has been collected. Examples of things you could categorize using nominal categories include gender, age, ethnicity, sexual orientation, and income. For example, we might want to code for gender. A common coding scheme for gender is assigning all males to one number and all females another number. Frequently we will see a scheme like females are coded 1 and males are coded 2 (or vice versa). The numbers have no meaning outside of identifying who is female and who is male. In nominal scales, numbers do not indicate rank order or preference. We commonly think of something with the number 1 as superior to number 2, but in a nominal coding scheme, 1 and 2 are merely identifiers and imply no rank order or preference. We could look at any set of respondent data and instantly know the gender of the subject. Nominal items do not have to be dichotomous in nature. We can identify more specifically than A and B or 1 and 2. If you were trying to find out about student eating habits and preferences at the college dining center you might have a survey that categorized students by the amount and type of meat that they consumed. In this case we might have a nominal scale that looked like this:

1. Omnivores
2. People who eat no "red" meat (poultry and fish only)
3. Pescetarians
4. Ovo-lacto vegetarians
5. Lacto-vegetarians
6. Vegetarians who use honey, but no milk
7. Vegans
8. Fruitarians

While the numbers in this list represent a range of eating behaviors, starting with those who consumed the widest range of food products and ending with those whose diet is the most restricted, in a nominal scale, the numbers would have no meaning other than to give each eating behavior a label. You could reverse the numbering scheme or jumble it up and it would make no difference. The numbers are used strictly to name and aid in the coding of the data. It is also useful to remember that if there is no "distance" between items on a scale, the scale is likely nominal. Red curry, yellow curry, green curry, and masaman curry are useful designators when discussing Thai curries, but there is no numerical distance between them.

The third scale of measure that we use in quantitative research is ordinal. The ordinal scale is a rank-order scale (Adler and Clark, 2003). An ordinal scale allows you to make judgments about people based on a variable or amalgam of variables. If you were interested in how much high-fructose corn syrup (HFCS) is in different people's diets, you could survey their consumption habits (perhaps using a dietary recall study instrument) and from that extrapolate how much HFCS was in their diet. Once you had determined the amount of HFCS each respondent had reported consuming, you could then create a scale using scale items labeled Very High Consumption, High Consumption, Moderate Consumption, Low Consumption, and Very Low Consumption. Based on how much HFCS respondents consumed you would then place them somewhere on your scale. As a consumer of research, the problem with ordinal scales is that, while the groups are rank ordered, we don't know by how much the ranks differ. In ordinal measure there is no requirement that all the categories have even spacing. In this example the highest consumption category could be twice as high as the next group, or five times, or even ten times. The fact that the groups differ in the amount consumed is interesting and might be important, but without knowing what the differential is, it would be hard to make any judgments about the data. We frequently see ordinal scales in journalistic reporting of food habits but we are often not told how the categories are arrived at or what the numerical differences between categories are. While this often makes for interesting reportage, it would not be useful for most research writing.

The next type of measure we use in quantitative research is interval measure. The interval measure scale is similar to the ordinal scale in that it is also a rank order scale; but with interval measure, categories are based on numerical categories like absolute number differences or percentage differences (Adler and Clark, 2003).

These categories are evenly spaced numerically so we know just how much the categories differ. We can tell much more about the respondents because of these evenly spaced categories. Interval scales have another feature that ordinal scales do not, a zero point. On interval scales the zero point is arbitrary and may not indicate an absence of the condition, but even so we can make some judgments about comparison and association. If we were to continue the example above, we would have a better idea of the comparative amounts of High Fructose Corn Syrup consumed because the categories would tell us relationally how much more or less one group consumed than the other.

The fifth type of measure we use in quantitative research is the ratio scale. The ratio scale has all the properties of the scales discussed previously, but it includes a true zero as part of the measure (Creswell, 2005). In an interval scale, zero is an arbitrary measurement point that does not indicate the lack of a condition. In ratio scales, the presence of a zero point indicates the lack of a condition, in our example this would be a total lack of High Fructose Corn Syrup consumption. Ratio scales are very useful because they tell us ratios of difference. On a ration scale, for example, we could assign the following numbers to HFCS consumption levels:

Zero Consumption = 0
Very Low Consumption = 1
Low Consumption = 2
Moderate Consumption = 3
High Consumption = 4
Very High Consumption = 5

Because the scale expresses ratios, we could tell at a glance that someone in the High Consumption of HFCS category consumed twice as much as someone in the Low Consumer category. Although our example here has no need for negative numbers, there may be occasions for the presence of negative numbers when using ratio scales.

STATISTICAL ANALYSIS THAT CAN BE USED WITH THE FOUR SCALES OF MEASURE

With binary scales we can use addition to see how many of the elements in our sample have the attribute and how many do not, but that is the practical limit of analysis you can perform on this data. While this may be interesting and important data for the research project, this type of data in itself would likely not constitute a strong enough data set for an academic research project, but it could be helpful in reportage and to add interest to your food studies project.

If you use one of the other four types of scales of measure in your project, there is some type of statistical analysis you can run on your data set. If our data is nominal we can use a few nonparametric statistics when examining them (Gliner and Morgan, 1999). Nonparametric statistics are used when we are dealing with data that does not have a normal distribution, a frequent condition when dealing with nominal data. The most common statistic associated with nominal data is the mode. The mode of a data set is its most commonly occurring value. For example, in a global analysis of Chinese restaurant menus, the mode would be the name of a dish or type of a dish that occurs the most frequently in your list of items. Another statistical test that can be run on nominal data (as well as on our other scales, except binary) is a chi square test (Charles and Mertler, 2002). When we have two or more nominal scale items and various possible responses to a survey item, we can use a contingency table to see how specific responses tally with the nominal items and can run further statistics to see if differences are significant. For example, imagine you are looking at whether college students primarily eat at home/dorm or in the cafeteria and you also want to look at those numbers in relation to students who are omnivores versus vegetarians (and vegans) to further study these preferences. A simple 2 x 2 contingency table for 100 students may look like this:

	Cook at Home/Dorm	Eat in Cafeteria	Total
Omnivore	20	55	75
Vegetarian	10	15	25
Total	30	70	100

From this table we see that most students eat in the cafeteria rather than cooking at home or in their dorms (in fact, over twice as many). But we also see that while over thrice the number of omnivores cook at home rather than eating in the cafeteria, only 50 percent more vegetarians eat in the cafeteria rather than cook at home or in the dorm. Further tests can tell you whether this difference is statistically significant and to what level.

Ordinal scales are the next highest-ranking instruments of measure. As we said earlier, ordinal scales indicate rank. If you performing a sensory analysis where tasters were asked to rank the hotness of six curries, their answers would be displayed using an ordinal scale. We wouldn't know how much hotter the one ranked the hottest was than the next hottest or the least hot. The difference between 1 and 2 might be very great and the difference between 5 and 6 not much at all. Once we have the data, we could perform a number of statistical tests on the data, including rank order correlation, calculation of the median and the mode, and a nonparametric analysis of variance (Gliner and Morgan, 1999).

Interval scales are like ordinal scales except there are equal distances between the points on the scale. In our example if we had asked our respondents to rate each of the six curries on a scale of fiery hot, very hot, hot, only slightly hot, mild, and not spicy whatsoever, we would be using an interval scale. Much of the survey research used in public life and academia uses a similar type of scale, which is known as a Likert scale.

The Likert (pronounced Lick-ert) scale is named for psychologist Rensis Likert, who popularized its use in research. Likert scales show level of agreement or disagreement with a condition or preference. In addition to all the statistical analyses already mentioned, once we have degrees of difference established we could begin to use parametric statistics such as the mean and the standard deviation and analysis of variance, and we could perform correlations and regressions (Gliner and Morgan, 1999). The strongest form of measure we have discussed is the ratio scale. All forms of statistical analysis can be performed on data measured on a ratio scale.

VALIDITY AND RELIABILITY ISSUES IN QUANTITATIVE RESEARCH

Reliability and validity of data are at the heart of quantitative research. If our research outcomes cannot be accurately analyzed and assessed then the research is without value. If our outcomes are to be accurately analyzed then they must be both valid and reliable. Validity is essentially a measure of quality in research (Best and Kahn, 2006). Questions of validity are questions about the soundness of your research. There are a number of types of validity in quantitative research, of which the two most important are internal validity and external validity (Best and Kahn, 2006). Internal validity speaks to the soundness of your research design; did your study or experiment actually measure what it was intended to measure? If you are attempting to study cause and effect in your research, then internal validity of your research is critical.

There are numerous threats to internal validity (Gay, Mills, Airasian, 2006); some of the more common ones include:

1. Time—Any number of events can occur over the course of your study, especially if you are performing an intervention of some sort and there is a significant time lag between the pretest and the posttest. Any of these events could affect the outcome of your experiment while having nothing to do with your intervention.

    For example, imagine you ask for a three-day dietary recall on a Wednesday for the previous three days—Sunday, Monday, and Tuesday—with one cohort of subjects. Later, a snow storm causes you to miss a Wednesday. Whether you ask about Sunday, Monday, and Tuesday on the following day (a Thursday) or ask, on Thursday, about the previous three days—Monday, Tuesday, and Wednesday—the data's validity would be compromised. Do you have as clear a memory what you ate three days ago as what you ate four days ago, and do your eating habits on Sundays closely mimic your eating habits on weekdays?

2. Subjects—People can affect the internal validity of your study. If some of your subjects drop out during the interval between the beginning and end of the study (attrition), it may affect the outcome. Also, if your pretest and posttest aren't different, scores may be better on the posttest due to what is called the practice effect, an improvement in scores because the subjects have seen the test items once

already. A third subject effect is related to group assignment. If groups were poorly constituted at the beginning of the study, it could affect the results. Randomization of selection can reduce problems with this effect.

A common example of a subject challenge to validity is attrition in long surveys. Imagine you have devised a survey to query adolescent girls who self-identify as having or having recovered from an eating disorder. Because of the emotionally trying nature of the topic as well as general time constraints of the subjects, it is conceivable that the most fragile subjects—those with the most serious or most recent eating disorders—would be emotionally fatigued by the survey itself and might drop out. While you might have carefully chosen your initial sample to provide a fair representation of your population, after attrition you may be left with a skewed sample.

3. Content—There are several issues surrounding content that may affect the internal validity of your study. The most basic of these is called face validity. This is the common-sense look at your instrument or intervention. Does the instrument or intervention appear on cursory examination to do what the researcher intends it to do? This is not a scientific measure, but a quick evaluation of face validity can keep you from wasting time using an inferior or incorrect procedure or instrument. More specific and scientific than face validity is content validity. Content validity speaks to the relevance of the items you are measuring to the topic of your study as well as the manner in which they are presented. If your subjects find your instrument confusing or ambiguous, you may not get valid answers. The most important indicator of the validity of your instrument is construct validity. An instrument with high construct validity would be that gives you a high degree of certainty that the instrument is measuring the theoretical construct that it is claiming to measure. As an example of content validity, imagine you want to ascertain whether a subject eats natural foods. Since *natural* has a very limited legal definition in many countries, how are you defining the term? And is it the same way the subject would define *natural*? Do you mean purchased from a natural food store? Whole grain? Organic? Not processed? No artificial ingredients? Unless the question clearly asks what you intend it to ask, the item will lack content validity.

External validity speaks to the generalizability of your findings. Is what you measured unique to the group you measured, or would your findings be able to be generalized to a larger population? Generalizability of findings is a common goal in quantitative research endeavors. Polgar and Thomas (1997) refer to the two types of threats to external validity as population issues and ecological issues:

1. Population issues—these are issues regarding the ultimate generalizability of the results generated by your sample to the larger population of the study. In quantitative research we are usually attempting to have our sample stand in for

a larger population, therefore our sample must carefully mirror that population so we can infer things about the population based on what our sample tells us. If our sample is not an accurate representation of our population, we are unable to make these inferences.

As an example of a population problem, let's imagine you are conducting a survey of awareness of food assistance programs for low-income Clevelanders. To save money, you decide to conduct a telephone survey rather than a face-to-face survey. While your sample might be large enough to be statistically sound, it lacks external validity because you've made a key error in your research design—by conducting a telephone survey, you eliminate subjects who do not have a working phone and the homeless, both populations presumably important in a survey studying a low-income population.

2. Ecological issues—these are issues of how much the conditions that we conducted our research under differ from the real-world conditions to which we want to make our inferences. If the conditions under which we conducted our experiment are so different from those in the real world of our population, then we might not be able to say that what happened in our experiment would happen in the real world. This would affect our claims to generalizability, generally a significant issue in experimental research.

Food studies is especially prone to problems of ecological validity because cooking and eating are not usually done in laboratory settings. While there are nutrition studies where subjects commit to taking all of their meals in the lab and forsaking all others, due to the cost and disruption such an intervention requires, tools like food journals and dietary recalls are more commonly used to determine what a person eats. But subjects being busy, ashamed, lazy, or confused can lead to inaccuracies in the recording of a food journal, for example, and can provide some very misleading results.

Reliability is a measure of consistency and representation (Best and Kahn, 2006). Quantitative research relies on instruments or interventions or observations to generate data. Reliability in quantitative research means that the application of the instrument or intervention will produce scores or measurements that will be stable over repeated administrations. A reliable instrument is one that will accurately reflect what it measures time after time. A common way to test reliability is to perform what is called a test-retest procedure (Gliner and Morgan, 1999). As an example, if the curry eaters in your study complete the curry survey instrument, and later you give them the same survey and scores are very close for each subject in the sample, the instrument could be said to have high reliability. In most instances, the closer the test-retest scores are, the more reliable the instrument is. If you are using an instrument to collect data that is already in existence (created by another researcher and used to collect data for their study), there should be information about the reliability of the instrument available. If you are creating a new instrument, then testing it for reliability will be one of the parts of the research process for you.[1] Reliability is a precondition for validity, because a measure that is not reliable cannot be valid, although reliability does not ensure validity (Cormack, 2000). To give an example from the world of foodservice, if you had a portion scale that consistently registered 17 ounces as 16 ounces, your measure would be reliable in that it consistently gave the same result, but it would not be valid, as it consistently gave an incorrect result. This is why instruments or observation techniques must be both reliable and valid.

WORKING IN THE FIELD VS. WORKING IN THE LAB

While most qualitative research happens in nonlaboratory settings, research using quantitative methods often occurs in laboratory settings. The distinction between the two is often referred to as lab research vs. field research. The goal of both methods is to collect data that aids in the understanding of the issue or question of interest (Conducting Field Research, 2008). Sometimes it suits the researcher's purpose to conduct an experiment in a lab setting to give the researcher control over as many extraneous and confounding variables as possible. The researcher hopes that by controlling these variables she will be able to make stronger statements about causality.

In the world of science research, lab research is considered the gold standard. But in food studies research sometimes it isn't possible, or even desirable, to work in a lab setting when you are using a quantitative experimental research technique. Some experimental researchers choose to work in the field because they want the research to occur in a naturalistic setting. While you may have control over confounding variables in a lab, you may wind up creating conditions that are detrimental to your research. Some researchers feel that it is easier to make claims about generalizability of results when the experiment has occurred in a setting that is, or closely replicates, a natural setting in the real world. You may be able to get a very good sense about how a research subject feels about the flavor of a slice of pumpkin pie if you put them in a sensory booth with only a red light, so color variations in the custard are masked and they are basing their judgment solely on the flavor. But in the real world other elements are as important as flavor, and visuals are critically important to our enjoyment of food. In an experiment conducted by one of the authors, a glass of orange juice was poured from the container in front of taste panelists. Panelists were asked to rate the desirability of the glass of orange juice prior to being asked to drink it. But before the panelists were allowed to drink the orange juice, it was colored black with food coloring. (This occurred in plain view of the panelists.) Then the panelists were asked again to rate the desirability of the juice. The desirability of the juice plummeted after it had been colored black and some subjects would not taste the juice at all. The visual characteristics of the orange juice were very important in the panelist's enjoyment of the product. As noted earlier, the lab setting gives the researcher more control over the setting and it also makes it easier for the researcher to use probability sampling and random assignment to groups, thus making the research design more purely experimental. But some would argue that the artificial nature of the setting and strict procedural controls could cause participants' behaviors and attitudes to change to some degree, perhaps significantly (Adler and Clark, 2003). On the other hand, doing experimental research in the field gives the researcher less control of the participants and any external influences that might affect the resulting data.

INTERNAL AND EXTERNAL VALIDITY IN LAB AND FIELD RESEARCH

For many years, a truism has circulated to the effect that laboratory studies rate high on internal validity, but low on external validity and that the opposite is true for field studies. Students of research have been told that while lab studies are good at telling us whether or not a manipulation of the independent variable caused a change in the dependent variable, they do not readily generalize to the real world. On the other hand, if you tested your hypothesis in a naturalistic setting, you could likely be more certain of its generalizability, but less confident that the change in the dependent variable was caused by the manipulation of the independent variable. Research by Anderson, Lindsay, and Bushman (1999) has to some degree laid this fallacy to rest. These researchers performed a meta-analytic review of matched pairs of lab-and-field effect studies in psychology and concluded that lab research (at least in psychology) is effective in terms of external validity and that field research in psychology is effective in terms of internal validity.

QUANTITATIVE RESEARCH DESIGNS USED IN FOOD STUDIES

Experimental Research Design

Experimental research is considered to be the most rigorous of all types of research. If your goal is to make some commentary about causality, then an experimental research design will be your best choice. To be able to make inferences about cause and effect, three conditions must be met (Polgar and Thomas, 1997):

1. The cause must precede the effect.
2. The size of the effect must vary (though not necessarily one-to-one) with the causal factor.
3. Any other potential causes besides the one being suggested must be satisfactorily ruled out.

Experimental research designs give us the most control over conditions and variables, which results in a well-designed experiment having the highest level of internal validity. The key phrase in the preceding sentence is *well designed*. Many conditions must be met for a research experiment to be able to make claims regarding cause and effect. In the simplest of terms, the objective of an experimental design is to be able to say that because of the intervention (program, drug, etc.), a specific outcome occurs. In research terms, the researcher is attempting to prove that the manipulation of the independent variable is the cause of the change in the dependent variable. To make it even more complicated, you also need to be able to show that if the intervention is not given then the outcome does not occur.

One of the strongest experimental research designs is known as the Pretest-Posttest Control Group Design (Campbell and Stanley, 1963). This type of design tests two different groups—known as the experimental group and the control group—where one group (experimental) gets the intervention or the treatment and the other group (control) does not. The design is intended to test the effect of the independent variable on the dependent variable. The independent variable is the treatment or intervention that the experimental group is subjected to, while the control group does not get the treatment or intervention. The dependent variable is the outcome.

Once you have decided to test the effect of an independent variable on a dependent variable, the first step in creating a pretest-posttest control group study is to determine your population. Once your population has been identified, you select your sample. If your population is very large—say every student at a major public university, selecting your sample will be more difficult than it will be if your population is smaller. Your sample is supposed to be representative of your population, and getting access to all members of it from which to select your sample is usually difficult. You may have to choose from a smaller subset of the population from which to select your sample. If your population were all of the members of the U.S. Marine Corps, it would be difficult to come up with a truly random sample because of the geographic spread and transient nature of the organization. You might have to settle for what is known as a convenience sample, for instance choosing your sample from the Marine Corps members who are stationed at the base closest to your place of residence. This is known as a convenience sample and will affect the degree to which you can make claims to generalizability. If you can get a sample that represents the entire population, this makes claims to generalizability much stronger.

Once you have been able to identify the elements of your sample, you will need to sort them into experimental and control groups. Your goal in setting up the groups is to minimize differences in the two groups. One way to do this is to use a simple random sampling technique. This way every element of your sample has an equal chance of being selected for either the control group or the experimental group. If you are concerned that there is some imbalance in your sample, you may want to use a matching technique to assign members to a group (Adler and Clark, 2003). In the matching method, you gather information about various characteristics or attributes of all of the elements in the sample and then try to come up with pairs of elements whose attributes match exactly (or at least as closely as possible). If your sample size were 70 elements, you would make 35 pairs that matched as closely as possible. After you have selected the pairs, you then split the pairs, making two groups who are closely matched in attributes mirror images of each other. One group would be randomly assigned to be the experimental group and the other group would become the control group.

After you have established your groups, you would then give all elements of both groups the pretest to establish the baseline for the dependent variable for both groups. After establishing the baseline, you would give the experimental group the treatment or intervention, but not the control group. After the treatment (the independent variable) has been given and allowed whatever time it has been allotted to have its intended effect, both groups are tested again. The researcher then measures the differences between the groups. If the groups have been carefully controlled and extraneous and confounding variables have been accounted for, the researcher can make some inferences about the effectiveness of the treatment on the outcome—the effect of the independent variable on the dependent variable. In pretest-posttest control group designs specific threats to internal validity such as maturation, testing effect, history, and selection bias are more carefully controlled than in other methods (Adler and Clark, 2003).

Similar to the pretest-posttest control group design is the posttest-only control group experiment. In the posttest-only group design all of the sample selection and assignment elements are the same as in pretest-posttest control group design, but there is no pretest given to the sample elements (Adler and Clark, 2003). The disadvantage of this design is that the researcher has no initial baseline measure of the two groups from which to make claims of degree of effectiveness of the treatment. The advantage of this design is that research subjects cannot improve their performance on the posttest by being familiar with the material in a pretest phase. According to Gall, Gall, and Borg (2005), this allows the researcher to isolate the effect of the intervention more precisely.

If the previous two methods are done with what are known as nonequivalent groups, the research is referred to as quasi-experimental (Creswell, 2005). These designs would then be called pretest-posttest with nonequivalent groups design and posttest only with nonequivalent groups design, respectively. In quasi-experimental research designs, the researcher still controls the manipulation of the independent variable very closely, but does not randomly assign research subjects to experimental and control groups, though the subjects are put into these categories. This method of assignment reflects realities of research in the public sphere. If you were doing research on nutrition education at a primary school, it is unlikely the superintendent of the institution would allow you to regroup students into randomly assigned classes for the purposes of your research agenda. You would have to make one class your experimental group and the other group your control group. The disadvantage of this approach is that there may be some extraneous variables between classes that you are unaware of and therefore unable to institute a control for. If, in your nutrition education study, one classroom happened to have a teacher who was very opinionated about dietary practice and conveyed this to the students, this could affect the outcome of your study. These kinds of issues are not insurmountable, and if you can demonstrate in the report of your study that the groups were essentially equivalent in many ways, you can still make some inferences about causality in your research report, though not nearly as strongly as if you had been able to conduct a true experimental study.

Nonexperimental Research Design

Nonexperimental research designs are useful in quantitative food studies research because in the real world we want to know about things, but we don't always have the means to randomly assign subjects to groups and manipulate variables to make assertions about causality. With food research, especially, it is difficult and expensive to experimentally control for all possible variables that may affect the outcome. Kerlinger (1986) defines nonexperimental research as:

> systematic empirical enquiry in which the scientist does not have direct control of independent variables because their manifestations have already occurred or because they are inherently not manipulable. Inferences about relationships between variables are made, without direct intervention, from concomitant variation of independent and dependent variables. (p. 348)

The two primary differences between experimental designs and nonexperimental designs are the manipulation of an independent variable and random assignment to groups. Both of these conditions are present in experimental research and missing in nonexperimental research. While this makes inferences about causality much weaker in nonexperimental designs, it doesn't mean that these designs are not useful in carrying out food studies research. Many of the reasons a researcher would choose to use nonexperimental designs fit well with what we are attempting to discover in food studies research.

Nonexperimental approaches to quantitative research go by a number of confusing and sometimes inappropriate names. Burke Johnson in his 2001 article entitled "Toward a New Classification of Nonexperimental Quantitative Research" has suggested a relatively straightforward and simple way to classify nonexperimental research using the dimensions of research objective and time. These classifications are very useful for considering nonexperimental designs in food studies research. The first way Johnson categorizes nonexperimental approaches is by research objective. The three most common research objectives are descriptive, predictive, and explanatory. If the research is aimed mostly at describing and documenting a phenomenon and does not aim to manipulate any of the variables in the study, then the research objective is descriptive. If you were attempting to answer the question of what is the dietary intake of incoming freshmen living in on-campus housing, your research would be descriptive. If the research is conducted to predict some event or phenomenon in the future, then the research objective is predictive. For example, if you were trying to determine what factors contribute to the likelihood of success of new farmers' markets in urban areas, this would be predictive research. If the research is conducted to explain how or why a phenomenon operates or what factors within the phenomenon cause it to change or evolve, then the research is explanatory. If your research was aimed at explaining why the USDA requires raw milk cheese to be aged a minimum of 60 days prior to sale, your research would be explanatory.

According to Johnson, the other way to categorize nonexperimental research is by time dimension. The three time dimensions are cross-sectional, longitudinal, and retrospective. In cross-sectional research, data is collected from the participants at one point in time (or in a very brief time span, but with just one collection per element) and comparisons are made. If you wanted to compare issues of race, age, or gender against other variables in a study of food consumption, a cross-sectional approach would be useful. In longitudinal research, data is collected at several points in time and then examined for change over time. A minimum of two time points is required for longitudinal research and some longitudinal studies have many collection points and go on for years. The Wisconsin Longitudinal Study began in 1957 and continues today, and the Harvard Adult Development Study has been going for more than seventy years. Longitudinal studies can happen one of two ways. A trend study looks at a phenomenon over time and uses the same questions, but with a new sample each time (Creswell, 2005). The purpose of a trend study is to examine public attitudes to a topic over time. If you wanted to study changing consumer attitudes toward genetically modified food products in the United States and Europe, you could issue a survey every two or five years and compare the results with those of prior studies. The other way to conduct a longitudinal study is to conduct a panel study (Creswell, 2005). A panel study is a survey that looks at the same sample over various points in time to measure changes in the sample. If you were interested in how children accepted new foods into their diet over time, you could establish a cohort of children and survey them every year to see how and when they accepted new food items. Panel studies can yield powerful data sets since you are measuring changes at the most basic and measureable level, but they are subject to attrition as participants drop out or even die. The third time dimension of research is retrospective. Retrospective research is research that begins in the present and works backward. If you were interested in the development of a food trend such as how farms became "certified organic," you might want to conduct a retrospective study in which you look at the current state of the phenomenon, then survey individuals to learn how and when they got involved and how their involvement has evolved.

Johnson suggests that the two dimensions, time and research objective, be viewed in a matrix so researchers can see how the three elements of each dimension relate to the other dimension. To do so gives us nine possibilities for fashioning a nonexperimental research study. When you have decided on which two dimensions of nonexperimental research best fit the research questions you are answering, you can go on to fashion your study based on the chart that follows.

Research Object	Time Dimensions		
	Retrospective	Cross-Sectional	Longitudinal
Descriptive	Retrospective, Descriptive Study	Cross-Sectional, Descriptive Study	Longitudinal, Descriptive Study
Predictive	Retrospective, Predictive Study	Cross-Sectional, Predicitve Study	Longitudinal, Predictive Study
Explanatory	Retrospective, Explanatory Study	Cross-Sectional, Explanatory Study	Longitudinal, Explanatory Study

(adapted from Allen, 2008)

SURVEY RESEARCH IN FOOD STUDIES

One of the most widely used and most useful quantitative methods in food studies is survey research. Almost everyone who is reading this book has participated in a survey at some point. Surveys and questionnaires are a daily part of life. The most obvious examples of survey research are the political opinion polls that we see the results of nearly daily in our national medias, but survey research is everywhere and is useful in a multitude of research applications. Survey research is somewhat different from other quantitative research methods in that most quantitative research is intended to offer rigorous explanations for behaviors or phenomena while survey research is designed to identify beliefs and attitudes of respondents, particularly in the area of trends (Creswell, 2005). It is this propensity that makes survey research a particularly useful tool in food studies research.

Survey research uses questionnaires or interviews or other types of instruments to collect information (Hutchinson, 2004). Survey research is done frequently in many types of social science research because of the ease of collecting and analyzing the data. If your population is small enough or responsive enough, you may be able to survey your entire population (conduct a census) rather than depending on a sample that may or may not be representative of your population (Salant and Dillman, 1994). You can design your survey instrument to be administered in person, over the telephone, by mail, or even over the Internet. There are two basic types of survey instruments, the questionnaire and the interview. A face-to-face administration of the survey instrument where the researcher asks the questions and records the responses is referred to as an interview. If the researcher or other individual associated with the research does not administer the instrument, but allows the participant to complete it on his own, it is referred to as a questionnaire. Clark-Carter (2004) lists three formats for asking questions in survey research: the structured interview or questionnaire, the semi-structured interview, and the unstructured interview. The structured interview is very formal. Questions are carefully worded and each participant in the survey is asked the same question in the same order. For questionnaires that require only a numerical response, like those using Likert items, the researcher doesn't have to participate beyond distributing and collecting the instrument. The semi-structured interview is less formal than the structured interview. There will usually be a set of questions called a schedule or protocol that the interviewer wants answered, but the interviewer is not strictly bound to the wording of the questions or the order of administration. This allows the interview to flow more like a conversation and the researcher can pursue items of interest that are not on the schedule as they arise in the process of eliciting answers to questions.

Interviewer Effects

While establishing rapport with your interview subject has many advantages in qualitative research methods, it can have negative consequences in quantitative research, especially in interview settings. The way the interviewer frames questions or even intones them can cause the respondent to modulate their answers, affecting the end results. Other things that can affect interviewees' response include the gender of the interviewer, perceived differences in social class, and even the dress of the interviewer. All of these can lead the respondent to give a response they feel the interviewer wants to hear instead of a response that accurately reflects how the feel about the topic being researched. You can try to fashion your interview tone and style to minimize the influence of these effects, such as having a person of the same gender conduct an interview where you feel there may sensitive topics that a person would have a hard time discussing with a person of the opposite gender, but any data generated by a face-to-face interview will in some degree be influenced by these effects and discussion of the data will need to be framed with these considerations in mind. Some researchers feel that very delicate topics, such as ones that involve sexuality or consumption issues that may portray the respondent in a negative light, are best handled in survey format so the respondent has greater anonymity and will therefore be more likely to answer honestly.

Much survey research depends on the respondent filling out a questionnaire and returning it to the investigator. These self-completed survey instruments, sometimes referred to as self-reports (Adler and Clark, 2003), can come in various forms. On some occasions the researcher is present when the instrument is distributed, administered, and collected. This is a common way to administer surveys in educational or other group settings. Group-administered questionnaires are generally inexpensive and result in a good response rate. They also tend to be relatively inexpensive to administer because the researcher only has to visit a limited number of sites to get the requisite sample. In other settings the researcher will distribute the survey instrument and the respondent completes and returns it at their leisure. In the past a good deal of survey work was done via the postal system. Mail surveys are useful when your sample is widely dispersed and your instrument is relatively simple. Mail surveys are good for Likert-type surveys and less useful if you want to get the kind of data that comes from open-ended questions. Given the relative cheapness of using the Internet for questionnaire-type survey research, mail surveys are coming to be regarded as an expensive method of collecting data. Once you have purchased stationery, printing, and postage, each response can have a significant cost attached to it, especially if your response rate is low. If your initial response rate is too low, you may need to incur extra expenditure on a second or third mailing or contact sample elements by telephone or email to get to a desired response rate.

Telephone surveys are also a very common method of obtaining survey research data. Telephone interviewers can usually ask more questions than you would typically use in a written survey and a well-trained phone interviewer can elicit a certain amount of information from minimally open-ended questions. Telephone interviews are generally cheaper than mail surveys if the researcher does not have to hire telephone interviewers.

Internet surveys are the fastest-growing type of survey research. Survey research over the Internet has become extremely popular because of the ease of use, the low cost, the global span, and the ability to automatically categorize and even analyze data as it is input by the respondents. Some survey instruments use branching or skip patterns that have the interviewer use certain pathways depending on the answer given by the respondent. All of this can be automated in Internet surveys. Web surveys can be effective if you have a closely targeted sample or population like a professional group or social group that uses the Internet as a social-networking tool. Web surveys are less effective if you are trying to have your sample be representative of a very large population. Access to the Web grows every year, but access is still skewed toward higher-income, more-educated, and younger demographic groups (Garson, n.d.).

DESIGNING YOUR INSTRUMENT

The type of information you wish to elicit from your participants guides instrument design. Once you have decided on the types of questions you want to ask, you can make decisions about whether to use interviews or questionnaires and how to administer them. Closed-ended questions, questions that require one-word answers or require the respondent to pick an answer from a predetermined list of options, are well suited to questionnaire-type techniques, while open-ended questions are better suited to interview techniques. The content of your questions will inform your choice of survey methodology. Creswell (2005) says there are three basic content areas commonly addressed using survey research: personal questions, attitudinal questions, and behavioral questions. Personal questions establish the characteristics (demographics) of the elements of your sample, including age, gender, ethnicity, level of education, level of knowledge about a topic, level of income, and level of participation or consumption in related behaviors. Information about characteristics or demographics is a common feature of food studies research surveys. These types of questions allow you to make comparative statements about people you have surveyed. For instance, do people with higher incomes report more frequent greenmarket attendance than those with lower incomes? Attitudinal questions relate to attitudes, opinions, and beliefs of the participants. These types of questions are often measured with Likert item–type scales where the respondent indicates the degree to which they agree or disagree with the statement posed in the item. In a study of gender and home cooking you may want to ask a respondent to agree or disagree with a statement like "Cooking for my family gives me a sense of pride" to learn some of the attitudes respondents have toward home cookery. Behavioral questions can elicit information about whether or not a respondent engages in a behavior and to what degree. To continue the previous example, you could then go on to ask, "How many meals per week do you cook in your home?"

Writing survey questions is much harder than you might imagine if you have not written any of these types of questions before. Clear and precise wording is critical if you want to elicit clear and consistent data. Interviewers have an advantage over questionnaire writers in this area because if the question is unclear, the interviewee can ask for clarification on the spot. This is not possible, or at least highly unlikely, if the respondent is answering a mail or Web survey in a different state or country. The most common flaw of survey question writing is lack of clarity. If the respondent cannot figure out exactly what you are asking, they will answer in a fashion that relies on their interpretation of the question. Double negatives are especially troubling and should always be rewritten as a direct query. For example, rather than asking a subject if she disagrees that she has not stopped cooking since beginning college, ask if she continues to cook. As a rule of thumb, the wordier the question the less likely it is to be clear to the respondent. Jargon should be avoided in survey item construction. As a food studies scholar you are likely well versed in the jargon of both this area of study and academic jargon in general. This is not the case with members of the general public and jargon causes both confusion and intimidation in many respondents. Surveys should ask just one question at a time. Questions with multiple purposes or clauses will confuse respondents and affect the quality of the resulting data; avoid this flaw by writing in a direct, declarative manner. Avoid using terms or phrases that are emotionally or politically charged. Asking someone if they believe in eating baby bunnies will elicit a much different response than asking if they have ever eaten rabbit. Leading questions, that is, questions that imply a correct answer by how they are phrased or worded, should be avoided as well. Pilot testing of the questionnaire, or at least getting expert advice on the content, wording, and question order will allow you to correct errors early in the research process and save much anguish later (Creswell, 2005).

Question order is a consideration when writing survey items. You don't want to put off your respondents right away, especially if you are going to ask sensitive questions at some point in the survey. Save these types of questions for the later parts of your instrument. Start your survey with background questions or questions that establish some demographic baselines. People can answer these questions easily and quickly and this gives them confidence about answering the questions that lie ahead. If your survey consists of both closed-ended and open-ended questions, try to put the closed-ended ones first if possible and save the open-ended ones for the end. This may not always be possible, as you also want to put questions that are related to each other in the same part or section of the survey, but as a general rule of thumb, it is useful. Respondents tend to interpret questions in context to other questions that are nearby so if questions probe related topics it is best to keep them together, even if it means mixing open- and closed-ended questions. While you want emotionally charged questions to come near the end of your survey, you may want to use the strategy of using a few innocuous "cool-off" questions after the charged ones so respondents don't end their participation in a highly charged state (Adler and Clark, 2003).

SELECTING YOUR SAMPLE

Sample selection in survey research is a function of the population of interest. As we noted earlier, if the group is small, you may be able to survey every member, thus conducting what we call a census. If the population is large, you will want to select a sample of it to survey. For large populations you will want to use some type of probability sample, like the simple random sampling technique described earlier in the chapter, in order to assure your sample is representative of the population. In many instances a probability sample will be hard to obtain. You may be surveying a small homogenous group about their food consumption behaviors, in which case the use of a probability sample will not be available to you. The other type of sample frequently used in survey research is the nonprobability sample. Nonprobability samples are useful when you have limited resources, when you can't identify all the members of a population, or when you are conducting exploratory or descriptive research to learn about the nature of a phenomenon (Adler and Clark, 2003). Trochim (2006) divides nonprobability samples into two categories, accidental and purposive. Accidental samples are those where the sample is a set of elements collected purely for the sake of convenience. The terms *convenience sampling* and *haphazard sampling* refer to accidental samples. The food critic is an excellent example of someone who uses a convenience sample to make a judgment. Most reputable food critics make a number of visits to an establishment and sample a variety of dishes each time. From this sample of food from the menu and service from the staff, the critic makes a judgment about the establishment. The sad reality of most research studies is that there is a lack of motivated individuals who want to participate for the sake of advancing knowledge, and unless you are surveying a select group of individuals who are interested in your topic, you may have problems obtaining a critical mass of research respondents. The notices you see posted on your campus seeking volunteers for various studies speak to this problem. There may be good reasons for using an accidental sample, such as a lack of time or volunteers or the need to have a quota (a certain percentage of females or Hispanics), but generally it is better to use one of the other types of nonprobability sample if you have the ability to do so.

Purposive nonprobability sample elements are selected based on the purpose of the research being conducted. Examples of purposive nonprobability samples include snowball sampling, expert sampling, modal sampling, quota sampling, and voluntary sampling. If you have access to a very small number of subjects who have the characteristics you want, say knowledge of an esoteric subject, you may ask the subjects you survey to refer you to other people who have the knowledge and may be willing to participate in the survey. This tactic is known as snowball sampling or chain-referral sampling or network sampling. A similar mode of sampling is what is known as expert sampling. In expert sampling, you sample a known quantity of experts on a topic. This can be useful in early stages of research or in prestudies or pilot studies to make sure that the questions being asked in the later survey are useful or correct. Modal sampling is used when we want to focus on individuals who fit some particular profile. If we are only interested in people who never cook at home, it would be a waste of our research time to interview people who are avid home cooks. In modal sampling, we would first determine if a person eats all meals away from home and only include those who fit our mode. Quota sampling is used when you want your sample to at least resemble the population in terms of some demographic signifier. You might want your sample to reflect gender balance or racial balance in your population, but beyond that you need to use a nonprobability sample—this is a case in which you would use a quota sample. Voluntary samples are frequently used in survey research. In voluntary sampling, people self-select into your research, usually because of an interest in the research topic. These types of samples can skew your data if you are trying to find out what a larger population feels or thinks about an issue or phenomenon, but may be useful if you are trying to get a basic idea about a phenomenon.

RESPONSE IN SURVEY RESEARCH

How many elements of your sample that respond to your request and complete the survey and whether or not those who do respond to it do so completely are two critical issues in survey research designs. Ideally, you would like to have every element in your sample complete the instrument completely and thoroughly. The reality is that this will almost never happen, especially if your sample is large or geographically disparate. Some of your elements you will not be able to contact because their contact information is out of date, some elements will refuse to participate once they have been contacted, and some will not participate (or only partially complete your instrument), even though they have expressed a willingness to do so (Colasanto, n.d.) Nonresponse is an important issue in survey research because the lower the response rate, the less likely it is that the responses that were collected and recorded are representative of the population being surveyed (Schueren, 2004). When the results of survey research are reported, one of the important details is what the response rate to the survey was. The most basic form of response rate is calculated by dividing the number of elements who responded and whose response was used by the total number of elements in the sample. This number is then expressed as a percentage (Johnson and Christensen, 2008). For years it was said that a 70 percent response rate was needed for research acceptability; a 60–70 percent response rate was usually a requirement to get results of survey research published in scientific journals; and a 50 percent rate was required for social science journals (Mundy, 2002, Dillman, 1978). While some organizations, like many agencies of the U.S. government, require a 75 percent or higher response rate on funded research, recent research has indicated that these numbers may no longer be the benchmark for survey research. Meta-analysis by Baruch (1999) suggests that the average response rate for academic survey research is just over 55 percent and that response rates have been declining over the past half century. An experiment conducted by the Pew Research Center in 1997 was designed to measure differences in data in opinion surveys. Using identical surveys measuring a number of social and political attitudes, the center used techniques that resulted in a 36 percent response rate in one application and a 61 percent rate in the second application. They found few significant differences between two applications of the survey, with only one or two exceptions (Colasanto, n.d.). Replication of the study in 2000 showed similar results. So it may not be necessary to achieve a high response rate as long as your respondents are representative of the population under consideration. Achieving a high response rate is costly in terms of both time and money. If an element in your survey has not returned the instrument in a certain amount of time (a time period to be determined by the researcher), then a follow-up contact must be made, either by telephone, mail, or email. Such efforts cost the researcher money, though email is considerably cheaper than the other two options. If 50 percent of your sample responds to the first request for participation, it may cost you as much or even more to get another 20 percent to participate.

There are many reasons that people may choose to not participate in a survey. Many times people feel that participation will take too much time or is not a worthwhile use of their time. If you can find a way to make participation important to the respondent, this will likely be the best way to ensure a high response rate. Survey instruments are often too long and too confusing in the eyes of participants. Survey fatigue is a common ailment in the survey business. Questionnaire length has been linked to response rate, with longer questionnaires having a lower response rate than shorter ones (Kaldenberg, Koenig, and Becker, 1994). Some other strategies for increasing response rates include:

Incentives—If you can offer the respondent a physical or monetary incentive (or at least the chance of one, like an entry to a drawing), you can generally increase your response rate. This can be an expensive way to increase participation if resources are limited. If you are expecting people to respond by regular mail, enclosing a postage-paid return envelope will improve response rates dramatically. If you are conducting phone surveys, have a toll-free number to respond to unless all elements in the sample are local calls.

Pre-announcement—A brief pre-announcement of your upcoming survey can alert people to the nature and importance of the survey that is to follow. This is most effectively done by the use of a simple post card or email. If possible use letterhead or a logo from the institution that you are affiliated with. In Fox, Crask, and Kim's

(1988) meta-analysis of mail survey results, this was the single most important factor in inducing response. This announcement may not be as effective in telephone surveys as it may annoy the respondent that you are going to have to disturb them again to actually conduct the survey.

Timing—When the element in your sample receives the research instrument can have an affect on response rate. E-mail surveys show a higher response rate when delivered in the middle of the week as research has determined that survey requests delivered in Monday and Friday's e-mail have a lower rate of response (Molasso, 2005).

Persistence—Some respondents need multiple follow-ups before they complete and return the instrument. This is less of problem with telephone surveys, but a common one with mail and e-mail surveys.

In addition to response rate, nonresponse bias must be considered if the response rate is low. Nonresponse bias is the idea that if you have a low response rate to your instrument (or even a middling response), then those who respond may not be representative of the population as a whole (Adler and Clark, 2003). There are various ways to see if this is going to be an issue with your study. One of these methods is to do some aggressive follow-up with a few of the nonrespondents in order to obtain information about them that will tell you if they are in some way different than the responders. If the elements of your sample that respond represent, say, more women, or have a lower average age, or have a different racial makeup, then the data you have gathered may not represent your population very well. If your aggressive follow-up doesn't work, then you may be able to check the information from those who have responded against your larger population to see if they are representative of the larger population. A third way to check on nonresponse bias comes from examining the data using what is known as the wave technique. If the responses from early responders are in line with those from later waves of response (late responders are generally considered to be similar in nature to nonresponders) then it is more likely the data you are gathering is representative of the population at large.

ANALYZING SURVEY DATA

The end goal of most quantitative research studies is to make assumptions about a population from a whole. As we have noted, it is usually not easy to survey an entire population unless the population is extremely small and confined to a small geographic area. This is why we use samples to stand in for the population. If we can survey the whole population, a census, we can easily come up with a parameter (a number that defines or quantifies a certain characteristic) for a population. A statistic is a similar number that comes from the sample we have surveyed. From statistics, we make inferences about parameters. We may want to know how many fat calories are consumed daily in Scotland, or how many minutes a day is spent on meal preparation in Brisbane, or how much the average Floridian spends on fresh fruits and vegetables. To do this we survey a sample of Scots or Brisbanians or Floridians, and based on the results of our survey, we calculate a statistic from which make our inferences about the population as a whole.

Likert Items and Likert Scales

In food studies research we often measure rather abstract constructs like flavor intensity or perceptions of authenticity. These are not concrete constructions like parts-per-million concentrations in pharmaceutical research. When we want to know about some particular characteristic of an item or attitudes about the item, we tend to use a *Likert item* to measure it (Gliner and Morgan, 1999). A Likert item is a question that allows for bipolar responses. There are generally five or seven possible responses (though sometimes we see nine), ranging from *strongly agree* to *strongly disagree* with various points, including a midpoint marked *neither agree nor disagree* (Gall, Gall, and Borg, 2005). Sometimes in food research this scale would range from *like very much* to *dislike very much* with a midpoint of *neither like nor dislike*. There is much debate over how many points to have in a Likert item. There may be good reasons to have seven or nine points to choose from in the scale, but using five points in the item usually suffices for most research. There is also some discussion in research circles about whether the middle *neither agree nor disagree* choice should be omitted from Likert items (Black, 1999). If the middle choice is eliminated it results in what is known as forced choice. Researchers advocating for this omission feel that no one is entirely neutral on any topic and that a choosing a neutral option represents a form of not making a choice for whatever reason; they therefore want the research subject to be forced to make a choice.

Likert items are not generally used by themselves, but are used as a part of a larger set of items, collectively known as a Likert scale or Summated Rating Scale. One of the most common misnomers in research is the use of the term *Likert scale* when the speaker or writer actually means Likert item. Likert scales are sets of Likert items that are generated to provide a sample of all opinions or attitudes about the topic under research (Gliner and Morgan, 2000).

An example of a Likert item in food studies might be:

Please indicate how you feel about the following statement:
I prefer home cooking to dining in a restaurant.
   Strongly disagree   Slightly disagree   Neutral   Slightly agree   Strongly agree

Use of Likert scales with multiple items will enhance the validity and reliability of your research about people's feelings and attitudes toward your topic. Likert scales are one of the most widely used forms of measure in social science research.

Definitions for Chapter

Variable—Any condition, characteristic, or attribute in a study that can take on more than one value.

Independent variable—The variable that is manipulated in a quantitative study for the purpose of influencing or affecting a change in the dependent variable or outcome.

Dependent variable—The variable that is caused to be changed by application of the independent variable.

Parameter—A numerical summary of a characteristic, trait, or quality of a population.

Statistic—A numerical summary of a characteristic, trait, or quality of a sample. A statistic is a stand-in for a parameter when the entire population cannot be surveyed or if it is impractical to do so.

Nonparametric statistic—a statistic that is calculated when the distribution of the variable is unknown.

6A A CONVERSATION WITH JEFFERY SOBAL

Jeffery Sobal is a professor in the Division of Nutritional Sciences at Cornell University in Ithaca, New York, and a member of the Cornell Graduate Fields of Development Sociology and Epidemiology. Before coming to Cornell, he was an associate professor at the University of Maryland School of Medicine in the Department of Family Medicine, and prior to that he was an assistant professor at Gettysburg College in the Department of Sociology and Anthropology. He received a B.A. in biology in 1972 from Bucknell University, a Ph.D. in sociology in 1978 from the University of Pennsylvania, and an M.P.H. in behavioral sciences and nutrition in 1983 from Johns Hopkins University. He teaches and conducts research about the application of social science theories, concepts, and methods to food and nutrition. His research interests include the sociology of food, eating, and nutrition; social aspects of obesity; food choice processes; commensality; and food and nutrition systems. He has co-edited three books with Donna Maurer: *Eating Agendas: Food and Nutrition as Social Problems (1995); Weighty Issues: Fatness and Thinness as Social Problems (1999); and Interpreting Weight: The Social Management of Fatness and Thinness (1999)*, authored and co-authored over fifteen book chapters, and published over 160 articles in professional journals. His current projects focus on patterns of obesity in relationship to marital status, stigmatization of obese individuals, and obesity as a social problem. He also works on conceptualizing the food choice process, studying commensal eating relationships, and analyzing the food and nutrition system. He co-teaches an undergraduate course at Cornell titled Social Science Perspectives on Food and Nutrition and teaches a graduate seminar at Cornell called Social Science Theories in Nutrition.

JD: Can you talk a little bit about the kind of work you do?
JS: Sure. I originally was trained as a biologist and then became a medical sociologist and also got trained in public health and epidemiology. So

I try to mix all of these things together. I do qualitative work, a lot of depth interviews. Less ethnography. But a lot of the work I do is survey research or analysis of big data sets that examine lots of different questions, a lot of them around body weight. But a lot of them about foods, perceptions of foods, social definitions of foods, things like that. So I work with undergraduate students and have had honors students present at ASFS [the Association for the Study of Food and Society] conference and publish their work. We do a lot of student surveys. So it's a way of examining how some of the things I'm interested in are manifested among students. We also do mailed questionnaires to the local area or larger areas. We also analyze a lot of large data sets that either are public opinion polls that are publicly available or government data that are available.

JD: And how did you make the transition from being in biology through medical sociology and now into food or food studies?

JS: It's kind of just a shifting of interests. Originally I wanted to be a marine biologist just like Jacques Cousteau. And I went to college and took every biology and oceanography course that I could. And it was interesting enough but it looked like I was going to be studying invertebrates or fish for the rest of my life. And then I took a social psychology course with a really dynamic teacher and said, "This is so much more interesting than working with invertebrates," that I got interested in social psychology and from there I got interested in even more macro perspectives and decided to get a Master's and Ph.D. in sociology, with a specialty in medical sociology. And there I did both qualitative and quantitative work even as a grad student. So I did a qualitative study of shopping malls that I almost did my dissertation on. This is back in the 1970s where shopping malls were just starting to make it big. So I did participant observation at malls, and interviewed people, and counted people, and things like that. And then I kind of got interested in combining my knowledge of biology with sociology in medical sociology. I actually wasn't involved in food until I went to a big conference at Penn State. It just looked interesting, called, "Nutrition: Personal and National." So I went there and there were about 100 people there and everybody else was a dietitian, nutritionist, biochemist, physician, you know a life scientist or healthcare person. And once I said I was a sociologist they started asking me all of these questions, saying, "We know about cholesterol, why won't people listen?" Or, "Can we do this to the food supply and would people tolerate it?" I kept just having to say, "I don't know." It's a new area I thought would be interesting. But I knew I had discovered an interesting area that would combine some biological and life science issues with social science issues. I always knew that if you wanted to learn something you should teach a course about it, so I volunteered to teach a course on the sociology of food and eating. And this is back in 1979. I was teaching at Gettysburg College. And they said, "Oh that sounds pretty novel, why don't you go ahead and do it?" And it was really fun and the students loved it and I loved it and that really got me started in this area.

JD: It seems like there aren't many people doing mixed methods or both quantitative and qualitative studies in food.

JS: That's a hot area within the qualitative evaluation and educational research areas. Mixed methods. I guess I don't actually do mixed methods as such. I do both methods but I don't necessarily tightly mix them. So there are a lot of people that will publish one paper where they do a survey and they do a bunch of depth interviews and they try to relate those to each other. I've found that a lot of those end up being bad quantitative and bad qualitative stuff because you're forcing them together. So we do decent qualitative work and decent quantitative work on the same topic but we don't necessarily try to mash them together. I see them as different lenses or different ways of looking at the same topic. Several of the previous years of the ASFS conference, I was one of two or three quantitative papers that I saw at the meeting, so I feel like it's a minority position which is different from what it was at the earliest ASFS meetings where there were a lot more nutritionists, epidemiologists, and survey people around. And it wasn't seen as food studies then. It was seen as really a food-and-society type of focus. So there has been a change in the people that attend the meetings. And I guess I would see food studies as different from food and society. I think it's kind of a nebulous, evolving area. Food and society, at least as I've seen it, represents more social science perspective that would include much more quantitative and positivistic analysis, whereas food studies seems to be more linked with the humanities, and bringing in a lot of the methods like historical analysis, qualitative, ethnography, autoethnography, things like that, as well as discourse analysis, textual analysis, things coming more directly out of the humanities.

JD: What do you think are some of the reasons for that shift over the last couple decades?

JS: This is some of the stuff that will go in the book I've been working on. I think some of the differences [are] that there are other places for the quantitative people to go, so epidemiology and nutrition and health sciences have been more open and welcoming to people studying food behavior, food patterns, things like that. And also the major social science disciplines have increasingly developed their own groups and focus on food, eating, nutrition, agriculture. So there are other places and I think some people have retreated back into their disciplines rather than working in an interdisciplinary area. So overall I see food quantitative research as being an important but a minority perspective in food studies as food studies currently exists. And I think it's important to include, partially for consuming other literature. So everyone should know about quantitative research methods and to some extent, statistical and quantitative data analysis and presentation just so they can read things from economics, from experimental psychology and things like that. So even if people don't do it themselves, I think they need to be somewhat quantitatively literate just like I think all of the hard-nosed nutritionists need to be qualitatively literate so they can read those literatures. So that's part of it and then the other part is that it offers another window into the world. Another perspective to make positivist or postpositivist assumptions about how the world works and then to collect quantitative data and analyze it offers a different focus, a different concentration on a variables-based approach as opposed to an interaction- or cognition- or setting- or contextually based approach.

JD: I'm wondering if you can comment on some quantitative methods that seem especially promising or apt for food studies.

JS: There are lots of existing data out there that can get mined quantitatively. So there are lots of surveys, collections of official records, all kinds of things that are just crying out for people who do food things to examine. All the way from doing quantitative analysis of the media where you're not just doing qualitative textual analysis but you're doing media counts of how many articles there have been about this and how that's changed in popular magazines from one time period to another. So I think there's a lot of existing data that really deserves to be mined. I think a mainstay is surveys and questionnaires. Just to be able to conduct really relatively simple surveys of topics of interest. So if you're looking at comfort foods, you survey 100 people and ask them what foods they think are comfort foods, what makes a food a comfort food, and you've gone probably a lot further than you could go in doing twenty or maybe thirty qualitative interviews in terms of characterizing the core, the broad phenomena. You still need to do, I think, the qualitative stuff, to look at the dynamics and the beliefs and the intensity, but I think that it should be complemented by quantitative stuff. There's a lot of opportunity for systematic observation. Just literally sitting there and counting people. And seeing how many people over a two-hour period go into the salad bar line or the fried food line at cafeterias and then maybe looking at their gender and things like that and then doing some interviews later to follow that up. But it's really pretty straightforward stuff that would answer and address the broad perspective you could get from observation or surveys as opposed to the focused perception or interpretation you would get from doing qualitative interviews. So observation, straightforward surveys with a lot of open-ended questions but fixed format questions, and analyzing available data. I think there's a lot of opportunity—it's really untapped.

JD: And those are methods that I think are very accessible.

JS: I think they're highly accessible. And I think the other part of it is to get some training. I am reluctant to have students to do qualitative work unless they've taken a course in that. And it isn't that hard to get training, even at conferences there are a lot of intense one-day workshops in how to get started in surveys or quantitative stuff or content analysis or focus groups.

JD: I wonder if you could talk about what you see as the difference between a disciplinary approach, like a sociology of food, and a food studies approach.

JS: I'm not sure there is a real difference. I think it's kind of a play on words that the interdisciplinary stuff is undisciplined. Which is in some ways a strength, in that they're freer to explore new and different things and not get sanctioned by rigid gatekeepers in their discipline, but they also don't bring the power and the experience of a disciplinary tradition with them. So when anthropologists do ethnography, they do it in a much more powerful way I think than someone who has self-learned ethnography. Just reading Carole Counihan's work I can just see the richness of 100 years of anthropology in there as opposed to if I tried to do an ethnography, I just wouldn't have that tradition behind me. So disciplines can be limiting but they offer some strength, but there also is the freedom and the creativity of what I would see as a food studies approach. It's really hard to situate food studies—where it is and how it really relates to the disciplines at this point. We actually don't even have a strong description of what food studies is and what it incorporates.

JD: What advice do you have for someone who is reading this who decides they want to get into the quantitative study of food and society?

JS: I guess my advice would be to collaborate. Certainly if you're a graduate student or an undergraduate student or even a young assistant professor and you're working on a problem or you're interested in a problem that you think would benefit from doing a survey or doing a content analysis, find somebody that does that method and has successfully done it in the past and published using it and say, "Hey I've got the topic, I'll put in the effort, but I need your methodological expertise. Will you work with me?" And that gets you a lot of the way there. And once you've done it, you can see where to go from there and you may get some additional training, do additional reading and develop your skills. But the real challenge I think is diving in and doing it once. So collaboration is really a hugely important thing. And it doesn't have to be someone at your institution. It's nice to have someone you can have contact with on a regular basis because I think there's no substitute for being able to walk down the hall or to the next building and saying, "I was working on this and I don't know where to go from here." And they sit down and look at the data and they say, "You should try this. Let's do this now." But it can also be done at a distance. So there are lots of people wandering around that have done quantitative work at the ASFS conference and many would be willing to collaborate on things.

7 OBSERVATIONAL METHODS IN FOOD STUDIES RESEARCH: ETHNOGRAPHY AND NARRATIVE

Don't think, but look.

Ludwig Wittgenstein

Some of the most widely used methods in food studies research fall under the rubric of observational research. *Qualitative observational research* is an umbrella term for a large basket of methods used by qualitative researchers to try to understand the motivation, meaning, and context behind the actions, behaviors, and rituals of cultures, groups, and individuals. These observational research techniques go by many names, and there is much overlap between the techniques. What they have in common is they are naturalistic forms of inquiry that usually occur in the field that do not rely on experimental research designs to provide a data set. Many of these are used in food studies research. Two of the most common types of observational research methods used by food studies researchers are ethnography and narrative. These two methods are widely used in food studies research because they tell the stories of people as they obtain, prepare, and share food. With very little modification these techniques can be used in phenomenological and ethno-methodological studies of food as well.

ETHNOGRAPHY IN FOOD STUDIES
WHAT IS ETHNOGRAPHY?

The best description of ethnography comes from examining the original Greek roots of the term. Our word *ethnography* comes from the Greek terms *ethnekos* and *graphein*.

Ethnekos referred to anyone who was not Greek—"other people" or outsiders—and *graphein* is the Greek verb "to write." Ethnography, therefore, literally means to write about people outside our own culture. In the early days of anthropological endeavor, the term *ethnography* usually referred to the activities of those who went out in the field[1], often far out into the field, traveling up the Amazon in canoes or hiking into the mist-shrouded forests of New Guinea, to report on "primitive" cultures, those untainted by contact with the modern world. It wasn't long before *ethnography* was also used to refer to reports of those intrepid explorers who ventured into the areas inhabited by the European or American or austral "primitive," the urban slums, or the rural "hollers" of the western poor (Erickson, 2002). As the twentieth century progressed, ethnography was used in more situations and ever closer to 'home' than the pioneers of the method might have ever imagined. Today we have stretched the meaning of the term to include even glimpses within ourselves, as is the case with auto-ethnographies.

Ethnography is a way of studying people, cultures, enterprises, and phenomena in a natural setting. It is a naturalistic form of inquiry that is conducted in the field. Creswell (2005) gives us a succinct definition of the ethnographical enterprise when he describes it as "qualitative research procedures for describing, analyzing, and interpreting a culture-sharing group's shared patterns of behavior, beliefs, and language that develop over time" (p. 436). To understand the culture of a group not our own (and, some would argue, even our own group), we "must deal with three fundamental aspects of human experience: what people do, what people know, and the things that people make and use" (Spradley, 1980, p. 5). Spradley uses the terms *cultural behavior, cultural knowledge,* and *cultural artifacts* to describe these three aspects of human experience. As an ethnographer in the field, you can use these three aspects of the human experience to try to gain an understanding of the culture, group, or phenomenon you are interested in. Food is a topic that is ideally suited to being studied from these three perspectives. The preparation, serving, sharing, eating, and enjoyment of food all have their roots and representations in these three areas.

Ethnography is different than many other types of research because it places the researcher in the field and has her actually participating in the activities that she is interested in. To do this, one of the early pioneers of ethnographic technique, Bronislaw Malinowski (1922), urged ethnographers to interact closely with the culture in question in order to grasp the "native's point of view, his relation to life, to realise his vision of his world" (p. 25). Ethnography is not so much an individual, particular research method, but rather a collection of research methods bundled together to help us understand the meanings that people in a group or of a place give to the things they themselves do or value. Atkinson and Hammersley (1994) tell us that ethnography is a form of social research that explores particular, individual forms of social experiences by gathering unstructured data in the field from a relatively small group or limited number of participants, and then interpreting the meanings of these behaviors in some type of report. If you choose to do ethnography for your research project, thesis or dissertation, you will use multiple research methods including participant observation, interviewing, and document analysis (to name just a few) in order to gain an understanding of the matter that brought you to the field in the first place.

CHARACTERISTICS OF AN ETHNOGRAPHIC STUDY

While each ethnographic study is unique there are some characteristics that tend to be common to many studies.

Ethnography is, *de facto,* fieldwork—as ethnographers, we want to find out what is happening in a natural (and frequently chaotic and disordered) environment, not an orderly and controlled artificial environment. Imagine a dinner table rather than a sensory analysis lab. The culture of the site is a critical element that needs to be used as an element in the understanding of the specific thing we are interested in and therefore becomes a critical element of the study.

Ethnographies are highly descriptive—Geertz's (1973) famous call for "thick description" is nowhere more relevant than in the ethnographic report. The ethnographic report must be highly detailed so the consumers of the research can assess for themselves if you are making an accurate representation of the situation in your analysis. The description needs to transport the reader to the scene and allow them a clear picture of the situation in their mind's eye. A "thick description" places the problem in its natural setting and provides context for the analysis to follow.

Thin Description vs. Thick Description

One of the most famous phrases in all of qualitative research is "thick description," a term coined by Clifford Geertz in his 1973 essay, *Thick Description: Toward an Interpretive Theory of Culture.* Thick description is different than traditional, or thin, description. Thin description is the reporting of facts without placing them in the context that makes them important. Thick description is a description that allows the reader to understand intentions, meanings, circumstances and to get a true context-sensitive sense of the place being described. Thick description tackles the difficult task of being a "written representation of a culture" (van Maanen, p. 1). Thick description not only describes the physicality of a place, but also its emotions, feelings, experiences, and circumstances. If your research is intended to be purely descriptive, then writing masterful thick description is a goal unto itself, but if you are striving for a deeper analytical result, thick description will be the base that you build on.

Ethnographies use multiple methods—a good ethnographer uses many methods to garner information about the topic at hand. The three most commonly used methods in ethnography are participant observation, interviewing, and document collection, though any method that adds to the understanding of the phenomenon of interest could be used. Recipes, food-centered interviews (see interview with Carole Counihan, p. 171), and observation of food habits are all common in food studies ethnographies.

Ethnography is a holistic endeavor—while most ethnographers are examining a specific group, situation, or phenomenon, the research is done in the context of a larger whole. Individual actors in any situation are motivated by both internal and external cues—to ignore the larger environment in which the actors exist inhibits the understanding of behaviors and actions. Observations made in the field are context-sensitive and so must be considered in the context of the field. A study of restaurant cooks cannot be divorced from the restaurant setting itself or the other actors (suppliers, servers, owners, diners).

Ethnography focuses on meaning—as ethnographers we want to understand the meanings and interpretations that come from the process of people interacting and negotiating their daily lives. An ethnographer will realize that identity and meaning are never static and that what we are creating is at best a snapshot of a place in time, hopefully a meaningful one that will aid in our understanding of the world around us (Stewart, 1998: Creswell, 2005; Fetterman, 1998; Tedlock, 2000).

ETHNOGRAPHY AND FOOD

Ethnography is one of the great implements in the food scholar's toolbox because it allows the researcher to gain an understanding of a person or group's social meaning of ordinary activities. Most social groups have shared behaviors revolving around the manner in which they select, gather, prepare, and share food. As food rituals and behaviors are some of the primary activities in private and public life, ethnography can help us gain understandings of the greater meanings of these activities. We may or may not be able to make larger inferences based on the understandings we gain from ethnographic research, but the ethnographic process can give us great insight into the food habits of culture-sharing groups. An excellent example of food ethnography is folklorist Kathy Neustadt's *Clambake* (1992), a look at the clambake in Allen's Neck, Massachusetts, a small-town event that has been going on for over 100 years. Neustadt attempts to understand what meaning the clambake has for the people who put it on and for the people who come to take part in it. Using a theoretical focus, she examines the way in which the event serves as a way to give the community identity, but to do this she has to examine the history and lore of clambakes in general and this one in particular; how the working group that puts on the clambake functions;

in what ways the menu has changed and in what ways it has stayed the same; and the technical particulars of a successful event from gathering seaweed and making pies to selling tickets and cleaning up. By examining as many aspects of the phenomenon as possible, she is able to offer an explanation of some of the social meaning of this clambake.

TYPES OF ETHNOGRAPHIES

Approaches to ethnography have changed a good deal in the last 100 years or so. When the early giants of ethnography, pioneers like Franz Boas and Bronislaw Malinoski, went out into the field, the ideal was a realist ethnography that attempted to be an "objective report" of what the ethnographer had observed. In contrast to many ethnographies today, early ethnographies were narrated in the third person, and the material that was reported was supposed to represent the "facts" of what was happening the field. In realist ethnography, little is offered in the way of personal reflection, points are made through the use of "closely edited quotations" (Creswell, 2005, p. 438), and the ethnographer remains in the background. The realist ethnography is generally an outside-looking-in approach to the representation of culture, and the interpretation at the end of it reflects the outsider's interpretation of the events portrayed in the report. This was in line with a positivist view of the time that social science was to fit in the empirical scientific mold that reigned in the "hard" sciences like chemistry or biology. Today the realist ethnography has frequently given way to a much more reflexive style of ethnography where the self-referential "I" is often seen in the final report and the author acknowledges her biases and prejudices as part of the final reporting. Some disciplines still favor the traditional realist ethnography, but there are a much wider variety of options open to the modern ethnographer. In the *Handbook of Qualitative Research,* Tedlock (2000) lists a number of forms that modern ethnographies take including life history, memoir, narrative ethnography, auto-ethnography, ethnographic novels and other fictive genres, critical ethnography, and field diaries.

RESEARCH DESIGN IN ETHNOGRAPHY

Research design in ethnography should begin as soon as you have selected the topic for your research. The research design process commences with the selection of a problem, situation, or phenomenon to be examined. Once you have stated, in a question form, what it is you want to know about this problem, the research design phase should begin. Your research questions will help you to make decisions regarding how you will gain access to the field, what kind of data collection methods you will use, how you will analyze the data you will collect, and what format the final report will take. Take the time to think about all of the elements of these considerations and begin to outline them on paper as a roadmap for your research project. This process will give your project structure and a starting point. It also gives your project some limits and parameters. If you are one of the joyful ethnographers, you will encounter a seemingly endless number of things that would be interesting to follow up on. These distractions, while often fascinating and fun to follow up on, can distract you from your primary topic and result in unfocused research that takes up an inordinate amount of your time.

Write out your research questions in such a way that the aims and objectives of your research are clear to you and to the ultimate consumer of your research. You may have a single research question or you may have multiple research questions, but avoid having a laundry list of questions, as you want to focus your research as closely as you can. For example, O'Connor (2008) asked the question, "What narratives and identities are embedded in the traditional Hawaiian luau?" Your choice of research field will usually be a direct result of the question that you ask. Most of you will have a question about what is happening in a specific place, so the field is *de facto* decided.

Your data collection methodologies are another component of your research design. In ethnography traditional methods of data collection include participant observation, interviews, and document analysis, but you may want to include other methods such as food recall journals or photography of food products or events. Specifically note each of the methods you intend to use and how you will obtain the data. If you are going to use participant observation, decide on what particular type of observation will work best for your study. The same applies to interviews—will you use highly structured interviews, semi-structured or unstructured?

Some of your answers to questions about field selection and data collection methodologies will depend on the resources available to you. In addition to money, make sure you consider time a resource. Time, money, and access are the primary limitations on what you will do. Unless you have a great amount of personal funding to spend on the project, the technological and time resources you will have to commit to the project will be limited. Research grants are available to conduct food ethnographies, but they will limit what and where you can do your research. Departments of agriculture and other governmental agencies will often fund research with nutritional implications, but their annual grant programs have strict parameters in the areas of populations, scope, and topics. In recent years projects around obesity, food safety, and child nutrition have been funded with some regularity, but other topics received scant attention. There are grants in the arts and humanities, but they tend to be as scarce as the proverbial hens' teeth. Arts and humanities grants aimed at historical preservation and primary school–level educational activities have gotten the highest levels of funding in the United States in recent years.

The amount of time you will have to spend on collecting data for a food studies–oriented ethnography will likely be limited as well. Very few of us are able to go live in the field for extended periods of time collecting data. As a student considering food studies ethnography, you likely have a time line that dictates how much time you can devote to your project. If you are doing a brief ethnography for a class project, this could be as short as a few weeks, and if you are considering ethnography for your thesis or dissertation, you may still only have a year or so to plan, execute, analyze, and write the report. Don't let these thoughts discourage you: one of the joys of food studies research is that there are many interesting projects in one's own back garden, so to speak.

Access to the field is another critical element in ethnographic research design. Reflect upon how you are going to get into the field. Is your field a place where you have ready access, some place you already work or participate in the activities, or do you have a friend or colleague already in place to provide entrée? If not, you will need to earn access, either formal or informal, to enter the field. This can sometimes be easy to obtain, but sometimes not, and in either case requires a plan. While some fields are easily accessed by talking with members of the group you want to find out more about, others are notoriously difficult. As researchers, we are often interested in the food habits and preferences of children, but gaining access to places that provide access to children can be extremely complicated and time-consuming. Most school districts require formal requests with copies of questionnaires attached and will require that all members of the research teams successfully complete a criminal background check before the request will even be considered. If the request is approved then the parent or guardian of each child you wish to interview or observe will also need to give you written permission to engage in the research.

Things to Consider When Choosing a Site for Study

Burgess's five criteria for site selection (1984, p. 61):

Simplicity: A site that is simple to assay at first, but allows for movement to more complex situations and sub sites.

Accessibility: The site must permit you entry and access.

Unobtrusiveness: The researcher must be able to maintain somewhat of a low profile at the site.

Permissibleness: A site that you are able to get permission to enter and allows you free access to people, situations, documents, etc., that you need.

Participation: A site where you will be able to engage in activities in order to gain perspective.

Once your site selection has been made, you will also need to plan what your role in the community will be. There are many forms of observation, from detached observer to participant observer to member of the community. Different observational roles have different advantages and disadvantages, and your role may change once you are actually performing your fieldwork, but you need to have a plan prior to entry.

Another issue related to the field is when to leave it. What is going to be your signal that you have collected the data you require and that it is time to retire from the field? The best signal that it is time to leave the field is that you feel you have collected enough data to answer the research questions you have posed for yourself to answer.

When you return from the field, you hopefully will have a great deal of data to analyze. What is your strategy going to be for analyzing the data? Do you have an idea of the coding scheme you will use? How much are the form of the final report and the intended placement of the report going to influence how you analyze and present your data? Consider these issues, beginning with the creation of research questions and ending with the presentation of the data, and construct a rough research design. Work with your advisor or collaborator(s) and have a good plan before you venture out into the field.

THE ETHNOGRAPHIC PROCESS

There is really no one correct way to "do" an ethnography. So much of what you do and how you do it will be shaped by the questions you write, the site you gain access to, the methods you choose for data collection, and the reality that every ethnographic project is truly unique. Don't let the idea of there being no standard formalized structure for conducting an ethnographic project scare you from attempting an ethnographic study of a food studies topic. For many researchers, ethnography allows a degree of freedom rarely found in other methodologies. This type of researcher appreciates the flexibility in shaping research to the situation at hand that ethnography allows. As an ethnographer you are in the field observing events and situations that are the result of human endeavor, with all the joys and problems that implies. What makes ethnography so attractive to many researchers is the fact that it is conducted in the field where there are many uncontrollable (and interesting) variables, not in a laboratory. You may get into the field and find information that sends you back to drawing board. While this prevents ethnography from being a neat A-B-C, 1-2-3 sequential type of research, these new discoveries are factors that make this an interesting style of research. This lack of structure means that ethnography may not be the ideal type of research for everyone, but for those who enjoy these potentialities, it can be extremely rewarding.

While there is no official standard on how ethnography should be conducted, analyzed, and reported, we can offer a general set of considerations that may help you with the organizational phase of your project.

1. Consider the intent of your study. What is it exactly you want to explain or illuminate in your final report? Committing this idea (or set of ideas) to paper and getting feedback will help clarify issues for you.
2. Write your research questions. As with other types of research, writing tightly focused research questions will help you organize your project and provide criteria for analysis.
3. Select an appropriate research design. This often will follow directly from the research questions that you ask. (See the "Research Design and Ethnography" section earlier in this chapter.)
4. Seek approval to conduct the study. You will need to get approval from two places if you intend to work with people. The first is your own institution's Institutional Review Board, what is often referred to as Human Subjects (see the Chapter 3, "Ethics and Responsible Behavior in Food Studies Research"). The second is the place or group where you intend to do your research.
5. Obtain access to sites and participants. This will follow to some degree from the previous step; gaining access can be as simple as asking a person's permission to a lengthy application and review process, something that is common if you wish to conduct research in institutional settings.
6. Collect your data. Use as many informants as is practical. Spending as much time as possible in the field will ensure the highest quality and quantity of data to work with.
7. Organize and analyze your data. This will be a matter of organizing, coding, and analyzing what you bring back from the field. If you are writing a critical ethnography, then you will need to identify changes that need to occur and create a plan for advocacy that you will describe in the final report.

DATA COLLECTION IN ETHNOGRAPHY

There are numerous ways to collect data for ethnography, but as we mentioned earlier in the chapter, the three most commonly used methods of data collection in food studies ethnographic research are participant observation, interviewing, and document collection. Data collection in ethnography is a time-intensive endeavor. Every facet of fieldwork and analysis in ethnography requires a commitment of time, from gaining access to the site to doing the observation and interviews to analyzing the data you collect.

Wolcott's Take on the Ethnographic Process

Harry Wolcott (1999), in his examination of the ethnographic process *Ethnography: A Way of Seeing*, relabels the triumvirate of observation, interviewing, and document collection as experiencing, inquiring, and examining. Wolcott feels participant observation should reflect everything that can be experienced by the senses, not just sights and sounds, and that these sensory experiences are an important part of the final report. He prefers the term *inquiry to interviewing* because he feels it better represents the scope of what the researcher should be doing in the field, being an active inquirer about all the researcher experiences. Lastly he prefers the term *examining* to *document collection* because he feels the latter term that may lead the researcher to confine his or her efforts to archival document research when all manner of physical artifacts tell important stories about the situation under investigation.

All the elements of collecting data in the field are collectively referred to as field-work. Fieldwork can be long or short in duration. The usual rule of thumb is, the more unfamiliar the situation, the longer your time in the field will be, but as with all rules of thumb, this is not true in every case. Sometimes your fieldwork does not happen all at once, but rather in a series of visits. You may only have access to the field at scheduled times or as your informants have room on their schedule for you. If you are researching food habits at a factory canteen, you would have to time your visits to coincide with meal periods set by the factory owners and likely perform many visits to obtain sufficient observational data to make assertions in the discussion section of your research report. Research done on a food festival that occurs on an annual basis will dictate a definitive set of dates (or time span) in which certain elements of your data collection must occur. In some instances you may want to leave the field and an-alyze the data you have collected and get a sense of what is happening before return-ing to the field to conduct more finely tuned observations or interviews. Fieldwork will continue until you run out of time or money or informants or until you feel you have exhausted all the data-gathering possibilities. If you see returns diminishing or you are observing the same patterns over and over, then the fieldwork phase is likely over and you can retire to your home base and begin analyzing your data.

Observation is one of the key elements of nearly every form of research. From nuclear physicists observing the subtle interaction of atomic particles to the psy-chologist observing the behaviors of children at play, observation plays a critical role in a wide range of disciplines. But in many disciplines these observations are done at a distance. The physicist will often see the behavior of particles through the screens of electron microscopes, and the psychologist will observe from behind a two-way mirror in order not to influence the behavior of the child at play. In ethnography we need to participate in the culture or group we are interested in to gain access to the meanings behind the actions. While there is much to be learned from merely seeing what people do, the richness of ethnographical research lies in understanding *why* people do things they do. By joining in the activities of the group and working alongside the members, we can more easily gain access to their interpretations of their activities and discover the social meanings of the activities they participate in and the objects they ascribe value to. In Miller's research (2006) on the meal served by the women's auxiliary of St. Wenceslaus parish during the Czech Fest in Wilson, Kansas, the researcher actually worked in the kitchen alongside the group members preparing and serving the food. By doing so, he could experience the physical work involved and be party to the discussions had by the workers as they prepared the food, thereby giving him additional insights into the process. By being involved with our subjects we are hoping to discover what they feel and experience as they go about the actions we are interested in discovering more about. We refer to this type of engaged observation as participant observation.

One thing to remember as you engage in participatory observational activities is that your presence among your research subjects will change the dynamic of what is happening. Think about what happens when a new person is introduced into your own personal social network. People are often initially guarded in what they say in the presence of a new person and may not act typically while under the gaze of this stranger. Simply by being there, the new person changes the traditional dynamic of the group. In the case of the meal served at the Czech Fest, the researcher was the first male who had ever donned an apron and made kolaches to serve at the meal. By being an outsider and a male, the dynamic of the process was altered and this alteration had to be accounted for by additional reflexive material in both fieldnotes and the final report. Ideally, these changes are neither drastic nor long-lived, but your presence will have an effect. The reflexive piece of your ethnographic report will have to include some of your perceptions relating to the effect you feel you had by participating in the group. On occasion some researchers deal with the group dynamic change by attempting to craft an identity as a member of the group. In anthropology, this attempt to become a group member or becoming over-identified with the group is referred to as "going native." As a researcher it is important to maintain a balance between being enough of an insider to gain access to the information you need to perform your research, and being an outsider, so you can maintain some level of objectivity and your critical faculties.

The ethnographer can learn a great deal by merely watching or participating in a situation, but rarely can the observer be a witness to or a participant in everything that influences the processes or outcomes under study. This means our gaze will be focused in some areas and not others. We all enter the field with a set of biases, prejudices, and conceptions no matter how much we would like it to be otherwise. This can influence where we turn our gaze, where we focus our attention. In focusing on certain areas, we may miss elements critical to our later analysis and interpretation. While engaging in participant observation we need to be careful of focusing our gaze on the odd, the aberrant, and the anomalous. These are the elements that tend to stand out in a situation, but generally speaking, unless our study is of the odd or aberrant (the holiday meal as opposed to daily dining), we are trying to understand the average and everyday.

While participant observation is a critical element of the ethnographer's method, it is only one leg of the stool. Because what we observe can be so strongly influenced by who we are, we use other techniques for collecting data as well. The second most common data collection tool is the interview. The layperson often confuses the terms *interview* and *questionnaire,* but the two are distinctly different items. A questionnaire is a form that is filled in by the person answering the questions. An interview is administered either in person or over the telephone directly to the person whose information we seek to gather. Questionnaires are generally used in mail and e-mail applications and can yield some valuable results when structured and applied correctly. A questionnaire will generally be highly structured and usually elicits shorter answers to the questions being posed. When we are engaging in ethnographic research we tend to rely more on interviews than questionnaires. We do use forms to guide our interviews, forms that we refer to as schedules or protocols.

Interviews take various forms, with the most commonly used ones being the highly structured interview, the semi-structured interview, and the lightly or unstructured interview. Think of interview forms as a spectrum, and the various types of interviews as being places on the spectrum. Exactly which point on the spectrum your interview form will be depends on the type of information you want to elicit and the people you are interviewing. The types, or classifications, of interviews are based on the specificity of the questions being asked, the degree of standardization of the wording, and the order of the questions being asked. The highly structured interview is the most ordered of these categories. The questioning in a highly structured interview "uses an interview schedule with closed questions, with explicit instructions to interviewers about when to prompt and what to say in order to ensure the (questions) take the same form for everyone" (Brewer, 2000, p. 66). This ensures the responses given by the respondents can be measured against a standard and have not been influenced by the way a question has been put to the respondent.

Semi-structured and unstructured interviews are widely used in food studies research because they allow for more explanation of the respondent's meanings. The lack of a rigid protocol allows the researcher to probe areas that arise in the course of the interview that may not have been considered in the development of the interview protocol. These types of interviews may have a number of specific questions that have been worked out in advance, or they may rely on a list of topics that the researcher is interested in, and then the researcher guides the interview in directions informed by the information elicited in the process of conducting the interview. In many cases the semi-structured and unstructured interview take the form of a conversation with the research subject rather than a formal question-and-answer format. The benefit of these less-formal approaches is that the respondent is allowed to answer in greater depth and with less structure to their answer, allowing the researcher to probe or ask supplementary questions that may shed more light on the topic of interest or illuminate unforeseen areas of interest. Often some very interesting revelations occur when the respondent is allowed to stretch out as they give their answer.

Which of the interview styles you choose for your research project will depend on both the topic you are investigating and your particular skills and proclivities as a researcher. Highly structured interviews tend to be easier to conduct because the interview schedule gives the researcher a tight framework for asking questions and getting shorter, more limited responses. Inexperienced interviewers often feel more comfortable with a highly structured interview format because it helps them conduct the interview in a linear and timely manner and they tend to experience a greater sense of control over the process. When a researcher wants to get a more limited range of information from a large number of people, or when a research project has multiple interviewers, the highly structured interview is an appropriate device. When analyzing the data after the interview phase is over, the researcher can more easily compare responses from highly structured interviews than from less-structured ones.

Food studies researchers often use a less-structured interview style because they feel it allows them to use probes and prompts to dig deeper into the response given by the interviewee and thereby gives "access to people's meaning-endowing capacities and produces rich, deep data in the form of extracts of natural language" (Brewer, 2000, p. 66). Conversations about food often contain informative digressions that will allow the researcher to discover additional information about the importance of the food phenomenon under investigation. Less-structured interview techniques require greater interviewing skills and depend more on the ability of the interviewer to make a personal connection with the person being interviewed so that the respondent feels comfortable spinning out answers and speaking to issues that the interviewer can later analyze for meaning and importance. This is especially true when discussing emotionally sensitive topics like food. A less-structured interview format is dependent on the ability of the researcher to recognize social cues, the ability to know when to probe and when to remain silent, and the ability to know when a vein of interest is exhausted and the topic needs to be changed or supplementary questions asked.

A common problem with both questionnaires and interview protocols is the fact that sometimes the questions are eliciting answers other than what the researcher wants to know about. What usually happens in these instances is that the respondent is interpreting the question in a different manner than the researcher intended. This is especially problematic with questionnaires that are not administered in person. Sometimes this problem can be overcome by asking the question in a number of different ways, but not always. The best solution is to try to couch all your questions in the most unambiguous language possible. Pilot testing the questions, or least having them evaluated by an experienced researcher, can go a long way toward alleviating these types of problems (Salant and Dillman, 1994).

Respondent interpretation is not the only problem the researcher will encounter when administering a protocol or questionnaire. Another set of problems lie in the fact that people don't always tell the truth when they answer questions put to them by a researcher. Rarely do people lie for the purpose of wreaking havoc with your research, but they may not tell you the whole, exact truth for a number of reasons. Sometimes people are embarrassed by the behaviors they engage in. Researchers engaging in research of intimate topics such as sexual and eating behaviors will run into this fairly often. No one wants to be thought of as promiscuous or a glutton, so they will decrease the number or scale of incidences of behavior that they admit to. Nutrition researchers discovered many years ago that self-administered recall intake surveys often significantly underestimate the number of calories the subjects consume. To be fair, this may partly happen from lack of memory about a time period—who remembers every ort of food they put in their mouth every day? But it likely happens just as often because respondents are embarrassed to admit how much or how often they really eat during the day.

Social acceptance is another reason that a respondent may not be completely honest with an interviewer. This is a common phenomenon in face-to-face interviews. The respondent will tell the interviewer what they think they want to hear in order to be "socially accepted" by the person who is conducting the interview, a person who can appear as an authority figure just by the fact that they are conducting surveys. Respondents may also worry about the purpose of the research and feel that there will be consequences if they reply in certain ways. Taken together, most of these problems that can distort the findings of an interview are known as the "interviewer effect" (LeCompte, Preissle, and Tesch, 1993) and can have the cumulative effect of skewing your data set as people minimize the number and intensity of "extreme" food behaviors when they are talking to you about their consumption. Data skewing can't always be eliminated, but it can be moderated to some degree by instituting some controls such as matching socio-demographic profiles of interviewer and interviewee when possible or by having some sort of control in place when analyzing the data.

ANALYZING DATA

Once you leave the field it will be time to begin analyzing your data. This can take as much time as doing the research. The analysis process begins with organizing your data. Organize all of your fieldnotes, memoranda, reports, pictures, recordings, transcripts, and so on and see how all of the threads, exhibits, and minutiae begin to coalesce into a whole. Time analyzing data can be shortened by keeping data organized as you go along and by doing some initial organization and analysis in the field during times you are not doing observations, interviews, collecting documents, and so on. Get in the habit of writing yourself research memoranda while you are in the field. Pose questions, write reminders, and posit potential theorems to yourself. Talk to informants about what you think and feel about what you have discovered and ask them for validation about your ideas. If you have issues that can cause potential problems in the analysis phase, this is the time to find them and go back to your field and/or informants.

One of the principal ideas to keep in mind as you contemplate the analytical phase of this type of research is that ethnographic analysis is iterative; that is, it builds on ideas that come forward throughout the course of the research. If you have been keeping your data organized and have been contemplating it as you conduct the study, you may have some ideas for analysis before you sit down to do the work. Whether you have ideas in mind or not, your analysis will likely start by coding data. Coding is a process that will allow you to discover themes in your data. Codes are labels that we give to words or passages of information that we put together in like categories. Themes can come from two sources. The first of these are external sources. Coding that stems from external sources is generally referred to as deductive coding. Deductive codes are codes that come from the theoretical literature in a discipline, and the researcher searches for material in the data that fits a set of pre-established categories (Bernard, 2000). If you were doing ethnography of soup kitchens you might look at the themes found in the literature of the soup kitchen and then code your data to see if your research supports (or does not support) the research that already exists on the topic. The other type of coding is inductive. Inductive codes are those that emerge from a reading of the data conducted without reference to standard theories in the field (Bernard, 2000). If you took your data on soup kitchens and coded the data based on words, phrases, ideas, actions, processes, and on from your interviews and observations, that would be inductive coding. Some researchers suggest you start with some themes suggested in the literature review as a base, then start adding more as you continue to code data (Ryan and Bernard, 2000). Sometimes the use of descriptive statistics can help the coding process. If you have access to a qualitative software program like NVivo, NUD*IST, The Ethnograph, or SuperHyperQual, you can find out how often various codes are used and which areas seem to be most important in interviews and analysis. If your access is limited to a word-processing program like Word or WordPerfect, you can get the program to count how many times certain terms are used and get an idea of relative importance based on word count. These tools can steer you in the right direction when it comes to developing and considering codes, but in the end you are still dependent to a great degree on personal judgment in the process of coding data. The purpose of coding is to be able to see the emergence of themes and patterns of behaviors, language, and actions. These themes and patterns are the basis for the interpretation that will happen when you write the final report.

You may want to include the scrutiny of photographs, maps, flowcharts, organizational charts, and so on in your analytical process. These types of exhibits, known by the collective term *visual displays* (Fetterman, 1998), can sometimes make clear things that we don't always get by observing people and listening to them. If you were conducting an ethnography of a food service organization it might be helpful to have an organizational chart mapping job titles and lines of report because these relationships will affect the way in which people relate to one another in the professional setting. In addition to studying visual displays, you will want to analyze any documents that you were able to obtain in the course of your fieldwork. In recent research in the area of community cookery, a series of community cookbooks were analyzed to see which dishes had been perpetuated in the different editions of the cookbook and which ones had fallen by the wayside (Miller, 2006).

In a vein similar to visual displays are what researchers refer to as key events (Fetterman, 1998). Key events give us a similar look into a culture, because so many important cultural meanings are imbedded into these events. These events are often metaphors for larger issues in a culture and actions that occur during the event are often symbolic of larger issues in the culture. For example, in considering Jewish American food culture (Deutsch and Saks, 2008), holidays and life cycle events, as well as everyday meals can be important entry points toward cultural understanding.

We said earlier that good ethnography uses multiple methods of data collection. If you have returned from the field with interview transcripts and notes from your observations and various documents you collected, then you can use a process known as triangulation to help with the analysis of your data. Triangulation is the use of different types of data sources (interview, observation, documents) in a study to verify reliability, clarify meaning, and identify the different ways in which the same phenomenon is being seen (Janesick, 2000, Stake, 2000.) As you find similar codes or themes in your different research areas, you compare them to see if there are similarities (or dissimilarities) occurring. Finding dissimilarity in no way invalidates what you are attempting to do. People see the world through different lenses and in doing so will create different interpretations of what they see. A good ethnography will account for varieties of perspective and incorporate them into the finished report.

A concept that has gained much ground in the world of qualitative research of late is *crystallization*. Richardson (2000) describes crystallization as a more complex way of looking at data; an approach that includes "an infinite variety of shapes, substances, transmutations, multidimensionalities, and angles of approach," so that we see data in a more complete and "deepened" fashion than mere triangulation (p. 934). Crystallization is an offshoot of the idea of interdisciplinary triangulation, a triangulation technique where the researcher goes outside their home discipline to find support for what has been observed in the course of their research. If we accept that multiple perspectives within a study are good things, then this is an extension of this logic into external perspectives. Valerie Janesick gives an example of interdisciplinary triangulation as delving into art and literature to support behavioral and social science conclusions (Janesick, 1994). Crystallization takes this idea to the next dimension and asserts that the multidimensionality and nearly infinite number of approaches to interpretation require that we leave behind the plane geometry of the triangle and move into the complex physical structure of the crystal and the way in which "what we see when we view a crystal...depends on how we view it, how we hold it up to the light or not" (p. 392). Using crystallization we would use as many perspectives as possible to inform our analysis of the phenomenon we have studied.

RELIABILITY AND VALIDITY IN ETHNOGRAPHY

Two concerns in many traditional forms of research are reliability and validity. Reliability and validity are much harder claims to stake in ethnography than in positivist areas of research. (See the discussion of reliability and validity in Chapter 6, "Quantitative Methods in Food Studies Research.") If we are using semi-structured interviewing or unstructured interviewing and observation as primary techniques, every time we enter the field we may have a slightly modified data set, so we would really have no way of measuring the reliability and validity of our instruments and results via traditional positivistic measures. One of the reasons for the ongoing tension between those researchers who favor quantitative methods and those who favor qualitative methods are the issues of reliability and validity and generalizability. Earlier in the chapter we noted the continuum of styles that fall under the rubric of ethnography. The researcher's selection of ethnographic style and method will, in many ways, shape the approach to analyzing the data that is collected in the field. Realist styles of ethnography are concerned with telling us what is going on in the field and presenting a more or less "objective" account of the phenomenon, *telling it like it is*, so to speak. At the other end of the continuum are the postmodern ethnographers who contend there is no objective reality and that what the ethnographer sees and chooses to present in her report is a result of selectivity (conscious or unconscious) in what was observed, how it was analyzed, and how it was finally reported. Your philosophy on how much "truth" can be told in the ethnographic report will inform your theoretical stance and will shape your analysis and final report. Your philosophy and theoretical orientation will also shape your approach to the issues of reliability and validity. If your theoretical orientation is more toward the realist end, then you will want to consider these issues fairly directly and use traditional measures like long quotations, thick description, and, increasingly, audiovisual documentation when making your final ethnographic report. But these forms of presentation are also effective in other approaches.

If your theoretical orientation is more toward the postmodern end of the spectrum, you may wish to dispense altogether with using traditional terms like *reliability* and *validity* and replace them with what Janesick (2000) calls qualitative referents. One of the primary qualitative referents is the member-check. Using a member-check means having a member or members of the group you are studying review your analysis and see if you have captured their meanings correctly. Hammersley (1990) suggests using plausibility as a measure of validity; can the claims made by the researcher be considered plausible given what we currently know? A number of other researchers make the argument that best practices to assure the validity of your research (though they tend to use the term *relevance* rather than *validity*) revolve around relationships and perspectives (Cohen, Manion, and Morrison, 2000). The argument is that in postmodern research, legitimacy is best established by showing that you have demonstrated relationships between what you have observed and the world at large, that you have clearly stated the preeminence of the emic or etic point of view (or the balance between them and why you chose this balance), that you have clearly stated your place in the field and your biases, and that your reflexive elements reflect your process and how that may affect your final representations.

The Emic and the Etic

The terms *emic* and *etic,* coined by linguistic anthropologist Kenneth Pike in the 1950s, refer to the two primary perspectives that the researcher can use to study and portray a group or culture. *Emic* refers to the perspective or viewpoint of the group under study (Gall, Gall, and Borg, 2005), and, according to Fetterman (1998), is at "the heart of most ethnographic research" (p. 20). The participants in the research express emic perspectives in terms and language that are meaningful to them. A good way to see if you are truly capturing the emic perspective is to summarize the data and return it to the participant and ask them if it is what they meant or if it rings true to them. The perspective of group members is essential to understanding perceptions and actions within the group. Perceptions of group members collected by the researcher may not be descriptive of an "objective reality," but they will inform any analysis of the data that is collected. There can be as many perspectives on a situation as there are observers of it, and giving a voice to all of these perceptions and considering them as you do your analysis is crucial to understanding why your informants act and think the way they do.

The etic perspective is the external perspective on the situation being observed, the viewpoint of the researcher (Gall, Gall, and Borg, 2005). This is where analysis is made using external categories, values, and judgments, often based in theoretical constructs (in the case of food studies) from the various social sciences. The etic perspective may be meaningless to members of the group but can be useful when making an analysis based in the concepts and terms of a specific discipline.

While arguments are made for the primacy of either the emic or the etic when weighing evidence and conducting analysis, the reality is that they are just different places on the continuum of perspectives and that all perspectives need consideration. A common approach in ethnography is to start data collection and analysis with the emic and then incorporate the etic as the analysis takes form. The etic doesn't replace the emic as the analysis progresses, but supplements it, giving the researcher multiple perspectives for understanding.

WRITING THE ETHNOGRAPHIC REPORT

The first step to writing the finished ethnographic report is taken in the field. The daily transcription of your fieldnotes is the first step in the writing process. Fieldnotes are the "accounts *describing* experiences and observations the researcher has made while participating [in the research] in an intense and involved manner" (Emerson, Fretz, and Shaw, 1995; italics in the original). By transcribing your notes in the field and adding any thoughts you have about them while they are still fresh in your mind, you will be well on your way to having a basis for a final report. Fetterman (1998) calls fieldnotes "the brick and mortar of the ethnographic edifice" (p. 114). Combining data from interviews and observations with thoughts that occur in the field and in the transcription process incorporating suggestions from informants will give you a solid foundation for this edifice. A delay in writing fieldnotes risks the loss of valuable detail and richness, so this needs to happen on regular schedule.

Take notes as often as possible in the field. There are two good strategies for taking notes in the field. The first is to carry a small notebook and jot things down as they occur. If you do this, develop a shorthand that allows you to write short but efficient notes to yourself. Jottings with key terms and the use of symbols that are meaningful to you make a useful foundation for the transcription of fieldnotes. The second way to record fieldnotes involves using a voice recorder. Keep it handy and speak notes into it as research occurs. A voice recorder is very useful for the interviewing process. A voice recorder need not always be an additional purchase, though a good quality voice recorder is one of the ethnographer's most valuable tools.[2] Some Personal Digital Assistants (PDA) have this function, and one of the authors of this text has an MP3 player that has a voice recorder function that allows him to dictate notes to himself between sessions of listening to music. Which method and technology you choose will depend on your personal preference for note taking, your research budget, and which method will be most appropriate in the field you enter.

Make sure every day in the field includes a fieldnote session, preferably before you go out for dinner or drinks. The less time you have for jottings in the field during the data collection period, the more critical the daily postcollection fieldnote session becomes.[3]

As you sit down to write your report, one of your important initial considerations will be who your audience is going to be. Are you doing the research for a class project, a thesis or dissertation, a journal article, or a book? Each of these will require a different approach. Most schools have very specific formats for theses and dissertations, and you should be clear about these with your advisor very early in the research project, as they will affect everything from the research questions to the literature review to writing up the findings. If you are targeting your writing to a specific journal, then you need to familiarize yourself with the author guidelines for the publication (generally available on the journal's Web site) and do some reading in the journal to familiarize yourself with the general style used by authors in the journal. All academic writing will follow some specific model for style and citation; for instance, this book largely follows the stylistic conventions of the *Publication Manual of the American Psychological Association* (APA), 5th ed. The venue of your final report will determine which model you will use. For example, the journal *Food, Culture and Society* accepts submissions in both APA format, commonly used in the social sciences, and *The Chicago Manual of Style,* often used in history.

Venue will also help you decide what structure and approach you will use in the actual construction of the document. One of the joys of ethnography is the myriad ways in which it can be presented. Some authors take a highly scientific approach with a standard five-chapter format (introduction, review of literature, methodology, results, and discussion), while at the other end of the spectrum we are seeing many alternative approaches to the traditional research report, many based in art and literature, like biographies, dramas, and even poetry.

Regardless of the form of the finished report, in ethnography we usually take a theoretical-style or thematic-style approach to reporting research (Creswell, 2005). Thematic approaches focus the bulk of the discussion in the paper on themes that arise from the coding of the data. Theoretical approaches discuss the data in terms of existing social science theory or theory that has developed in the course of the data analysis (e.g., grounded theory). Once you have decided on an approach you can begin the job of writing the paper.

Given the broad spectrum of possibilities for the form of the final report in ethnography it is virtually impossible to say "Here are the specific things that belong in every ethnography." But if we think of what ethnography is, then there are a few things that will likely show up in most ethnographies. The first of these is lots of description. As we said early on in this chapter, ethnography is a highly descriptive endeavor. It would be hard to imagine a good ethnography without copious amounts of descriptive detail and illustrative quotes from informants; heed Geertz's call for thick description, but don't include quotations and descriptions that aren't directly supportive of your thematic or theoretical analysis.

Reflexivity, the practice of acknowledging what the researcher brings to the study and how that will affect her understanding of meanings constructed during the project, is a crucial element of the modern ethnography. The reflexive element in research requires us "to explore the ways in which a researcher's involvement with a particular study influences, acts upon and informs such research." (Nightingale and Cromby, 1999, p. 228). While realist ethnography purports to offer an objective report, most ethnographers today acknowledge the biases they bring to any situation and the lenses through which they view it, so a reflexive element should be a part of your report.

Interpretation is a critical piece of any ethnography. As we noted in an earlier chapter, there are millions of good stories in the world, but without interpretation, they are not research. Norman Denzin (1998), a famous figure in postmodern social science circles, went so far as to say "in the social sciences there is only interpretation" (p. 313). Data sets can be interesting but need interpretation to explicate their various levels of meaning.

Technical issues surrounding the accumulation and analysis of the data belong in an ethnographic report. Beginning with the choice of research design through data collection strategies and coding and ending with the findings of the study, the nuts and bolts of how this was accomplished is essential to establishing the credibility of the final report. While ethnographies are rarely, if ever, subject to replication for the purposes of verification, acceptance by the research community and other readers will depend on the sound use of methodology by the researcher.

Good Practices in Reporting Ethnographic Research

1. Set the scene well. Establish early if you are trying to claim greater relevance or generalizability or if you are limiting your conclusions to this situation only.
2. Explicitly set out the theoretical framework under which you are operating and the research was predicated.
3. Discuss your background research and expertise acquired before entering the field.
4. Discuss your research design and fieldwork strategies. Explain why the one you ended up using was the best for your situation.
5. Discuss the "grounds upon which knowledge claims are being justified" (p. 132), for example, length of time in field, breadth and depth of access to informants, and so on.

6. Discuss any problems that arose in the field and how they were handled.
7. Discuss how data categorizations were arrived at and why you felt they were justified. Let the reader know if these categories were ones you created or if they were "indigenous" (p. 132).
8. Provide many extracts of data from your findings in the report; that is, include many illustrative quotes and observations to support your conclusions.
9. Provide as much context as possible for your data and your findings.
10. If possible, talk about other interpretations of your data and why you chose not to accept them and why they were "inferior" to the ones you did choose.
11. Discuss anomalies; for example, if some respondents felt or acted in a manner outside what you are contending is the norm, why? Discuss the natural contradictions offered up by observations and interviews. (People are contradictory beings, how did this present itself in the field and how did it affect your research?)
12. In your discussion, discuss areas of omission, why the omission was made, and what bearing this may have on your findings. (Adapted from Brewer [2000])

In the end, ethnography should reflect the culture and way of life of the phenomenon, group, or culture that is being studied. For researchers who enjoy finding out about why people act in certain ways, believe in certain things, or perceive things the way they do, ethnography is an excellent research method. For the food studies researcher who wants to walk among the people who buy, cook, serve, respect, and enjoy food, ethnography is a wonderful research joy with many built-in rewards.

NARRATIVE RESEARCH IN FOOD STUDIES
STORYING LIVES: INTERVIEW AND NARRATIVE

Narrative research projects are investigations about people's lives through the stories (narratives) that they tell. Narrative researchers collect stories about people's lives and then analyze these stories to discover the deeper meanings of these experiences. Reissman (2002) describes narrative as "talk organized around consequential events" that people use to try to make sense of the experiences of their life (p. 219). Hopkins (1994) goes further and claims that "recounted experience" is a fundamental element in the development of an individual's social and personal identity. We use narrative approaches in food studies when we want to find out the meaning that food, food products, food rituals, food traditions, and other food-related behaviors have in individual's lives. In narrative research, we take the stories people tell us about food and their lives and attempt to provide insights into the lives of those who tell the stories, the narrators. Narratives are compelling sources for food studies research because food is an important component of most cultures, and culture is an "ensemble of stories we tell about ourselves" (Geertz, 1975, as reported in Fraser, p. 180). Narratives are the way that people express their conception and understanding of the world. If we can understand people's narratives, we can begin to understand their world. Most people have complex relationships with food and by allowing them to tell their stories, we give them voice in the idiom of food. Narrative research is a two-part process. The first part of this process is the telling of the story by the participant (and the collection of it by the researcher). The second part of the research is where the researcher analyzes the stories of the participant and retells them for the intended audience. In the retelling of the stories (along with our analyses of them), a process called *restorying*, we hope to shed light on important issues and inform and enrich the lives of readers of the research as well as the lives of those who have provided the stories to us (Gay, Mills, and Airasian, 2006).

Narrative research is a distinctive form of research because of the emphasis it places on a single individual, story, or experience (Creswell, 2005). People often order their memories and emotions in a way that tells a story. If, as food researchers, we listen to these stories and make an attempt to understand them, we can use these stories as a tool for understanding the human experience as expressed through the voice of food. How people think or feel about something, why they acted or reacted in a certain way, or why some process or product is important to them is frequently coded in their narrative. While narrative analyses are generally not concerned with issues of generalizability to some larger population, they can be a good way to learn about some phenomenon using the eyes of an individual to personalize it and thereby give it a human dimension. Each individual story is a piece of the human mosaic (Marshall and Rossman, 1995, p. 88). Various types of interviews and interview techniques have always been useful tools for the qualitative researcher, but narrative techniques at the same time go beyond the bounds of traditional ethnographic techniques by focusing on a single individual or story, while concentrating tightly on an area within the discipline by focusing on the story or stories of the individual of interest. Rather than accumulating multiple interviews and searching for fragments and themes that unite them, an individual story is scrutinized and parsed for the meaning it holds. While narrative focuses tightly on the individual and their story, in practice the narrative researcher can go beyond the interview and perform observations of the experience she wants to know more about as well as look at various objects, documents, and other physical artifacts that relate to the story be analyzed.

CHARACTERISTICS OF NARRATIVE RESEARCH

While narrative research has some elements in common with other qualitative techniques like ethnography, it has a unique set of characteristics that set it apart from them as well. As with most types of qualitative research these characteristics are not set in cement, and which characteristics can be utilized flexibly depends on the researcher and the nature of the project. Some of the characteristics of narrative research:

- It is individual-centered—most narrative research focuses on the stories of one person, not a larger group.
- It tends to be based on a written or oral account of the individual, not on observations by the researcher or other outside individual.
- Context and place are important elements of the finished report.
- The final report is not reported like an interview or ethnography, but as a purposeful restorying with strong analysis by the author.
- It features a strong emphasis on some type of chronology (temporal, consequential, thematic).
- The final voice of the narrative report reflects the voice of both the participant and the researcher and is a negotiated document that allows the participant to be sure their point-of-view is included.
- The finished document has a literary quality. Regardless of the chronology selected, the finished report will almost undoubtedly have characteristics of a novel or memoir. Human stories represent cares, struggles, and predicaments, and it is natural for narrators to sequence them chronologically. Therefore the finished document will be at least partially literary in nature. (Connelly and Clandinin, 2000; Young, 1987)

The Two Types of Narrative Research

Donald Polkinghorne, in *Narrative Knowing and the Human Sciences*, splits narrative research into two primary categories, descriptive and explanatory. Descriptive narrative research aims to "render the narrative accounts already in place which are used by individuals or groups as their means for ordering and making temporal events meaningful" (p. 161). Explanatory narrative research has as its aim, the construction of a narrative account that explains why a situation, event, or phenomenon occurred or unfolded in the way that it did (p. 161). While the field of food studies has seen more descriptive narrative research to date, explanatory narrative research holds great promise as a research technique in this area.

Descriptive narrative research documents what is expressed by an individual and then tries to establish the meaning and significance contained in the story. Polkinghorne asserts that the stories told by members of a community establish the significance of past events and anticipate the consequences of future actions. But this significance is rarely reported in a straightforward manner. The researcher's job is to sort out conflict and confusion within the narrative, which he says is often "similar in form to a modern novel, with flashbacks and with portions of the story out of chronological order" (p. 163). Polkinghorne likens the process of narrative research to formal empirical research wherein the researcher performs detection, selection, and interpretation of data.

Explanatory narrative research is conducted to answer a question that begins with "Why?". In food studies there are many of these "why" questions, and explanatory narrative research may be a good method for answering them. Explanatory narrative research is retrospective. If you are interested in the why of a phenomenon, you could gather many different narratives of decisions and events, compare them to the current state of the phenomenon, and select from them to analyze and report on why you think the phenomenon is the way it is.

TRUST AND OTHER CHALLENGES IN NARRATIVE RESEARCH

As a type of field research, narrative will pose many of the same challenges as other types of field research like ethnography. Some of these issues include access to the individual and the site as well as gaining the trust of the individual and creating a rapport and partnership with them. Field research always entails an element of giving up control; the field is not a laboratory, but very often narrative research is characterized by the locus of control being located in the person telling the story, not the researcher, a position that can be hard for some researchers to be in (Gay, Mills, and Airasian, 2006). Trust is a significant issue in narrative because the researcher is usually only dealing with a single individual or event. In some types of qualitative interview research, if an informant is unwilling to participate or the researcher is unable to form a bond with a participant, there are other informants to fall back on. This is not the case in narrative research. The singular nature of the individual of interest means it is critically important for the researcher to develop a relationship of trust and respect with the person whose story they want to record. As with all types of field research, time will be an issue. Narrative frequently requires more time than you might expect given that you will be dealing with just one individual. Gaining access to the individual and building the trust needed for the person to feel comfortable discussing potentially intimate issues can take a good deal of time, commitment, and patience. Narrative is a highly personal approach to research that can reap great rewards as you get to know someone's story in detail, but it requires a great deal of sensitivity on the part of the researcher to make sure it is an experience that rewards the participant as much as the researcher. The final report needs to reflect the voice of the participant, not the voice of the researcher. In many types of food studies research, we have anonymity as a crucial element of our research stance. This anonymity will be harder to preserve in narrative approaches since the whole of the effort revolves around a single person or episode. As a researcher, you will need to either take these extra steps to preserve anonymity or get the individual to sign a release indicating it is permissible for the researcher to reveal details that may lead to the uncovering of the participant's identity or allow the participant to be formally identified in the report. While the choice always lies with the participant, the authors have found that in practice, there are many occasions where the participants are willing to be formally identified and associated with the research project, especially if they feel the project reflects well on their family or community.

A researcher who wants to use the narrative approach should keep in mind that the story being told belongs to the participant and not the researcher. Experts in the area of narrative research (Connelly and Clandinin, 2000; Ollerenshaw and Creswell, 2002; Gay, Mills, and Airasian, 2006) stress the collaborative nature of the process from beginning to end. While the end result of the process will be a restorying of the material with the researcher's analysis as a significant component, the fact remains it is the participant's story that is being told. Narrative is a useful research style in food studies because it can give voice to those in the community who often don't have a chance to tell their story. As a narrative researcher your goal is to empower the participant to tell his or her story, and the participant must feel that he or she is a partner in this enterprise, not a subordinate.

SOURCES OF NARRATIVE

One of the aspects of narrative research that makes it useful for food studies scholars is the many sources of narrative that one can analyze. Reissman (2002) points out the ubiquity of narrative, "Telling stories about past events seems to be a universal human activity, one of the first forms of discourse we learn as children" (p. 219). While discussions of narrative often focus on the interview, there are other rich sources of narrative as well, what Ken Plummer so famously called the "Documents of Life."[4] Plummer urges researchers to use not only the interview, but biographies and autobiographies, documents like diaries and letters, and various memoirs and oral histories as rich sources of narrative material (Plummer, 2001). All of the following are useful as sources of finished forms of narrative:

Biographies and autobiographies
Oral histories
Popular memoirs
Testimonios
Bildungsroman
Ethnic history collections and stories
Diaries, letters, and other personal documents
Auto-ethnographies
Ethno-psychology texts
Individual-centered ethnographies

Interviews with individuals about their lives

(Connelly and Clandinin, 2000; Reissman, 2002; Gay, Mills, and Airasian, 2006)

RESTORYING IN NARRATIVE

Restorying is the key concept in analyzing and reporting the stories we gather while collecting our data. While narratives are important for the perspective they provide, they require interpretation to provide context and understanding. This is where the restorying process comes in. Creswell (2005) defines restorying as "the process in which the researcher gathers stories, analyzes them for key elements of the story (e.g., time, place, plot, and scene), and then rewrites the story to place it in a chronological sequence" (p. 408). As people tell stories about their lives, they frequently do so in a random and nonsequential order—this is the nature of storytelling. When we report their stories we need to develop the logical links between elements and themes, between people and places and relationships and activities that have been described in the stories, thus the need to "re-story" the stories we have been told. The restorying process is a continuation of the process that begins when we collect our initial data via interviews or reading of documents. Once we have our data in a written form (transcriptions if we have conducted interviews) we can begin to code it to look for themes. Once some basic coding has occurred, the researcher can begin to think about which chronological scheme is best for organizing the data.

Most scholars agree that sequence is an important element of narrative. The most common sequencing scheme is time (temporal sequencing). In temporal sequencing, events are ordered they way the occurred by the clock or the calendar. This is probably the most common form of story telling and the most common way to restory a narrative. Another sequencing scheme is referred to as consequential. In a consequential sequencing scheme, elements of the story are ordered by the effect on other elements of the story. Whether to sequence from least important to most important or vice versa is a decision that is made by the researcher based on the material, but consideration should be given to the literary nature of the finished product when making this decision. The third type of sequencing is thematic. The themes (inferred or explicit) conveyed in the story are related and using the relationships between uncovered themes can be an effective method of sequencing. (Young, 1987; Reissman, 2002).

Part of the restorying process involves contact with the participant. While the researcher restories to make sure the final report is coherent and logical, in the end the story belongs to the teller and it is the responsibility of the researcher to make sure that after restorying, the story is that of the participant and not the researcher (Smythe and Murray, 2000).

THE NARRATIVE PROCESS IN FOOD STUDIES

The research process in narrative shares some qualities with other forms of qualitative research. You will be dealing with verbal information as opposed to numbers. You will have to be able to interact with individuals while collecting their stories. You won't be entering the field with a hypothesis, but you will need to emerge with a data set that becomes the restoried narrative. Narrative is different from ethnography because you will be dealing with a single individual. All of your data will come from a single storyteller, not a larger group. You must be ready to forge a relationship with one individual, yet have the distance from that person to see what is clearly going on in the situation you want to learn more about. We suggest the following steps as a useful approach to narrative research in food studies, but as with all qualitative research methods, there may be a need to make some adjustments once you are in the field.

Steps in the narrative research process in food studies:

1. Identify a phenomenon or situation or area of interest to you where food is central to the activity or is at the core of the phenomenon.
2. Select an individual who can tell you more about this area.
3. Consider how you will get access to this person and how you will convince them to participate in your research. Do you have the time and resources to get the access you will need to get a detailed set of stories on which to base a narrative?
4. Develop an interview protocol. While interviews can range in organization from the highly structured to the loosely structured, you need to have some sort of idea of where the interview is going to go, if only to insert prompts as the narrator strays from the topic of interest.
5. Collect the story. In narrative, this is done primarily with interviews, but you may need to get some supporting documentation as well. As we noted in the previous section, there are many types of documents that will support and add richness to a narrative. In food studies we may be able to collect recipes, community cookbooks, memoirs that deal with food, newspaper and magazine accounts, historical documents, and other, similar types of documents.
6. Transcribe the interviews and organize the collected supportive documentation.
7. Perform analysis on the collected material. Coding of data in narrative is similar in nature to how it is performed on ethnographic data and other types of qualitative data. Multiple levels of coding will enhance the quality of the resulting data.
8. Organize the coded material and begin the restorying process. Remember that this material "belongs" to the narrator, so checking in with them to ensure that the final story represents them as well as you is critical.

9. After restorying the narrative, consider issues of veracity and rework the narrative if required.
10. Write the final report.

INTERVIEWING IN NARRATIVE RESEARCH

Interviewing is the most common data collection technique in narrative research. Many of the styles of interviewing used in other types of qualitative research (structured, semi-structured, unstructured, and nondirective) are used in narrative research. Narrative research tends to work best when using the less-structured forms of interview technique. When people are telling stories about the things that are important to them (and food is important to nearly everybody), they will usually provide lengthy narratives with little or no prompting from the interviewer. How the story is paced, what tones and volumes are used, and what is emphasized or deemphasized are all valuable clues to what meaning the narrator is attempting to convey. Most storytellers will offer some evaluation and/or interpretation of their narrative. They usually have some point to make by telling the story and they want to be sure that you are getting it (Reissman, 2002). This is an important consideration, but make sure you are listening for the subtexts as well.

Transcription

If you are using the interview technique, you will need to have the interview transcribed. The person who actually conducts the interview is usually the best choice to type it up, but some researchers hire a transcriptionist to do this. The benefit to doing this is the speed at which the finished transcript can be returned to the researcher for coding and analysis—for a person with average listening and typing skills with no specialized equipment it can take as long as four to six hours of transcription for every hour of interviewing. Transcription can be a tedious process and professionals can get interview transcripts turned around and back in the researcher's hands quickly. These professionals usually have transcription tools that speed the process and are skilled at listening and converting the spoken word to text. If you have the financial resources to pay for this service (and it can be expensive) it may be worthwhile to pay someone who can have the material back to you in a relatively short time frame that allows you to begin coding while the interview is relatively fresh in your memory. The advantage to doing it yourself is the familiarity you have with the material. If you have conducted the interview, you already know the terminology and idiom the participant is using to tell their story. This answers many questions an outside transcriptionist may have about the finished product. If you are transcribing your own data, you can add critical notes about the nonverbal aspects of the interview, including the storyteller's emotions or moods, gestures, and intonations, which may give further clues to meaning that are important to understanding the words on the page. If you hire a transcriptionist, you should add notes about these things as soon as you get your transcripts back, while they are still fresh in your mind.

ANALYSIS IN NARRATIVE RESEARCH

As we noted previously, analysis begins early in the narrative research process. We begin to analyze our data as soon as we begin to code it. Since narrative is concerned with life stories, we tend to focus our analysis on the "emotional, moral, and aesthetic qualities" of the story being told (Connelly and Clandinin, 1990, p. 11). Reissman (2002) reminds to us to ask, "Why was the story told that way?" (p. 218). In the creation and deliverance of a food-based narrative, the teller not only tells what happened, but attempts to impart some (or all) of the meaning it holds for them. When a narrator tells you the food-related story that is important to them, you can look closely at the cultural background of the narrator and examine the language they use to tell the story for clues to the meaning they are attempting to convey. To some degree, your analysis of a narrative will be informed by your epistemology and the social science background you have in addition to working in the field of food studies. This is a normal condition of research and can be useful as a basis for examining the information being exposed as a result of your analysis.

Sometimes examining the language of the storyteller for linguistic function is a useful beginning for analysis of narrative. Linguistic approaches are useful in extrapolating meaning from the words we get from the narrator. Finch (1998) suggests that language has four primary functions (he calls them the macro functions); ideational, interpersonal, poetic, and textual. Ideational functions are those functions that allow language to be used as a way to form concepts. Interpersonal functions are expressions of the way the speaker or writer uses language to project their ideas and emotions and represent themselves to others. The poetic function refers to our ability to use language in a creative way. Metaphors, phrasing, humor, and dialect specific expressions (to name a few) all are ways we creatively express meaning when we speak and write. The textual function of language refers to the language user's ability to create a cohesive and coherent text. This allows for expression of complex and lengthy (ideas.) By analyzing the story the narrator tells with these concepts in mind, you can begin to intuit the meaning the narrator is attempting to convey. In addition, *where* a narrator chooses to begin and end a narrative can "profoundly alter its shape and meaning" (Reissman, 2002).

Not all narratives have an easily determined chronology, so one of the chores of the researcher choosing to use narrative methods will be to determine which type of chronology will best tell the story in the restorying process. Remember that narrative is a holistic form of research and that you will need to make connections to other events in the narrator's life and to events that have happened in society surrounding the event being described in the narrative account. Keeping these things in mind will add to the quality of the reported analysis.

Coding of data in narrative is similar to coding in other types of qualitative research; the researcher wants to find themes that are presented in the data and this is best done in the beginning using a line-by-line reading of the material (Fraser, 2004). If you are heeding Connelly and Clandinin's instructions to focus on the emotional qualities of the story you will want to be sure to code the nonverbal parts of the data collected as well. The storyteller's reaction to probes, nonverbal exhibits of tension, reactions to other characters in the story, and similar phenomena are all important clues to the emotion of the story. Actions and actors outside the *mise en scene* always have an effect on the action and should be considered in any analysis of the story.

Connelly and Clandinin (2000) in their excellent text, *Narrative Inquiry*, emphasize the literary nature of the analysis in narrative research. They tell us to look for elements of plot, character, scene, place, time, and point of view when we code and analyze our data (p. 131). Why the narrator uses any or all of these to frame his or her story will give you clues about the meaning they are trying to convey. Rosenwald and Ochberg (1992) tell us, "How individuals recount their histories—what they emphasize and what they omit, their stance as protagonists or victims, the relationship between the teller and the audience—all shape what individuals can claim of their own lives" (p. 1). As you begin to code data think about the hopes and desires, the feelings and perspectives, the point-of-view and the environment of the narrator. Refer to your fieldnotes if you are analyzing interview data so you can use your impressions of the moment to aid in your analysis. For some researchers, photographs that aid in recalling the environment are useful (Connelly and Clandinin, 2000).

As you perform analysis of narrative, it is often helpful to go back to the respondent and share your impressions with them. Ask them if they feel the work as it has developed so far accurately represents what they feel is happening in the situation. As we noted earlier, the story belongs to the narrator and they need to feel it tells their story, but there may be elements that the participant doesn't recognize because they are an actor in the story and they have an emotional stake in the restorying and final outcome. You don't have to eliminate elements the narrator objects to if you feel they are honest assessments of the situation, but keep in mind that the finished document will be a negotiated document to some degree.

REPORTING NARRATIVE RESEARCH

As Connelly and Clandinin (2000) so eloquently put it, "sometimes our field texts are so compelling that we want to stop and let them speak for themselves...but we cannot stop there, for our inquiry task is to discover and construct meaning in those texts" (p. 130). Your work has to both honor the story told by the narrator and be useful in the academic and social community at large. The researcher needs to come up with a finished product that is a both a representation of the phenomenon or situation and adds to the greater literature. As with other reports of research, it is always useful to think about where you think the final report is going to appear. Will you be presenting the research at a symposium, in an academic journal, in a popular journal, or in a book? Ask yourself—where does the research fit in the larger field of food studies? In food studies we are lucky that we are not as frequently constrained by the impersonal, scientific approach to reporting. In food studies journals it is more often acceptable to feature the personal nature of the work, to include yourself in the narrative, and to write in a more literary style than the more formal and impersonal style required by many academic journals. This loosening of constraint allows the narrative inquirer to write in a style that best explicates the material.

Some of the things that should show up in your report include:

Thick description of people, places and things

Analysis of the situation that renders clear relations between actors and events

An order sequence of events (though the chronology does not have to be strictly temporal) (Connelly and Clandinin, 2000)

As with all types of research, you need to make clear claims as to the significance of the research. This is what is often referred to informally as the "so what?" issue. Ask yourself how this research fits in the arena of food studies research and how it contributes to the larger field. Can connections be made with more overarching areas of social significance? Sometimes our research is descriptive and serves to open a new area of interest within food studies. Other times we are creating new theory or contributing to existing theory. Make these issues clear as you write the research report. Since narrative is one of the methods that are sometimes not well understood by reviewers of research, be prepared to justify your reasons for choosing narrative as a research method.

Most research reports contain a section (or at least a statement) regarding the veracity of the material contained in the report. Establishment of veracity in narrative research is an uncertain enterprise. How do we tell a "good" narrative from a "bad" one? Critics of the narrative method point out that in the telling of stories, there is much opportunity for people to create a fictitious version of events, a possibility that they claim invalidates much, if not all of the research.[5] Establishing the veracity of our informants can indeed be a difficult task. Jane O'Dea (1994) points to three areas where inaccuracy may color what is told to us by informants. The first is the complexity of any "real-world" situation. The phenomena we examine in food studies research are complex and situational. Food is an intimate topic and issues surrounding it are open to numerous interpretations. The second area is what she refers to as sentimentality. Narrators can play up aspects of a situation that present themselves in a more favorable light, while playing down those that present themselves less favorably.

Lastly, she makes the point that the literary nature of narrative leads narrators to form stories that are compelling and frequently moralistic, conditions that sometimes require narrators to bend the material to fit the artistic covenant. While veracity in narrative forms of food studies research cannot be established in the same way that it is in experimental research, time and effort spent in the analysis considering and addressing these issues and the use of reflexivity in the reporting phase of narrative research can support your claims to the veracity of your report and enhance its acceptance by the consumers of research.

Narratives are ways of expressing the meanings that people give to events, situations, and phenomena as told in the "story" format. Given the story format, there is necessarily an element of interpretation in the narrative enterprise. This doesn't give us an account that is truthful in the positivist sense, but does give us an understanding of how someone experienced something and their emotional reactions to it and an understanding of how it shaped them as a person. In this sense, narratives are truthful. Traditional positivist measures of veracity are not particularly useful when assessing narratives, and even accepted methods of assessing validity in qualitative research like triangulation and crystallization may not be helpful when analyzing narratives, which often contain contradictory statements and conflicting ideas. Sometimes the narrator can leave out useful and even critical information. These may be sins of commission or merely omission. In the interview itself, or later in the transcription, you may think of questions that need to be asked in order to get a fuller picture. It is acceptable (and prudent) in narrative research to go back and ask these questions so the final report is the best representation of the phenomenon possible. Knowing that these items will come into play and asking thoughtful questions should help you render an account that is both useful for the food studies community and authentic for the narrator.

Narrative is a useful and interesting form of food studies research. As we attempt to give voice to the formerly disenfranchised, narrative allows their stories to be told. Food is a topic that is deeply intertwined in daily lives, yet the ordinary people who provide us with our daily bread have often not had their story told to the world at large. Narrative research provides an excellent forum for these stories to be told.

7A A CONVERSATION WITH CAROLE COUNIHAN

Carole M. Counihan is Professor of Anthropology at Millersville University, part of the Pennsylvania State System of Higher Education. She received a B.A. in history from Stanford University in 1970 and a Ph.D. in anthropology from the University of Massachusetts at Amherst in 1981. Counihan's research centers on food, culture, gender, and identity in the United States and Italy. Supported by a 2005–2006 National Endowment for the Humanities Fellowship, she authored *A Tortilla Is Like Life: Food and Culture in the San Luis Valley of Colorado* (University of Texas Press, 2009), which is based on food-centered life histories collected from Hispanic women. Counihan is the author of *Around the Tuscan Table: Food, Family and Gender in Twentieth Century Florence* (Routledge, 2004) and *The Anthropology of Food and Body: Gender, Meaning, and Power* (Routledge, 1999). She is editor of *Food in the USA: A Reader* (Routledge, 2002) and, with Penny Van Esterik, of the second edition of *Food and Culture: A Reader* (Routledge, 2008). She is co-editor of the scholarly journal *Food and Foodways*. Counihan was a visiting professor at the University of Gastronomic Sciences Masters Program in Colorno, Italy, during Spring 2009, where she began a new ethnographic research project on several local chapters of the Slow Food movement.

JD: Maybe we could start with your telling me a little bit about the kind of work you do and the kind of methods you employ and how you got in to food studies.

CC: Well, the main method that I use I call food-centered life histories. And that consists of tape-recorded or, now, digitally recorded, semi-structured interviews with willing participants on their beliefs and behaviors surrounding food production, distribution, preparation, and consumption. And that I have used with men and women in one extended Florentine family, which resulted in my book *Around the Tuscan Table*. And then I used it with women in the small town of Antonito in Southern Colorado, which is going to be my next book, coming out next fall, and that is called *The Tortilla Is Like Life: Food and Culture in the San Luis Valley of Colorado* (University of Texas Press, 2009).

JD: I'm also wondering a little bit about how you got into food studies from anthropology?

CC: Well, what happened was I, after I graduated from college, way back in 1970, I wondered what I was going to do with my life and I decided to take off and go live in Italy and have an adventure. I had been an exchange student at Stanford in Italy as an undergrad and a friend and I decided to go back to Italy after we graduated. And I spent about three years living in Florence and doing a lot of traveling. One of my travels took me to Sardinia and I was really blown away by the culture. And fascinated by it. And really taken by the generosity and real difference from anything I had known of the people. So I said, "I know what I'm gonna do with my life. I'm going to go to grad school and be an anthropologist!" So it's really Italy that got me into anthropology. I didn't have a single anthro course as an undergrad. I was a history major. And so I went from Italy to anthropology and then when I started in grad school I was thinking, "What am I gonna study? What am I gonna focus on?" and the lightbulb went off, "Oh, Italians talk about food all the time, whether you ask them about it or not. They love food. It's the center of their culture. I'm going to study food!" And this was triggered or really supported by the fact that I was a grad student at UMass (University of Massachusetts) and George Armelagos was there at the time. And George is a biological anthropologist but he was fascinated by food. He wrote the book *Consuming Passions* with Peter Farb, which I think came out in 1980. And he and Sylvia Foreman, who is a cultural anthropologist who was on my committee, both of them were alternately teaching a course called "Food and Culture," which I think must have been one of the first in the country. So food was in the air at UMass. So I think there was a little bit more acceptance of the topic than there might otherwise have been. And that certainly, as we all know, took a long time to become mainstream. Because I started my dissertation research in 1978, and at that time it was—nobody was doing food.

JD: Even in anthropology, which is maybe the most food-friendly discipline. That's surprising.

CC: Well I shouldn't say nobody because of course Levi Strauss had already done his stuff. And Mary Douglas had already done her stuff. And there were some classic ethnographies like Audrey Richards's work. Pretty much every anthropologist included a chapter on subsistence. So food was in there but it wasn't really considered a major lens of analysis the way I think it's become.

JD: I wonder if you could tell me what the difference is between a food-centered life history and an oral history or life history removed from food. What role does food play?

CC: Well, really what I think the difference is is that pretty much all of my questions start with food and they invariably spin out into all kinds of other things. You know—you ask about food, you end up hearing about death. Or you hear about all the important rituals. Or you hear about family and gender relations. But it's kind of the insert, the opener, and I think if you did a more general life history you might touch on food, depending on the person you were interviewing, but you might never get it. The person might never think to talk about food. Now if it's women you might eventually get something on it. But I think what is so valuable about the food-centered life history in my experience is that many women in particular, but many people in general, are very comfortable talking about it because, I don't know if you've had this experience, but if you ask people, you come in, you're the outsider, you're the professor, you're the researcher, and you ask them about something they may say, "Oh, don't ask me about that, I'm really not knowledgeable." But it almost never happens about food. If you ask women about food they feel like experts; they feel knowledgeable, and I think that makes it so rich because it's comfortable, and then what else makes it so rich is the fact that it does tie in to so many things. And I think you may have heard me say this—it's kind of a truism—it links the sort of objective, material realm, you know, how many peaches did I buy at the store today, how many acres of grain did I grow, and the subjective, personal, emotional dimensions. You know, "I feel fat. I'm sad, I can't eat. I fought with my husband and he threw the food against the wall" stuff. So it really covers such a wide range of realms of human behavior that I think it can be really rich.

JD: I'm wondering how you see the relationship between a disciplinary approach like an anthropology of food and a food studies approach, if there is such a thing.

CC: I think for me, methodologically, I work as an anthropologist. I think in terms of the discipline it's anthropologists really read other anthropologists mainly. Food studies people, we read all of each other. And so I think food studies is fundamentally interdisciplinary in subject matter, in thinking, in theoretical and analytical approaches. So I would say in my methodology I feel really grounded in anthropology. In my thinking I feel much more grounded in food studies.

JD: You mentioned some of the advantages of starting with food in your food-centered life histories. I'm wondering if you've seen challenges or problems in doing food studies work?

CC: I think the challenges of doing ethnographic work on food are similar to those of doing any kind of ethnographic work. And one is that people have their own agenda and they ramble, and so you are challenged to both listen and hear where people want to go with the interview but also to try to bring them back or reel them in to the topic. And I think sometimes with ethnographic interviews you get so much and then your challenge is to deal with it all. And of course you know the challenges of transcribing. It's incredibly time-consuming and what I find usually is about 5 hours to transcribe every hour of interview and so it takes a long time, it's not wondrously fun to transcribe but it's extremely important. So I think it's time-consuming not only to transcribe but once you have transcriptions to work with them, to figure out how to use them.

JD: I'm wondering what advice you would give to someone who wants to get into this work—ethnographic methods around food, whether it's interview, participant observation, or other methods.

CC: First of all, plan ahead and plan a lot more time than you think you'll need. Because there's many a slip twixt the cup and the lip and so plan a lot of time. Don't give up. Be persistent. We've all had interviews fall through time and time again but you just have to keep at it. Be flexible. Go with the flow. Serendipity plays a huge part in good ethnography and I wouldn't go so far as to say what somebody said to me when I was starting my dissertation research, which was, "OK, throw away your prospectus now." But I think you certainly, you want to have a very good idea of what you're looking for but you don't want to freeze out a whole realm of possible knowledge by being too rigid, and so what I encourage my students to do is have their research design, have their question, research question, generate a bunch of interview questions, and have them ready but start with the most open-ended and general questions possible because you may find all kinds of things that you've never even imagined, particularly when you're working cross-culturally. So the most general questions, "Tell me about your food habits," or "Tell me about what you eat," and then you have your more specific questions ready but don't start with them because you'll close down the interview.

JD: I'm wondering if there are some ethnographic methods that you think are particularly well suited to food, maybe some that you use, maybe some that you don't.

CC: That's a really good question because I love interviews and I think interviews are very well suited but, particularly one thing I've learned teaching here in Italy, sometimes with students who don't speak much Italian, and I have them all do ethnographic research, well their interview capabilities are very limited because of the language, so participant observation can be extremely rich, particularly if they're interested in sort of questions of space and place. I very often have them use photography, which again, I think is fabulous. There's so many things you can capture with photos. I have them do maps and diagrams. I had some students at Millersville. I had one student do a project on Food Not Bombs. And it was very interesting—she plotted out on the map where they cook, where they distribute, where they get food donations, and there's sometimes something really explicit when you plot stuff on a map or you draw, you know, a market, and show where the vendors are working. So, maps and diagrams. Another method that can be really revealing is what we call informant documentation. And this would consist of things that your informants produce or give to you. So this could be, "Write a description of your food," or "Keep a food log," or, "Do you have grandma's old handwritten recipe book?" that you can photocopy or photograph and bring in. Letters. Journals. This kind of stuff. All can present—depending on the project and depending on the quality of those documents—old photos, too—can be really rich. And just an aside, speaking of old photos, I remember Lois Stanford talking—she's a food anthropologist at New Mexico State—I remember her giving a paper and talking about using old photos in her research and she said, "You know, there's hardly any photos of the kitchens because people rarely took photos, they were expensive, and they wanted to be either in the living room or outside where the light was better." And I thought, "Wow." So if you can find photos of old kitchens they can be a rare and wonderful document.

JD: Is there anything that you wish I had asked that you would love to say about ethnographic methods in food studies?

CC: I would just close by saying it can be incredibly exhilarating. You know, I talk with my students about the ethnographer's rush. You know you get a good interview and it's just "wow," great.

8 USING MATERIAL OBJECTS IN FOOD STUDIES RESEARCH

The most commonplace object has the capacity to symbolize the deepest human anxieties and aspirations.

Ian Woodward, *Understanding Material Culture,* p. vi.

Goods that minister to physical needs—food and drink—are no less carriers of meaning than ballet and poetry.

Mary Douglas and Baron Isherwood, *The World of Goods,* p. 49.

Some of the richest sources of material to study in food studies are actual food objects. Not only can the food studies scholar study foodstuffs and their preparation, distribution, and consumption, but she can also look at all the material objects used in the growing, preparing, serving, and storing of food as well. Foodstuffs and all the implements used in their production, distribution, and consumption can tell us much about the culture that uses them. Skibo and Schiffer (2008) contend that "the manufacture, use, and disposal of any technology—past or present, simple or complex—is woven into a social, economic, and ideological tapestry that is, in many ways, unique to a particular place and time" (p. 1). Using the study and research tools of the material culture scholar can reap fascinating rewards in the field of food studies.

THE MATERIAL CULTURE APPROACH TO FOOD AND FOOD-ASSOCIATED OBJECTS

Most of the studies of objects in food studies research have their basis in what is referred to as the material culture approach. Material culture research is the cultural approach to the study of the human-made world (Skibo and Schiffer, 2008). Material culture research is based on the premises that (1) material objects are an integral part of most cultures, past and present, and (2) that these objects both represent and facilitate social relations and interactions within cultures (Martin, 1996). While a material object can be nearly anything that has been subject to human intervention or manipulation, in food studies research we tend to concentrate on common things that most people have interaction with on a daily basis. The current vogue for trophy kitchens, stores full of cooking gadgets, media networks devoted to nothing but food, and a seemingly endless stream of new food products and ways to consume them should provide a nearly inexhaustible mine of data for the food studies material culture researcher in the future.

While Hodder (2000) refers to material objects as "mute objects,"[1] objects are in fact far from mute. Objects have much to tell us about who made them, who consumed them, and the culture in which they have their home. One of the seminal scholars in material culture studies, Jules Prown, in his 1982 essay "The Truth of Material Culture: History or Fiction?" defines material culture research as "the study of material to understand culture, to discover the beliefs—the values, ideas, attitudes, and assumptions—of a particular community or society at a given time" (p. 1). He goes on to explain, "human-made objects reflect, consciously or unconsciously, directly or indirectly, the beliefs of the individuals who commissioned, fabricated, purchased or used them and, by extension, the beliefs of the larger society to which these individuals belonged" (p. 1). Material objects are thus far from mute, but rather represent vivid expressions of the domain of the mind. As Dant (1999) observes, "more of our daily lives is spent interacting with material objects than interacting with other people" (p. 15), therefore an examination of these objects should speak to us about the life of the person or the culture of the people who interact with them.

Material culture is about "the way people live their lives through, by, around, in spite of, in pursuit of, in denial of, and because of the material world" (Martin, 1996, p. 5). As we noted earlier, objects tend to occupy much more of our daily time and space than other human beings do. Nearly every waking minute of the day—from the time we turn off the alarm clock in the morning to when we reset it again at bedtime—objects mediate most of our transactions with our culture. Our commute, our work transactions, our personal relationships, and how we procure, prepare, and produce food are products of our interaction with the material world. If we accept the central role that objects play in the daily life of humans, we can use the object as way to better understand various aspects of social systems like political power and economic structure, as well as meanings that people use to give order to their own lives and the relationships that they have with others.

WHAT IS AN OBJECT?

The question above that heads this section may seem a bit silly; everyone knows what an object is, don't they? Perhaps so, but even Martin Heidegger had to ask the question, *What Is a Thing?* (1968), in order to lay the groundwork for his explorations between the physical and the abstract. Sometimes as researchers we have a tendency to consider the physical and the abstract to be two distinct areas with little overlap, what Carl Knappett (2005) refers to as the "Cartesian dualism" that "pervades much social science" (p. 3). Using research into the objects of the physical world as information systems, transmitters of values, badges of identity, symbols of social position, and even methods of transgression and resistance helps us bridge the gap between the binaries of this dualistic approach.

When we talk about material objects in food studies research we are talking about objects that have a definite corporeal, or physical, substance, and have been shaped by some type of human action (Waugh, 2004). The ranges of material objects that can be the basis of food studies research are nearly unlimited: nearly everything we eat and everything with which we produce, prepare, and consume food would fall under that definition. For example, a drinking cup in earliest times may have simply been an animal horn that was hollowed out to serve as a vessel to convey a liquid from a container to the mouth of the drinker. In most definitions of material culture, the animal horn itself would not be considered an object in the material culture sense and it would belong to the realm of the natural scientist to make inferences about the type of beast from whence it came, how old it was, and how it came to be in the place in which it was found. But if a human interacted with animal horn to make it into a drinking vessel, hollowed it out or carved some decoration on it as way of announcing this is a drinking vessel not merely an animal horn, it would enter the realm of the material object. As with many items we research, sometimes the boundaries and definitions of the topic or area of interest are porous and changing, and this is the case when we consider objects in food studies.

Some scholars may have very narrow definitions of what they would consider acceptable material objects to scrutinize, while others would make the range very broad. How much human modification of the material constitutes enough to consider it a material object instead of a natural one is a question that would likely be answered differently by different scholars. As we move forward on the time line from early hominid toolmakers to modern humans, this distinction becomes easier to make because the amount of design energy and material manipulation that goes into an object increases dramatically as we move forward in time; we no longer use a conveniently shaped tree branch as a hoe, rake, or broom; we use objects of intentionality and purpose, designed for specific tasks. To continue with the drinking vessel analogy, drinking vessels today take on numerous forms—they are shaped from metal, glass, plastic, or numerous other human-made materials, and have gone far beyond the simple animal horn in terms of form, function, and meaning. All types of drinking vessels serve to convey liquid to the drinker's mouth as their primary physical function. Beyond pure functionality though, drinking vessels have taken on a plethora of forms depending on the purpose of the vessel and the message that the consumer of the beverage wishes to convey. Today drinking vessels have all sorts of social connotations ranging from plain water or juice glasses for use in private family situations to sophisticated martini glasses and champagne flutes meant for public consumption and the broadcast of a certain social message. Interestingly, in a full circle of progress, Tuborg and other breweries make glass and ceramic drinking horns that replicate Viking animal-horn drinking vessels as a way to add a cachet of "authenticity" to the beer they brew.

Foodstuffs, that is, food itself as opposed to the various objects associated with its production and consumption, is one of the areas where it is harder to draw firm boundaries in deciding what is a material object and what is not. If we use the definition that a material object is that which has been modified by human manipulation, then where do plants and animals stop being subjects of the natural scientist and start being the subject of the social scientist? As Dant (1999) points out, once living beings cease to have life, they still retain traits that keep them from crossing into the category of the material object. He uses meat as a prime example of this boundary issue. "Food, especially meat, provides a particularly difficult anomalous form that is both material and not yet" (p.11). As food researchers, we can ask the question—at what point does the complex of muscles between the sixth and twelfth ribs located in the loin primal region sitting atop a cow stop being a natural object and become the material object, prime rib? And at what point does the material object stop being a material object? As Dant goes on to say, "Once eaten, the material becomes part of the consumer and cannot be distinguished as separate and material" (p. 11).

These are not always simple questions to answer. In the case of meat, one way to answer the question may be linguistically (an approach we will elaborate on later in this chapter); once the muscular and fatty tissues are removed from the cow and renamed beef, this may be the moment at which prime rib crosses the border into material object status. As with so many things, perhaps the commonsense approach is the best when trying to make judgments in border areas. Judgments might be made using common social denominators, common cultural beliefs, and commonly accepted definitions, or they might be made using constructed delimiters specific for the purpose of the study.

WHY STUDY OBJECTS?

The study of material objects is an interesting and effective way to understand all manner of food and food-associated objects as they relate to both historical and modern culture and consumption (Woodward, 2007, Carson, 1985). Every modern culture is chock-a-block with *things,* and most historical periods are well represented by the objects their inhabitants have left behind as well. Skibo and Schiffer (2008) tell us that the human animal, unique from other animals, "bathes constantly in an environment of our own artifacts" (p. 6).[2] By studying all the things that humans make, share, and consume, we can learn a good deal about both people and the cultures they live in.

Objects are one of the primary ways that members of a culture or society share beliefs, values, activities, and lifestyles (Dant, 1999, Prown, 1982). People use objects to understand both themselves and their place in their particular culture or society. Material objects are an easy way for individuals in a culture or society to communicate meaning to those within and without the group because there are common meanings associated with many goods in addition to the personal meaning that individuals ascribe to objects. Woodward (2007) says objects can be used to establish and negotiate identity; establish or challenge one's place in society; signify one's social affinities, perceived social status, or occupation; facilitate one's relationship with other individuals or groups; and facilitate changes of self-identity or reconcile a current self-identity.

Material objects tend to function at two levels. The first of these is the utilitarian function. When we buy a drinking vessel, our primary expectation is that it will hold liquid without leaking and that it will convey that liquid to our mouths in practical and sensible manner. The second function of the object is what might be termed the *communicative* or *representational* function. In this function we use the object to send our message or signal our aspirations. The meanings associated with the second function are not always easily determined if for no other reason than these meanings are extremely fluid. Meaning is ascribed to objects in a continuous, variable process much like the way meaning is used in abstract processes where we consider human lives, thoughts, and emotions. Food, food objects, and the consumption of food are subject to this continuous process. Imagine you are invited to a friend's house for dinner. The menu, you are surprised to see when you arrive, is champagne, raw oysters, and chocolate-dipped strawberries. The foods themselves have utilitarian functions—to provide nutrition. But they also communicate that your friend may want to become more than just a friend; they represent your friend's aspirations. Often actual qualities of the object don't matter greatly in the construction of meaning; the mere possession of them can empower the individual. A trophy kitchen in a McMansion may be little used, but the fact that the owner has made a great expenditure of resources to have one speaks volumes about the owner.

Douglas and Isherwood (1996) argue that no good has a meaning outside of the system or context in which it is found. They contend that we choose goods based on our social objectives, the personal meanings they have for us, and the messages that they send to others. In this approach, it is our worldview that will cause us to make selection and consumption choices, that objects have no meaning by themselves, but must always be considered in the context of the system in which they exist. This idea is beautifully illustrated in the following passage from *The World of Goods* that sums up one of Roland Barthes's meditations on how one's worldview will influence their choice of goods:

> Even the choice of kitchen utensils is anchored to deep preconceptions about man and nature…take the process of making coffee: you can use a pestle and mortar or a mechanical grinder. Brillat-Savarin preferred beans pounded by hand in the Turkish fashion, and gave several practical and theoretical reasons. But beyond these, Barthes discerns a poetic bias; the grinder works mechanically, the human hand only supplies force, and electric power can easily be substituted for it; its produce is a kind of dust—dry, fine, and impersonal. By contrast, there is an art in wielding the pestle. Bodily skills are involved, and the stuff on which they are bestowed is not hard metal, but instead the noblest of materials, wood. And out of the mortar comes not a mere dust, but a gritty powder, pointing straight to the ancient lore of alchemy and its potent brews. The choice between pounding and grinding is thus a choice between two views of the human condition and between metaphysical judgments lying just beneath the surface of the question. (p. 50)

Food and food-associated objects are not only used to represent aspirational messages but can also be used transgressively as a way to signal resistance. The co-author's grandmother, when in her teens, would take advantage of the Sabbath darkness in her Orthodox Jewish home to sneak out to the diner for BLT (bacon, lettuce, and tomato) sandwiches, signaling her resistance to her family's religious traditions to her secular friends.

By the use and display of objects, we express to others what we feel our identity to be and where we feel we are located in society. While each individual has unique and subtle variations in how they classify objects and how they make meaning through them, their classifications are also linked to collective consciousness at some level, allowing them to gain ideas of place, both their own place and the place of others, in a culture or society. Some items of material culture are specifically designed to represent and communicate our identity to others. If we entered a restaurant and saw an individual wearing a chef coat we would immediately make a connotation with the cooking trade. Marketers for years have understood the power of branded shopping tote. Carrying a shopping tote from Whole Foods broadcasts an entirely different message about the identity of the carrier than one from Wal-Mart. We can use objects to signal affinity with others, wealth, participation in a lifestyle, and other aspects of social identity (Woodward, 2007). While it may make little difference to the food system or our immediate health whether we individually buy hormone-free milk, certified organic milk, soy milk, or conventional milk, our decisions regarding these objects speak to our individual and collective identities and we can use these decisions to affiliate with a larger community. We can also use food-related items to cement our internal identity. Can you intuit a difference between someone who prefers to eat her ice cream from the carton rather than from a bowl? Someone who has lettuce, tomato, and onions in his produce bin versus kale, kohlrabi, and fava beans?

In the postmodern turn, consumption is considered to be the critical act of identity formation. Woodward (2007) notes that "consumption signif[ies] identity to an extreme...newness, beauty, and status are god-like in the minds of consumers, and are keys to forming one's identity" (p.135). Indeed, much of the success of the restaurant industry is attributable to this craving of "newness, beauty and status." While it is surely more cost-effective to dine at home, possibly healthier, and at times even tastier, dining out has import beyond nutrition to be an important signifier of identity, whether to ourselves or others.

OBJECTS AND DOCUMENTS

Objects can act as a supplement to the written record or act alone in being the basis for your research. While written records are extremely valuable in examining a phenomenon or period, they don't always give us a complete record. As O'Toole and Were (2008) note, "textual representations can be overly representative of the views of the privileged" (p. 617). Prown (1982) relates Henry Glassie's observation that only "a small percentage of the world's population is and has been literate" (p. 3) and suggests that records that are left by people in periods or places where a large segment of the population is not literate may be atypical representations of everyday life. Objects, on the other hand, are used by nearly everyone, literate or not, and therefore may be more representative of life in general than written records. Examinations of objects and material culture can give us an idea of what was happening in the lives of those who have had less access to ways of leaving a written record. Historically, the disenfranchised have had less voice in official documents and other written records. Various material items related to the production, consumption, and storage of food may be alternate ways to examine discourse by and between these groups, who often were silenced by the dominant interests who controlled access to traditional areas of official memory such as government documents, media representations, literature and the arts. As Hodder (2000) says, "the study of material culture is...of importance for qualitative researchers who wish to explore multiple and conflicting values, differing and interacting interpretations" (p. 705). Another difference between the study of objects and many of the other methods of research we have discussed in this text (interviewing, questionnaires, document analysis, etc.) is that these other methods are, in many ways, what people *say* about themselves. While what people say about themselves is always interesting and often useful, studies of the things that people interact with is different because it is a record of what people actually do—which can be different from what they say. For example, a perennial problem in food studies is the written recipe. Written recipes tell us whether certain preparations are valued, how they are communicated and perpetuated, and how they *could* be made, but they don't actually tell us whether they were used and with what frequency. Seeing Ferran Adria's cookbook on our bookshelf may indicate that we value his work but doesn't tell a historian a millennium from now whether we actually used it. Upon an archaeological investigation of our home kitchens, the lack of material objects called for in the book like vacuum sealers, Vita-Mix blenders, and small thermocouples may suggest that possessing the recipe does not necessarily correspond to cooking the recipe. All the things that people leave behind, both intentionally and unintentionally, give us myriad insights into the way they structure their lives and represent themselves to both internal and external domains.

ANALYSIS OF DATA IN THE STUDY OF OBJECTS

Many food-related items are experienced within social situations and therefore have certain common meanings attached to them in addition to any personal meanings an individual may ascribe to them. Oftentimes our knowledge of a specific cultural situation will allow us to intuit common cultural meanings quite quickly. In other instances we may need guides to help us gain this understanding. If we are unable to interview or otherwise communicate with members of the culture in question, we need to limit our analysis to what can be understood from the etic (outsider) viewpoint. But even when we can get the emic (insider) viewpoint by communicating, we need to be careful about making interpretations. As Hodder (2000) suggests, because personal meanings are based in feelings and emotions, "actors often seem curiously inarticulate" about their reasons for choosing and consuming the object in question (p. 703).[3] There are numerous reasons for this inarticulation. In many instances, as humans we have a hard time teasing out all of the strands of reasoning that guide our consumption. If we buy an espresso coffee maker, how much of the purchase can be assigned to the idea that we really love espresso or cappuccino and how much can be assigned to any aspirational desires or other emotional aspects of owning a really cool espresso machine? Do we buy the machine because we drink espresso frequently and want a machine to make the process more effective? Or do we buy it because we aspire to drink more espresso at our convenience and not rely on a lesser machine or the coffeehouse? We also have to be aware that some informants will not be totally truthful about their weighting of the rationale. There is still residual shame or embarrassment felt by some purchasers of aspirational goods, so they will talk up the utilitarian nature of the purchase while playing down status implications of ownership of the item. We don't always have this option when examining a historical artifact. If this is the case, try to find as much material that relates to the object as possible (e.g., historical documents and even literature of the period if available) in order to aid and support your analysis.

Begin your analysis by using a list of questions like the ones provided in the "Exercise in Material Object Analysis" that follows the list below.

As you begin to answer the questions, keep these ideas in mind:

1. The cultural perspective—Each object we study is the product of a particular cultural environment. When we interpret it as part of our research we are looking at it from our own cultural environment. The beliefs and tenets of our particular culture can cause us to make unconscious assumptions about the object that may be unwarranted. The first step in overcoming this hurdle is to recognize this problem and constantly attempt to lay aside your preconceptions in order to see the problem via fresh lenses. Prown (1982) advises that we attempt to put ourselves inside "the skins of individuals who commissioned, made, used, or enjoyed these objects, to see with their eyes and to touch with their hands, to identify with them empathetically" (p. 5), an approach he titles *sensory apprehension*. By being aware of your own biases and using Prown's sensory apprehensive approach, you can at least attempt to limit the amount of subjectivity that colors your analysis.

2. The polysemic nature of goods—Goods are mutable; that is, they often escape the intention of their creators (Knappett, 2005). While many goods are created with status motives clearly in mind, others are produced for utilitarian function. As a researcher you will have to consider which is which. To complicate matters even further, items often move across whatever boundary their creator intended them to stay within, and messages are often treated very flexibly by consumers of the object. The meaning of an object is not fixed in time or space. An item that is utilitarian one day is a status object the next (and vice versa). Societies, cultures, social networks, and individuals are constantly reclassifying objects. Even within the individual, the sign value of an object is subject to constant rescrutinization. The issue of boundaries can be especially problematic when goods are used as method or symbol of resistance or transgression.

3. Objects as fetishes—When performing your analysis of an object, you will need to resist the temptation to turn the object into a fetish. Objects create meaning at multiple levels both internally and externally. Some objects may become talismanic if they become vested with great amounts of social or spiritual meaning, but resist this interpretation if you do not have the supporting data.

4. Performance—Think about how the object was supposed to perform in its original conception. A researcher can determine a good deal about an object by

considering its performative qualities. Food objects with many decorative qualities are likely intended to have a greater role in transmitting information about the consumer who displays them than a simple utilitarian object. A highly ornate ladle used for serving soup from a tureen in a Victorian or Edwardian era dining room had an entirely different performance expectation than the ladle that transferred the soup from the kettle to the tureen in the kitchen did.

5. Avoid the binary—We have seen that much material culture research is aimed at bridging the gap between the physical and the abstract. Try to maintain that bridge as you conduct your analysis. Miller (cited in Woodward, 2007, p 101) tells us that consumption of goods is not inherently good or bad, oppressive or nonoppressive, alienating or not, but much more nuanced. People search for comfort, success, identity, mastery, and many other qualities through their consumption of goods.

6. Avoid discrimination against the mass-produced—This is somewhat related to the previous idea of avoiding the binary. As westerners we have a bias toward adulation of the custom-made or luxury good. While there may be a good deal of status and satisfaction to be gained from owning an AGA range, a Gaggia espresso machine, or a Masanobu knife, many people use mass-produced goods to create something meaningful and personal.

7. Embrace the commonsensical—Occam's razor has much to recommend it in a complex world. While parsimony is not *per se* always preferable to complexity, it may have use in the study of material objects. When examining food and food-related objects we are dealing with items at the baseline of human existence. Therefore at least consider the simple commonsense explanation before constructing an elaborate edifice of theory and rationale.

8. Food rots. Remember that in studying food, you're studying decaying tissue from animals and plants. While some foods like grains, animal bones, and dried corn husks survive for millennia and allow for tremendous insight into foodways of the past, other foods have long since disappeared.

Now that you have learned a bit about the material culture approach to food studies research, practice your skills by completing the following exercise.

EXERCISE IN MATERIAL OBJECT ANALYSIS

For this exercise, pick an object that is related to food in someway. After you have picked the object go through the following list, answering the questions posed.

What is the object? Does it have different nomenclature in other cultures or societies?
What is the object used for? What details support your suppositions?
When was the object made?

What materials were used to make the object? Does the choice of material support your guess as to the age of the object?

What is distinctive about this object that would differentiate it from similar objects?

For what functional purpose was the object created? If this is an older object, has its function in society changed over time?

When was the object used? Daily? Ceremonially or ritually?

Who created the object?

Who used the object originally? (If it is an older object whose function has changed, who uses it today?)

Can you estimate an original exchange value for the object? What about a current exchange value? (If the difference is dramatic—why so?)

What does the object suggest to you about the values, attitudes, and beliefs of the people who created and used the object? How does the object reflect the time and place in which it was created?

What further questions do you have about the object? What questions were raised in answering the previous questions? How would you go about finding information about the questions you were unable to answer? (Adapted from Teacher's Guide: What Is Material Culture?—March 3, 2008)

Biographies of Things

> Biographies of things can make salient what might otherwise remain obscure...what is significant about the adoption of alien objects—as of alien ideas—is not the fact that they were adopted but the way they were culturally defined and put to use.
>
> Igor Kopytoff—*The Cultural Biography of Things*

One of the strengths of the material culture approach is its ability to bridge the "Cartesian dichotomy between physical and psychic experience" (Douglas and Isherwood, 1996, p. 49). The anthropologist Igor Kopytoff suggests trying to bridge this binary between the physical and the abstract by writing a biography of an object. Kopytoff argues that objects have value beyond the simply economic and that because objects have what he refers to as a "social life," that the researcher can write a biography of the object. The writing of an object's biography can then tell us how it is valued by an individual, society, or culture.

This exercise in biography is an attempt to see beyond the object as a commodity, taking it through the decommodification (singularization) process to explicate its value to individuals and societies. The biography writing process is an expansion of Durkheim's sacred object theory wherein it is posited that societies singularize some items, giving them value far beyond simple exchange value. Food-related objects commonly get singularized in today's society. This can happen based on the object's iconic status, the fact that it may be a scarce commodity, or that it has some real or imagined property that is desired by the consumer of the product. Traits of singularity "go on show" to assert the "individuality and astuteness" of the owner (Woodward, 2007, p. 105). In the realm of food related objects we can point to items such as Chemex coffee makers, fancy Italian espresso machines, kitchenware by Alessi or Philippe Starck, and many other similar items as examples of how mass-market items get singularized by their consumers. Foods that are hard to get can get singularized as well. While we think of expensive foods like caviar in this category, common items can become singularized as well. During the 1960s Coors beer was not distributed east of the Mississippi River. Residents of western states were sometimes asked to bring Coors beer back to their friends in the eastern states as an item these people could then use for their social display. Some products get their singularization by the fact that the consumer can customize them. Burger King for years "customized" a mass-market food product by instilling in the customer the thought that you could "have it your way."

In writing the biography of a thing, Kopytoff directs the researcher to consider the following questions:

1. What, sociologically, are the biographical possibilities inherent in its status and in the period and culture in which it was made? Have these possibilities been realized in the thing?
2. Where does the thing come from and who made it?
3. What has its "career" been so far?
4. What do people consider the thing's ideal "career" to be? Has it been used this way or in some transgressive fashion?
5. What are the recognized ages or periods of the thing's life? If the thing has survived beyond its normal age or period, how has its "career" changed? What happens when the thing reaches the end of its useful life? (Adapted from Kopytoff, 1986)

Carson's Can of Pie Filling

The historian and decorative arts specialist Barbara Carson is an advocate of interpreting history through objects. She feels strongly that we need to relate objects to the people who made, sold, and bought them; to the activities people engaged in with the objects; and to what political, social, economic, religious and cultural assumptions motivated people to use the objects. In her article "Interpreting History through Objects" (1985), she bases her approach to interpretation on the familiar five W's (and one H) of journalism—who, what, when, where, why, and how. Using the example of a can of cherry pie filling, she shows us one method for interpreting the material object in the realm of food studies.

Carson's object in question is a 1 pound, 5 ounce (595 grams) can of cherry pie filling. She states the that obvious connections with the can are the making and eating of cherry pie. But using the "5W" method, she goes beyond the implications of nutrition and sustenance and explores people's historical actions and interest through the lens of the pie filling.

Carson restates the 5W's of historical interpretation as:

1. What is it?
2. What activity was it part of?
3. Who made, owned, used, or maintained the object?

4. How did people work together to make the activities happen or obtain the desired result or product?
5. How have things and circumstances changed from one historical period to the next?
6. Why have things and circumstances changed over time?

Carson's 5W's applied to a food object, a can of cherry pie filling.

1. What is it?—The "what" is the can of pie filling.
2. What activity was it part of?—It was part of the regular meal period with family and friends or could signal some special event like Independence Day celebrations. Cherry pie may especially significant to Americans since there is a strong association of cherries with George Washington. The tale of George Washington chopping down the cherry tree is one of the most renowned pieces of American folklore.
3. Who made, used, owned, or maintained the object?—If we take a commodity chain approach to the cherry pie filling, we see that the list of people associated with the product includes growers, canners, industrial product manufacturers, printers, food chemists, food store employees, cooks, garbage collectors, and refuse disposal site employees.
4. How did people work together to make the activities happen or obtain the desired result or product?—Some worked together in communal efforts of production to get the cherries in the can and to the store, others labored singularly to make the pie in the home, others came together to enjoy the fruit of the labor.
5. How have things and circumstances changed from one historical period to the next?—Two hundred years ago the commodity chain associated with this product was probably much shorter and much more localized than it is today. Today the chain may not even be contained within a single country. There are likely many more industrial processes and food miles associated with the product than there were in the past. Today's cook may no longer be the mother of the family, but the father.
6. Why have things and circumstances changed over time?—This is the hardest question there is to answer according to Carson. Answers in this instance will likely lie in changing tastes, revalorization of products, contestation of meaning, and the industrialization of the food supply (just to name a few).

8A A CONVERSATION WITH PSYCHE WILLIAMS-FORSON

 Psyche Williams-Forson is an assistant professor in the American Studies Department at the University of Maryland and is an affiliate faculty member of the Women's Studies and African American Studies Departments and the Consortium on Race, Gender, and Ethnicity. Dr. Williams-Forson is the co-founder and co-director of the Material Culture/ Visual Culture Working Group, an interdisciplinary group of faculty and graduate students engaged in research on objects and culture. Her research and teaching interests are in the areas of cultural studies, material culture, food, and women's studies along with the social and cultural history of the United States in the late nineteenth and twentieth centuries. Williams-Forson is the author of *Building Houses out of Chicken Legs: Black Women, Food, and Power* (University of North Carolina Press, 2006).

JD: Maybe you could describe a little bit about your work and your training.

PWF: Well I'm trained as a material culturalist so my first love of the study of food really comes at studying what objects mean to people and how objects speak in society. So every class I teach I come at it from the standpoint of what is the object, how do we contextualize objects, and then how do we understand their place in society and how that has changed over time. And mostly what I want is for students to not only understand how objects speak but the tools that you need to help listen to what they're saying. So a lot of the methods and toolkits that I introduce to students might deal with issues of power, coming from an archaeological point of view, because I really like the concept of power as heterogeneous and not only top-down but operating in different ways. I also have to teach them material culture methods. Usually the one I use does stem from a historian, but because it's the simplest and it's the most user-friendly. So those are some of the tools that I try to equip students with right upfront. And then we move into understanding how do you study gender, how do you study objects in gender, how do you study food as an object in gender. So then we open it up to, for example, now let's take a look at literature and see how that manifests, let's take a look at popular culture and see how that manifests, let's take a look at history. Sometimes we end up with particular food items, sometimes we're unpacking life experiences around food, but I tend to be open to all of that once they've got the necessary skills.

JD: So can you give me an example of how an object speaks?

PWF: Sure. A woman named Barbara Carson who did a lot of work in museum studies but also wrote an article that is very useful, "Interpreting Objects in History." What she does is explain to students when you go into a museum, you have a very short period of time as a curator to help your audience really grasp the point that you're trying to make. And what she ends up doing is using a cherry pie filling can, and she takes students through these various stages. And she says the first set of questions you want to ask are where did the cherries come from. So that's a perfect example of asking students to substitute another food item and answer these questions. Where does this food come from? Who planted it? Who harvested it? Who plucked it or picked it or what have you? And what's the next process. Somehow it has to go from the garden or the field into processing. Now let's take a look at all of those issues involved, so forth and so on until we get to the end. What happens after the can is discarded? Who picks it up? And then where does it go from there? So it involves so many different layers. And at each one of those stages of going through the particular object you can introduce numerous theories and methodologies. So object, starting with procurement. Let's look at procurement, say, from the standpoint of performance. That's a really good place to bring in Barbara Kirschenblatt-Gimblett's work on food as performance. If I said, "Who is doing the processing of these foods?" that's a great place to bring in Deborah Barndt's work on the tomato trail. So you're helping them engage this theory in very important ways but also they can see it as a process as well. And they're developing their own toolkit.

JD: And you're starting with that one object.

PWF: I start with one object, yeah. This semester when I teach it, I am going to use the Carson article and I'm going to say look at what she does with the cherry pie can and I map it on the board so they can see it. And I say, "Now you take an object. A food object. And you ask these same questions and you develop a composite in there." Where does gender fit in? Where does race fit in? Where does class fit into this discussion?

JD: What's interesting I think about material culture in food is that the objects—the material—are ephemeral in many cases. What you ate yesterday, what you ate 100 years ago.

PWF: Right. Because even though the food itself, the actual object, for the food that's closest to my knowledge, let's say we take the chicken. While the actual food may not exist, when you take it through that process, by the time you end up with what happens with the food once it's discarded, there are ways you can come in and have conversations around that. For example if you talk about the fact that chicken bones were discarded, that's a great place then to bring in conversations about the chicken bone express and that legend, and what that means. The fact that it was an urban legend that says you can always find where African Americans traveled looking at the trail of chicken bones that they left. So if we start with that legend, and we work backwards, we are unfurling so many different issues that are connected to that one food item. Which now puts us into a historical discussion, a pop culture discussion; it opens up all the kinds of things that I talk about in the book. So that may be a place then, at the end of that discussion, where I may slide *Building Houses out of Chicken Legs*.

JD: One of the things when I read your work that makes me crazy because I can't do it, is that when you do this kind of work in pop culture and material culture, the world is really your data set.

PWF: You're absolutely right. I get references every day. Often from people who are like, "Check this out." I hold on to it and maybe an article is in the works somewhere. But in terms of the amount of material that didn't make it into this book, you know there are practical considerations, of course, but I think even more than that it was what can I reasonably do at this point in time. And what all of these other references say to me, when people are throwing them out and saying, "Oh, did you see this?" or, "Oh, did you see this picture," it says to me there *is* so much more that can be done and someone else can pick up the ball and run with it. And come at it from a different point of view. One of the things about having an interdisciplinary degree is you are trained to think in these multiple layers at all times. And you're also trained to think intertextually. I have a literary background. My undergraduate, and a large portion of my graduate degree—even though I took it in American studies—focused on nineteenth-century literature. So even back then when I was reading these nineteenth-century novels, long before I decided I was going to do food as an object, these sort of references spoke to me. And I was like, "Wow, it's really interesting." So when you start working with this body of material, these kind of things just start coming back to you and you're like, "Yeah, now I have a better understanding of why that may have been put in this book or what the author may have been saying or trying to say by using references to various objects." The connections are sort of endless, I guess.

JD: You mentioned your disciplinary training in literature. And you could certainly be a literary historian, or you could also be a comp lit or English person and look at the literature itself. But the type of work you do in cultural studies could use the same data but has a different approach.

PWF: The difference I guess between me and the straight literary critic is that because I took an interdisciplinary degree, I have permission and license in ways that they may not feel that they have to think broadly about the way in which I want to interpret. What I'm reading when I made the decision to return to school, I really examined the Ph.D. in literature and in American Studies and I said, "I really like this more multiplicitous way, if you will, of coming at one piece of material." I like that fact that I can look at one thing from an archaeological point of view. "What do archaeologists say about this? What do sociologists say? What does the historian say?" Now the danger is you end up bringing to, say, history, some nonhistorical ways of thinking to the material. For example, and I have no shame in admitting this, I did a lot of the social history stuff but I had to go back and really consult with several historians, and I said, "Am I thinking about this, am I asking the questions that I should be asking of this material in order to get a really good read on it?" Because otherwise you're not using historical training and methods so you might not be asking the right questions. And the same is true archaeologically speaking. I consulted a couple of different archaeologists. And I said, "Help me with this. Help me think this through. Am I correct in arguing XYZ." I don't want to say it makes you second guess yourself as much I would perhaps say I think it gives you license to feel free to consult with those who have training in that area and say, "Here's what I'm thinking about. Help me to work this through a little bit."

JD: Shouldn't historians and sociologists consult with their colleagues even in a disciplinary study?

PWF: Absolutely. Absolutely. I think that in academia we're very protective of our work for all the reasons we feel we need to be. OK, so be that as it may, I think when you do interdisciplinary work some of that protection is there but a fair amount of it is also not there in the sense that you're used to consorting with people who have different knowledge than you. And that's a welcome part of your methodology.

JD: Can you tell me a little about how you got into food studies?

PWF: You know I was doing the material culture piece. But then I was a researcher for Hasia Diner. I was her researcher for her book *Hungering for America*. She was doing some work on Jewish foodways, and I started doing the research and I'm like, "I never heard of something called foodways." And I looked it up and I wondered if African American people have this—do black people have foodways? And when I started doing the research most of what I came up with was Jessica Harris's work. Which I liked and admired and enjoyed. But the more I read the more I realized these folks are talking about the food. I want to know about the behavior. Why is it that certain cultures eat certain foods? What do those foods mean to them? People can write ad nauseum about what they mean culturally but what do they mean to individual people and to groups what do they mean? The actual chicken piece didn't come until much later. But that's how I began looking at food.

JD: What sort of advantages or challenges, for that matter, do you see in working with food?

PWF: That's a good question. I think the benefits of doing it with food are several. One, for me at least, food is elusive in many ways. Because it's so taken for granted and, as you said, it's ephemeral. But it speaks volumes. The way that food operates. The kind of events that take place in and around food. And the kind of things that happens when people come together around food. And that's the thing I think that's exciting to me. How do you take a food event, for example, as Charlie Camp talks about, how do you take a food event and study it for what it reveals about people's behaviors? So you might say actually I am most interested in people's behavior or cultural behavior in studying culture and how culture gets enacted or acts out. And food becomes one more vehicle just like gender, just like race. Food for me becomes the lens through which I can do that.

JD: That's interesting because typically food is spoken of as the object rather than the lens. Do you think food then becomes a method in itself, or maybe an enhancement to a method?

PWF: I gave a talk early last semester to a group in a course on methods and the professor in the course said to me, "Talk to us a little bit about the difference for you between your method and your methodologies." And that's the quintessential question. What's the difference? I enjoy various different methods of getting at this information, and my methodology and the way that I do that is through a material culture or an American studies set of methods. Under the umbrella of food studies there are so many different methods you can employ.

JD: So your methodology is putting the food at the center of the study and using a variety of methods and theories to examine it.

PWF: Yes a variety of methods. But food becomes the center of analysis. And then how I approach that will include methods from women's studies, will include largely in that respect, intersectional methods where you cannot leave out race, you cannot leave out class, you cannot leave out gender, region, in many respects you can't leave out sexuality, depending on what I'm talking about.

JD: Is that methods or theory?

PWF: It's both. Because with intertextuality or intersectionality, which is a theory unto itself, there are particular methods that employ intersectionality. I think my work, the book, is a really good example of using various methods to get at intersectional analysis. There's race, there's power, there's gender, there's sexuality, and I employ a variety of theories under the umbrella, if you will, of cultural studies or intersectional analysis to get at our understanding of particular foods and their function in American society.

JD: For a novice researcher who wants to get into cultural studies or media studies what kind of wisdom would you give them?

PWF: Forget the labels. If you find that your passion is film and you like food representations in film, then go for it. Learn all you can about it and then figure out once you start writing it or writing about it, figure out whose school of thought or whatever or what tools are out there to best help you make sound arguments about that material. I didn't start out saying, "I'm gonna do this or I'm gonna do it like that." My first couple of drafts were a mess. But then when I looked back and took another look I said "Angela Davis is talking about music in a way that I really like. And I want to borrow her style and her way of thinking about music. I want to take her way of thinking about music in blues women—Billie Holiday, Bessie Smith—and I want to write about food like that." And so she helped me sort of rethink how I wanted to approach my writing. I wouldn't limit myself. And I think that's the beauty of interdisciplinary fields of study. You don't have to limit yourself. What I do think you have to do is be aware and ask lots of questions of the people who are considered experts in those areas to teach you how to ask really smart and sound questions so you can gather all of that material and then put forth a really good undertaking of it.

9 TECHNOLOGY TOOLS

All of the methods discussed in this book can be implemented with minimal technology support. Most research methods were in existence well before the advent of computers and recording devices. However, technology can make research easier and more effective in a number of ways. Technology tools can both enhance traditional research methods—such as allowing easy quantitative content analysis of historic cookbooks using a "find" feature in a digitized version—as well as enable new methods such as using geographic information systems to map farmers' markets by household income. This chapter discusses how technology tools may assist with the research process in a variety of areas and recommends sources for learning more.

FINDING, ORGANIZING, AND MANAGING LITERATURE

Perhaps your first interaction with technology to enhance the research process will be in finding and managing the sources in your early reading and literature review. The literature review, as discussed in Chapter 3, is still a challenging and, at times, tedious process, but it is significantly easier since the advent of electronic databases than it used to be.

Databases like ProQuest, ABI/Inform, Google Scholar, and many others allow you to search for articles by author, title, journal, key word, and subject. Some databases allow you to search not only these general fields ("casu marzu and production") but also for unique phrases within the abstract or full text of the article ("commodity chain analysis"). This allows you to find references that might not have come up earlier. For example, if you're researching the origins of the New York egg cream, an article from a Jewish Studies journal about immigrant labor making only a brief but important reference to the topic would have been missed by searches by key word or title but could be found with an advanced database search.

Once you've identified your sources, technology can assist again. When we learned to do research, it was by writing important points in the literature on separate index cards with the bibliographic information of the source written atop each card. Now, you can use widely available software, or even basic productivity software, to create your own database of important facts from your literature search. This type of software is called reference management software. These technology tools will also allow you insert a footnote or work cited in a variety of formats (MLA, Chicago, APA) with a click of a button, something that previously required a style guide and retyping for each paper using the same source.

Your institution's library may have a site license for one or more of these products that allows you to use it without additional charge. Many are commercially available as well.

Reference Management Software

Here are a few examples of reference management software, but do your own search on the topic to find many more:

■ RefWorks: "RefWorks—an online research management, writing and collaboration tool—is designed to help researchers easily gather, manage, store and share all types of information, as well as generate citations and bibliographies." www.RefWorks.com

■ EndNote/EndNote Web: "EndNote Web is a Web-based tool for managing and citing references in papers and creating bibliographies. Integrated seamlessly with EndNote desktop and the ISI Web of Knowledge^{SM} research platform, EndNote Web provides an online collaborative environment for existing EndNote users, and an entree for undergraduate students requiring a basic bibliographic solution." www.endnote.com

■ ProCite: "ProCite® [is] the industry standard software [tool] for publishing and managing bibliographies on the Windows® and Macintosh® desktop. Researchers, writers and students depend on these products to locate bibliographic data and create bibliographies for *curricula vitae,* manuscripts, grant proposals, term papers and other publications. These products automate the creation of bibliographies for over 1,000 scholarly publications, a tedious and error-prone activity when performed manually. Using these products, writers save countless hours of typing and interpreting style requirements of scholarly publications by simply selecting the publication by name and generating a perfectly formatted document." www.ProCite.com

■ Scholar's Aid. "Scholar's Aid is a specialized program conceived primarily for students and scholars who write academic documents. It was designed and written by a doctoral student who is himself engaged in research activities and who felt the need of a computer program that could facilitate the scholar's task." www.scholarsaid.com

■ Zotero. "Zotero is a free, easy-to-use Firefox extension to help you collect, manage, and cite your research sources. It lives right where you do your work—in the web browser itself." www.zotero.org

---

QUALITATIVE RESEARCH TOOLS

Perhaps the most important technology tool for qualitative research is the audio recording device. Now with a digital voice recorder, interviews, focus groups and other interactions can be recorded, transferred to a computer, and played back slowly on a media player for easier transcription. Voice recognition software can make transcription even easier, but it hasn't yet developed to the point where it can accurately transcribe a conversation with a participant who hasn't "trained" the software. Important sections of the recording can be tagged on the recording, and the recording can be edited with basic software to allow for clips to be played in an electronic document or conference presentation.

Qualitative researchers also use photography, video, or digital video to record focus groups, interviews, participants in various settings, or practices like cooking or meals. Like the audio recordings, this documentation can be analyzed with qualitative methodology, edited as illustrations in documents or presentations, or presented as documentary research. Media scholars are also having an easier time thanks to technology. In the early days of studying film or television, scholars would have to buy the film or visit a library to view it and, much later, could record using a video cassette recorder. But even in the videocassette days, we remember the frustrations of seeing an ad on TV that we would love to show to a class or incorporate into a research project and have to wait days to catch it again with the VCR queued to record. Now, millions of clips are available on the Web and can be embedded into digital documents, provided as URLs in texts, or shown in research presentations.

As in the literature review, qualitative data from transcripts, fieldnotes, photographs, and documents need to be segmented by discrete unit, analyzed, and organized before presentation. Qualitative research databases provide similar functions to reference management software, allowing you to apply one or more "tags" to various snippets of data, sort them hierarchically, and rearrange them as needed. For example, if you are given an interview quote like, "Making meatballs is something meaningful we can do together as a family," you might label this, "meat," "family," "togetherness," "cooking together." The software will place this quotation with other data into folders or categories similarly labeled. As your argument takes shape and your data folders become saturated, you may decide to add tags, delete tags, or re-name tags. Like reference management software, these electronic databases replace or supplement index card–based sorting that qualitative researchers used for decades. Newer versions of qualitative software also allow you to organize audio and visual data in the same way as text.

Qualitative Research Software

NVivo. "If you need to handle very rich information, where deep levels of analysis on both small and large volumes of data are required, NVivo 8 is your solution. It removes many of the manual tasks associated with analysis, like classifying, sorting and arranging information, so you have more time to explore trends, build and test theories and ultimately arrive at answers to questions." http://www.qsrinternational.com/products_nvivo.aspx

- Qualrus. "Qualrus is an innovative qualitative data analysis tool that helps you manage unstructured data. Use it to analyze interviews, organize field notes, categorize paintings or photographs, measure survey responses and much more." http://www.ideaworks.com/qualrus/index.html

- QDA Miner. "QDA Miner is an easy-to-use mixed-model qualitative data analysis software package for coding, annotating, retrieving and analyzing small and large collections of documents and images. QDA Miner may be used to analyze interview or focus-group transcripts, legal documents, journal articles, even entire books, as well as drawing, photographs, paintings, and other types of visual documents. Its seamless integration with Simstat, a statistical data analysis tool, and WordStat, a quantitative content analysis and text-mining module, gives you unprecedented flexibility for analyzing text and relating its content to structured information, including numerical and categorical data." http://www.provalisresearch.com/QDAMiner/QDAMinerDesc.html

QUANTITATIVE RESEARCH TOOLS

Much quantitative research technology is highly specialized. In qualitative research, nearly any type of media—text, audio recording, photograph, illustration, film—can be handled with qualitative research software. In quantitative, calorimeters, turbidity testers, viscosity meters, pH meters, water activity meters, and so on are all used in food research (mainly food science), especially for experiments, and at times are employed in food studies research as well. For example, you might design an experiment to determine the relationship between the psychological and sensory perceptions of terroir to see if the same wine labeled Bordeaux and Languedoc is scored differently by tasters in sensory analysis. To compare the results to an additional, objective data set, an aroma-meter may be employed.

Because of the general introductory nature of this text, the quantitative technology tools on which we will focus are those more widely used across quantitative research, namely software for statistical analysis. Statistical software has made research significantly easier. Even a calculation as simple as a mean of 100 Likert-scale responses that would have taken many minutes to be calculated by hand or inputted with a calculator can now be done in one click in even a basic office productivity spreadsheet. Advanced statistics like multiple regression analysis were often calculated over a matter of days rather than minutes. While any statistician will tell you that you should be *able* to make statistical calculations by hand in order to better understand the underlying theory behind the formulas, and that you certainly need to understand what you are calculating and why, statistical analysis software has transformed statistics from a tedious chore to a matter of design and strategy.

Quantitative Research Software

- SAS. "SAS provides a complete, comprehensive and integrated platform for data analysis, including solutions for data integration, analytics and business intelligence." www.SAS.com

- SPSS. "The SPSS Statistics family of products is the world's leading statistical software used by commercial, government, and academic organizations to solve business and research problems. Quickly and easily discover new insights from your data, test hypotheses and build powerful predictive models. SPSS Statistics has the flexibility you need, including access to a wide variety of data and file types, direct access to command syntax for power users and a range of deployment options that put the power of statistics where you need it." www.SPSS.com

- Systat. "SYSTAT is a powerful and versatile statistical software package. It employs a staggering range of powerful techniques to help conduct many types of research. Novice statistical users can use SYSTAT's menu-driven interface to conduct simple analyses and produce beautiful 2D and 3D graphics for presentations or reports. Advanced users can greatly speed up their research by using SYSTAT's intuitive command language, with the ability to save complex command macros. Those in need of advanced analysis can use SYSTAT's more sophisticated statistical routings, and create plots and charts that are instantly ready for publication. SYSTAT's menu and command interfaces are interlinked, allowing users the option of whichever method works best for them." www.systat.com

GIS: GEOGRAPHICAL INFORMATION SYSTEMS

By Joel Lindau, Colorado State University

Geographical Information Systems, or GIS for short, are changing the way we view the world. GIS have given us the ability to re-create maps and bring a new understanding to the area displayed. A look at a traditional map might exhibit streets, lakes, parks, and schools. When we add additional layers to these standard maps, such as population density, poverty levels, and ethnicity rates, we are able to create a more inclusive map and a deeper understanding of the planet in which we live. This in a nutshell is what GIS is all about.

The foundation for GIS has been around for thousands of years. Maps are the basis for understanding where things are in the world. In creating maps we utilize the concept of spatial design. Spatial design allows us to understand where things are located in the world. Within a GIS everything is spatially mapped. This is the geographical component of GIS. The second component of GIS, information, is based on data layers that make up what we see in the maps. These data layers might be transportation grids, utility services, community garden locations, school districts, or disability rates. Virtually any data that can be gathered spatially can be integrated into a GIS. This is what gives GIS enormous potential for use in different agencies. The third and final aspect of GIS, Systems, denotes the interconnection between hardware, software, data, and personnel used in creating a working GIS. These systems enable the entry, storage, manipulation, and display of huge amounts of data.

To understand how a GIS works, we need to appreciate why computers were built. The storage, arrangement, and retrieval of large amounts of information sit at the very heart of computer design. Elaborating on this theme, GIS rely on data entry of spatially referenced information. With advances in hardware and software devices like digitizers and scanners, the input of data is becoming easier and faster. Once the data has been entered, storage and manipulation software allow the user to design a GIS appropriate for their needs. Finally, when the data has been arranged, the designer can retrieve and present it in many different ways. LCD projectors, the World Wide Web, and color printers allow users to determine their unique presentation method.

It used to be that only large, private agencies had the resources to pay for GIS technology. Entities like Harvard, MIT, and the U.S. and Canadian governments were pushing the bounds of GIS mapping during the 1950s through the 1990s. But with the cost of hardware and software decreasing and schools producing more GIS-savvy programmers, more agencies than ever are utilizing GIS. Traditionally, GIS has been the domain of natural resource planning. Spatially mapping species habitats, land resources, and utilities management drove the creation of GIS programs. Today, however, interest from multiple fields is expanding the ways in which GIS is being used.

One example of how GIS is being used is its role in aiding the Colorado Food Bank Association (CFBA) to detect food deserts in urban and rural areas in Colorado. Food deserts exist where the population has limited access to healthy food choices. The CFBA in conjunction with Colorado State University has created a GIS of five counties in Colorado using the 2000 US Census and data collected by the food banks themselves. Data layers that can be mapped are childhood poverty rates, homes with no access to transportation, pounds of food distributed by specific food pantries, and percentage of free and reduced meals provided by schools, to name a few. By viewing this information as a map, the CFBA is able to locate populations in greatest need of their services.

In the future the CFBA would like to display this GIS on the World Wide Web. Once the system is available online, food pantries themselves will be able to access the information. With this GIS resource at hand, food pantry personnel would be able to inform clients on the spot with helpful information. For example, food pantry locations, hours of operation, services provided, and public transportation routes would be available by a click of the mouse. Not only would this help clients, but it would allow food pantries to better understand and accommodate the populations they are serving.

BIBLIOGRAPHY

Abarca, M. (2007). *Charlas culinarias:* Mexican women speak from their public kitchens. *Food and Foodways, 15*(3/4), 183–212.

Adams, G., and Schvanaveldt, J. (1985). *Understanding research methods.* New York: Longman.

Adler, E., and Clark, R. (2003). *How it's done: An invitation to social research* (2nd ed.). Belmont, CA: Thomson Wadsworth.

American Association of University Professors (AAUP). (n.d.) *Informal glossary of AAUP terms and abbreviations.* Retrieved February 18, 2009, from http://www.aaup.org/AAUP/about/mission/glossary.htm

The American heritage dictionary, Second College Edition. (1985). Boston: Houghton Mifflin.

Anderson, C., Lindsay, J., and Bushman, B. (1999). Research in the psychological laboratory: Truth or triviality? *Current Directions in Psychological Science,* 8(1), 3–9.

Anderson, K. (2003). *Handbook of cultural geography.* London: Sage.

Anslem Library (n.d). Retrieved October 21, 2008, from http://www.unc.edu/depts/wcweb/handouts/literature_review.html TYPES OF INFORMATION SOURCES.

Ashley, B., Hollows, J., Jones, S., and Taylor, B. (2004). *Food and cultural studies.* London: Routledge.

Atkinson, P., and Hammersley, M. (1994). Ethnography and participant observation. In N. Denzin and Y. Lincoln (Eds.), *Handbook of qualitative research* (pp. 249–261). Thousand Oaks, CA: Sage.

Avakian, A. (2005). *Through the kitchen window: Women explore the intimate meanings of food and cooking.* Boston: Beacon Press.

Bankert, E. A., and Amdur, R. J. (Eds.). *Institutional review board: Management and function.* (2nd ed.) Sudbury, MA: Jones and Bartlett, p. 130.

Barnum, B. J. (1990). *Nursing theory: Analysis, application and evaluation.* New York: Little, Brown.

Barthes, R. (1957/1972). *Mythologies.* (Annette Lavers, Trans.). New York: Noonday Press.

Baruch, Y. (1999). Response rates in academic studies: A comparative analysis. *Human Relations, 52,* 421–434.

Bateson, M. (1994). *Peripheral visions: Learning along the way.* New York: HarperCollins.

Belasco, W. (2002). Food matters: Perspectives on an emerging field. In W. Belasco and P. Scranton (Eds.), *Food nations: Selling taste in consumer societies* (pp. 2–23). New York: Routledge.

Belasco, W. (2007). *Appetite for change: How the counterculture took on the food industry* (2nd ed.). Ithaca, NY: Cornell University Press.

Belasco, W. (2008). *Food: The key concepts.* Oxford: Berg.

Berger, P. (1966). *The Social construction of reality: A treatise in the sociology of knowledge.* Garden City, NY: Doubleday.

Bernard, H. (2000). *Social research methods: Qualitative and quantitative approaches.* Thousand Oaks: Sage.

Best, J., and Kahn, J. (2006). *Research in education* (10th ed.). Boston: Pearson, Allyn and Bacon.

Black, T. (1999). *Doing quantitative research in the social sciences.* London: Sage.

Blaikie, N. (2000). *Designing social research.* Cambridge, UK: Polity Press.

Blaxter, L., Hughes, C., and Tight, M. (2001) *How to Research* (2nd ed.). Buckingham, UK, and Philadelphia, PA: Open University Press.

Boschma, G., Scaia, M., Bonifacio, N., and Roberts, E. (2008). Oral history research. In S. Lewenson and E. Herrman (Eds.), *Capturing nursing history: A guide to historical methods in research* (pp. 79–98). New York: Springer Publishing.

Brewer, J. (2000). *Ethnography.* Buckingham, UK: Open University Press.

Buck, J. (2008). Using frameworks in historical research. In S. Lewenson and E. Herrman (Eds.), *Capturing nursing history: A guide to historical methods in research* (pp. 45–62). New York: Springer Publishing.

Burgess, R. *In the field.* London: Routledge.

Burns, R. (2000). *Introduction to research* (4th ed.). London: Sage.

Busha, C., and Harter, S. J. (1980). *Research methods in librarianship: Techniques and interpretations.* New York: Academic Press.

Campbell, D. T., and Stanley, J. C. (1963). *Experimental and quasi-experimental designs for research.* Boston: Houghton Mifflin.

Carmines, E., and Zeller, R. (1991). *Reliability and validity assessment.* Newbury Park, CA: Sage.

Carrus, G., Nenci, A. M., and Caddeo, P. (2009). The role of ethnic identity and perceived ethnic norms in the purchase of ethnical food products, *Appetite, 52*(1), 65–71.

Carson, B. (1985). Interpreting history through objects. *Journal of Museum Education 10*(3), 129–133.

Categories of research that may be reviewed by the Institutional Review Board (IRB) through an expedited review procedure, November 9, 1998. Retrieved February 18, 2009, from http://www.hhs.gov/ohrp/humansubjects/guidance/expedited98.htm

Charles, C., and Mertler, C. (2002). *Introduction to educational research* (4th ed.). Boston: Allyn and Bacon.

Chen, M.-F. (2008). Consumer trust in food safety: A multidisciplinary approach and empirical evidence from Taiwan. *Risk Analysis: An International Journal, 28*(6), 1553–1569.

City College of New York (CUNY) policy on academic integrity 2004. Retrieved February 18, 2009, from http://web.cuny.edu/academics/info-central/policies.html.

Clark-Carter, D. (2004). *Quantitative psychology research.* Hove, Sussex: Psychology Press.

Code of Federal Regulations, Title 45, Public Welfare, Department of Health and Human Services, Part 46, Protection of Human Subjects (45 CFR 46). Revised June 23, 2005. Retrieved November 29, 2008, from http://www.hhs.gov/ohrp/humansubjects/guidance/45cfr46.htm.

Cohen, L., Manion, L., and Morrison, K. (2000). *Research methods in education* (5th ed.). London: Routledge Falmer.

Colasanto, D. (n.d.) *Planning and using survey research projects: A guide for the grantees of the Robert Wood Johnson Foundation.* Retrieved October 13, 2007, from http://www.rwjf.org/files/publications/RWJF_SurveyGuide_0804.pdf.

Conducting Field Research (Web site). Retrieved January 19, 2008, from http://writing.colostate.edu/guides/researchsources/fieldresearch/index.cfm.

Connelly, M., and Clandinin, J. (1990). Stories of experience and narrative inquiry. *Educational Researcher,* 19 (5), 2–14.

Connelly, M., and Clandinin, J. (2000). *Narrative inquiry.* San Francisco: Jossey-Bass.

Cormack, D. (2000). *The research process in nursing.* Oxford: Blackwell.

Crang, M., and Cook, I. (2007). *Doing ethnographies.* London: Sage.

Creswell, J. (2005). *Educational research: Planning, conducting and evaluating quantitative and qualitative research* (2nd ed.). Upper Saddle River, NJ: Pearson Merrill Prentice Hall.

Csikszentmihalyi, M. (1993). Why we need things. In S. Lubar and W. Kingery (Eds.), *History from things: Essays on material culture* (pp. 20–29). Washington, DC: Smithsonian Institution Press.

Dant, T. (1999). *Material culture in the social world: Values, activities, lifestyles.* Buckingham, UK: Open University Press.

Davis, A. L. (2006). The study population: Women, minorities, and children. In E. A. Bankert and R. J. Amdur (Eds.), *Institutional review board: Management and function,* 2nd ed. (p. 130). Sudbury, MA: Jones and Bartlett.

Denzin, N. (1994). The art and politics of interpretation. In N. Denzin, and Y. Lincoln (Eds.), *The Strategies of Qualitative Inquiry* (pp. 500–515). London: Sage.

Deutsch, J. (2004). Masculinities on a spit: Travels with a competition barbecue team. *MNEME: Revista de Humanidades, 3* (9).

Deutsch, J. (2005). "Please pass the chicken tits": Rethinking men and cooking at an urban firehouse. *Food and Foodways, 13*(1/2), 91–114.

Deutsch, J., and Miller, J. (2007). Food studies: A multidisciplinary guide to the literature, [bibliographic essay], *Choice,* 7–15.

Deutsch, J., and Saks, R. D. (2008). *Jewish American food culture.* Westport, CT: Greenwood.

Dey, I. (1993). *Qualitative data analysis.* London: Routledge.

Dillman, D. A. (1978). *Mail and telephone surveys: The total design method.* New York: Wiley.

Douglas, M., and Isherwood, B. (1996). *The world of goods: Towards an anthropology of consumption.* London: Routledge.

Ely, M., Vinz, R., Downing, M., and Anzul, M. (1997). *On writing qualitative research: Living by words.* New York: Routledge.

Emerson, R., Fretz, R., and Shaw, L. (1995). *Writing ethnographic fieldnotes.* Chicago: University of Chicago Press.

Erickson, F. (2002). Ethnography and education policy: A commentary. In B. Levinson, S. Cade, and A. Padawer (Eds.), *Ethnography and educational policy across the Americas: A view across the Americas.* Westport, CT: Greenwood Publishing.

Exempt research and research that may undergo expedited review, Office for Human Research Protections (OHRP), OPRR Reports, Number 95-02, May 5, 1995. Retrieved February 18, 2009, from http://www.hhs.gov/ohrp/policy/index.html#exempt.

Fetterman, D. (1998). *Ethnography: Step by step* (2nd ed.). Thousand Oaks, CA: Sage.

Finch, G. (1998). *How to study linguistics.* Houndmills, UK: Palgrave Macmillan.

Fink, A. (1998). *Conducting research literature reviews: From paper to the internet.* Thousand Oaks, CA: Sage.

Flick, U. (2002). *An introduction to qualitative research* (2nd ed.). London: Sage.

Fox, R., Crask, M., and Kim, J. (1988). Mail survey rate: A meta-analysis of selected techniques for inducing response. *Public Opinion Quarterly, 52,* 467–491.

Fraser, H. (2004). Doing narrative research: Analysing personal stories line by line. *Qualitative Social Work, 3*(2), 179–200.

Galgano, M., Arndt, C., and Hyser, R. (2008). *Doing history: Research and writing in the digital age.* Boston, MA: Thomson Wadsworth.

Gall, J., Gall, M., and Borg, W. (2005). *Applying educational research: A practical guide* (5th ed.). Boston: Pearson, Allyn and Bacon.

Gallant, D. R. (1996). *Human subjects at Harvard: A brief overview.* Unpublished manuscript, Harvard University, Cambridge, MA.

Garson, D. (n.d.) *Survey research.* Retrieved June 28, 2008, from http://faculty.chass.ncsu.edu/garson/PA765/survey.htm.

Gay, L., Mills, G., and Airasian, P. (2006). *Educational research: Competencies for analysis and applications.* Upper Saddle River, NJ: Pearson, Merrill, Prentice-Hall.

Geertz, C. (1973). Thick description: Toward an interpretive theory of culture. In *The interpretation of cultures: Selected essays* (pp. 3–30). New York: Basic Books.

Gesine, G. (2009). Food and politics: Nazi agrarian politics in the occupied territories of the soviet union. *Contemporary European History, 18*(1), 45–65.

Glaser, B. (1978). *Handbook of quantitative research.* Thousand Oaks, CA: Sage.

Glassie, H. (1999). *Material culture.* Bloomington: Indiana University Press.

Gliner, J., and Morgan, G. (1999). *Research methods in applied settings: An integrated approach to design and analysis.* Mahwah, NJ: Lawrence Erlbaum.

Gluck, S., and Patai, D. (1991). *Women's words: The feminist practice of oral history.* New York: Routledge, 1991.

Goetz, J., Preissle, J., and LeCompte, M. (1984). *Ethnography and qualitative design in educational research.* London: Academic Press.

Guba, E. G., and Lincoln, Y. S. (1998). "Paradigms in Qualitative Research." Chapter 6 in K. Denzin and Y. S. Lincoln (Eds.). *The landscape of qualitative research: Theories and issues.* Thousands Oaks: Sage.

Hammersley, M. (1991). A note on Campbell's distinction between internal and external validity. *Quality & Quantity, 25*(4), 381. Retrieved November 29, 2008, from Academic Search Premier database.

Hammersley, M. (1990). *Reading ethnographic research.* London: Longman.

Hansen, S. (2008). Society of the appetite: Celebrity chefs deliver consumers. *Food, Culture and Society, 11*(1), 49–67.

Hart, C. (1998). *Doing a literature review: Releasing the social science research imagination.* Thousand Oaks, CA: Sage.

Hauck-Lawson, A. (2004). Introduction to special issue on the food voice. *Food, Culture and Society, 7*(1), 24–25.

Hauck-Lawson, A., and Deutsch, J. (Eds.). (2008). *Gastropolis: Food and New York City.* New York: Columbia University Press.

Heidegger, M. (1968/1967). *What is a thing?* W. B. Barton, Jr., and V. Deutsch, Trans.). Chicago: H. Regnery.

Hiestand, W. C. (1986). Conceptualizing historical research. In P. Moccia (Ed.), *New approaches to theory development* (pp. 105–117). NY: National League for Nursing.

Hilton, A. (1998). *Dissertation preparation and presentation.* Leicester, UK: De Montford University Press.

Hitchcock, G., and Hughes, D. (1989). *Research and the teacher.* London: Routledge.

Hodder, I. (2000). The interpretation of documents and material culture. In N. Denzin and Y. Lincoln (Eds.), *Handbook of qualitative research*, 2nd ed. (pp. 703–715). Thousand Oaks, CA: Sage.

Hopkins, R. (1994). *Narrative schooling: Experiential learning and the transformation of American education.* New York: Teachers College Press.

Hutchinson, S. (2004). Survey research. In K. deMarrais and S. Lapan (Eds.), *Foundations of research: Methods of inquiry in education and the social sciences* (pp. 284–301). Mahwah, NJ: Lawrence Erlbaum.

The intelligent scholar's guide to the use of human subjects in research (ISG). Revised August 1, 2008. Retrieved November 29, 2008, from Harvard University Faculty of Arts and Sciences Web site: http://cuhs.fas.harvard.edu/ISG.html.

Janesick, V. (1994). The dance of qualitative research design. In N. Denzin and Y. Lincoln (Eds.), *Handbook of qualitative research* (pp. 209–219). Thousand Oaks, CA: Sage.

Janesick, V. (2000). The choreography of qualitative research design: Minuets, improvisations, and crystallization. In N. Denzin and Y. Lincoln (Eds.), *Handbook of qualitative research,* 2nd ed. (pp. 379–399). Thousand Oaks, CA: Sage.

Johnson, B., and Christensen, L. (2008). *Educational research: Quantitative, qualitative, and mixed approaches.* 3rd ed. Los Angeles: Sage.

Johnson, R. (2001). Toward a new classification of nonexperimental quantitative research. *Educational Researcher, 30*(2), 3–13.

Jones, I. (1997, December). *Mixing qualitative and quantitative methods in sports fan research* [33 paragraphs]. *The Qualitative Report* [On-line serial], 3(4). Available at http://www.nova.edu/ssss/QR/QR3-4/jones.html.

Jones, J. H. (1982). *Bad blood: The scandalous story of the Tuskegee experiment—When government doctors played God and science went mad.* New York: The Free Press.

Jordanova, L. (2000). *History in practice.* London: Arnold.

Kaldenberg, D. O., Koenig, H. F., and Becker, B. W. (1994). Mail survey response rate patterns in a population of the elderly. *Public Opinion Quarterly, 58,* 68–76.

Kaplan, S. L. (1996). *The bakers of Paris and the bread question 1700–1775.* Durham, NC: Duke University Press.

Keeter, S., Kohut, A., Miller, A., Groves, R., and Presser, S. (2000). Consequences of reducing non-response in a large national telephone survey. *Public Opinion Quarterly, 64*(2), 125–48.

Kellner, D. (1995). *Media culture: Cultural studies, identity and politics between the modern and postmodern.* London: Routledge.

Kerlinger, F. (1986). *Foundations of behavior research* (3rd ed.). New York: Holt, Rinehart, and Winston.

Kingery, W. (1996). *Learning from things: Method and theory of material culture studies.* Washington, DC: Smithsonian Institution Press.

Knappett, C. (2005). *Thinking through material culture: An interdisciplinary perspective.* Philadelphia: University of Pennsylvania Press.

Kopytoff, I. (1986). The cultural biography of things: Commoditization as process. In A. Appaduri (Ed.), *The social life of things: Commodities in cultural perspective* (pp. 64–94). Cambridge, UK: Cambridge University Press.

LeCompte, M., Preissle, J. and Tesch, R. (1993). *Ethnography and qualitative design in educational research.* San Diego, CA: Academic Press.

Leedy, P. (1993). *Practical research: planning and design* (5th ed.). New York: Macmillan.

Malinowski, B. (1922/1961). *Argonauts of the western Pacific.* New York: E. P. Dutton.

Marshall, C., and Rossman, G. (1995). *Designing qualitative research* (2nd ed.). Thousand Oaks, CA.: Sage.

Martin, A. (1996). Material things and cultural meanings: Notes on Early American material culture. *William and Mary Quarterly, 53*(1), 5–12.

Marx, M. (1976). Formal Theory. In H. Marx, and F. Goodson (Eds.), *Theories in contemporary psychology* (pp. 234–260). New York: Macmillan.

McMillan, J. H., and Schumacher, S. (1997). *Research in education: A conceptual introduction.* New York: Longman.

Miles, M., and Huberman, A. (1994). *Qualitative data analysis* (2nd ed.). Thousand Oaks, CA: Sage.

Miller, J. (2006). *Jiternice and Kolaches: Food and identity in Wilson, KS.* Unpublished doctoral dissertation, Colorado State University, Fort Collins, Colorado.

Mills, L., Gay, G., and Airasian, P. (2006). *Educational research: competencies for analysis and applications* (8th ed.). Upper Saddle River, NJ: Pearson Merrill Prentice Hall.

Molasso, W. (2005). *Ten tangible and practical tips to improve student participation in web surveys.* Retrieved January 11, 2009, from http://studentaffairs.com/ejournal/Fall_2005/.

Moyer, J. (1999). *Step-by-step guide to oral history.* http://www.dohistory.org/on_your_own/toolkit/oralHistory.html.

Mundy, D. (2002). Solution corner. *Science Editor,* 25(1), 25–26.

National Commission for the Protection of Human Subjects of Biomedical and Behavioral Research. *The Belmont Report: Ethical principles and guidelines for the protection of human subjects of research,* Office of the Secretary, April 18, 1979. Retrieved November 29, 2008, from http://www.hhs.gov/ohrp/humansubjects/guidance/belmont.htm.

Neustadt, K. (1992). *Clambake: A history and celebration of an American tradition.* Amherst: University of Massachusetts Press.

Nightingale, D. J., and Cromby, J. (1999). *Social constructionist psychology: A critical analysis of theory and practice.* Buckingham, UK: Open University Press.

Novick, P. (1988). *That noble dream: The "objectivity question" and the American historical profession.* Cambridge, UK: Cambridge University Press, 1988.

O'Connor, K. (2008). The Hawaiian luau: Food as tradition, transgression, transformation, and travel. *Food, Culture and Society, 11*(2), 149–172.

O'Dea, J. (1994). Pursuing truth in narrative research. *Journal of Philosophy of Education, 28*(2). 161–171.

Ollerenshaw, J., and Creswell, J. (2002). Narrative research: A comparison of two restorying data analysis approaches. *Qualitative Inquiry, 8*(3), 329–347.

O'Toole, P., and Were, P. (2008). Observing places: Using space and material culture in qualitative research. *Qualitative Research, 8*(5), 661–634.

Paltridge, B., and Starfield, S. (2007). *Thesis and dissertation writing in a second language.* London: Routledge.

Payton, O. D. (1979). *Research: The validation of clinical practice.* Philadelphia: F. A. Davis.

Pearce, J., Hiscock, R., Blakely, T., and Witten, K. (2009). A national study of the association between neighbourhood access to fast-food outlets and the diet and weight of local residents. *Health & Place, 15*(1), 193–197.

Phillips, D. C. (1994). Telling it straight: Issues in assessing narrative research, *Educational Psychologist, 29*(1), 13–21.

Plummer, K. (2001). *Documents of life 2: An invitation to a critical humanism.* London: Sage.

Polgar, S., and Thomas, S. (1997). *Introduction to research in the health sciences.* Melbourne: Churchill Livingstone.

Polit, D., and Beck, C. (2006). *Essentials of nursing research: Methods, appraisal, and utilization.* Philadelphia: Lippincott, Williams, and Wilkins.

Polkinghorne, D. (1988). *Narrative knowing and the human sciences.* Albany: State University of New York Press.

Prentis, E. D. and Oki, G. S. F. (2006). Exempt from institutional review board review. In E. A. Bankert and R. J. Amdur (Eds.), *Institutional review board: Management and function*, 2nd ed. (p. 93). Sudbury, MA: Jones and Bartlett.

Presnell, J. (2007). *The information literate historian: A guide to research for history students.* New York: Oxford University Press.

Prown, J. (1993). The truth of material culture: history or fiction. In S. Lubar and W. Kingery (Eds.), *History from things: Essays on material culture* (pp. 1–19). Washington, DC: Smithsonian Institution Press.

Ray, K. (2008). Nation and cuisine: The evidence from American newspapers ca. 1830–2003. *Food and Foodways, 16* (4), 259–297.

Reissman, C. (2002). Narrative analysis. In A. Huberman and M. Miles (Eds.), *The Qualitative Researcher's Companion* (pp. 217–270). Thousand Oaks, CA: Sage.

Refsgaard, K., and Magnussen, K. (2009). Household behaviour and attitudes with respect to recycling food waste: Experiences from focus groups. *Journal of Environmental Management, 90*(2), 760–771.

Richardson, L. (2000). Writing: A method of inquiry. In N. Denzin and Y. Lincoln (Eds.), *Handbook of Qualitative Research,* 2nd ed. (pp. 516–529). Thousand Oaks, CA: Sage.

Ritzer, G. (2004). *The McDonaldization of society.* Thousand Oaks, CA: Pine Forge Press.

Rosenwald, G., and Ochberg, R. (1992). *Storied lives: The cultural politics of self-understanding.* New Haven, CT: Yale University Press.

Rousmaniere, M. (2004). Historical research. In K. deMarrais and S. Lapan (Eds.), *Foundations of research: Methods of inquiry in education and the social sciences* (pp. 31–50). Mahwah, NJ: Lawrence Erlbaum.

Rozin, P. (1999). Food is fundamental, fun, frightening, and far-reaching. *Social Research, 66,* 9–30.

Ruane, J. (2005). *Essentials of research methods: A guide to social science research.* Malden, MA: Blackwell Publishing.

Ryan, G., and Bernard, H. (2000). Data management and analysis. In N. Denzin and Y. Lincoln (Eds.), *Handbook of qualitative research,* 2nd ed. (pp. 769–802) Thousand Oaks, CA: Sage.

Salant, P., and Dillman, D. (1994). *How to conduct your own survey.* New York: Wiley.

Salazar, M. L. (2007). Public schools, private foods: Mexicano memories of culture and conflict in American school cafeterias. *Food and Foodways, 15*(3/4), 153–181.

Schlereth, T. (1985). *Material culture: A research guide.* Lawrence, KS: University Press of Kansas.

Schueren, F. (2004) *What is a survey?* Retrieved July 13, 2008, from http://www.whatisasurvey. info/.

Seale, C. (1999). *The quality of qualitative research.* London: Sage.

Shank, G. D. (2002). *Qualitative research: A personal skills approach.* Columbus, OH: Merrill Prentice Hall.

Shannon, K., Mahmud, Z., Asfia, A., and Ali, M. (2008). The social and environmental factors underlying maternal malnutrition in rural Bangladesh: Implications for reproductive health and nutrition programs. *Health Care for Women International, 29*(8/9), 826–840.

Sheumaker, H., and Wajda, S. T. (2007). *Material culture: An encyclopedia.* Santa Barbara, CA: ABC-CLIO.

Skibo, J., and Schiffer, M. (2008). *People and things: A behavioral approach to material culture.* New York: Springer.

Smith, P. (1995). *Art education historical methodology: An insider's guide to doing and using.* Kalamazoo, MI: SRAE Monograph.

Smythe, W., and Murray, M. (2000). Owning the story: Ethical considerations in narrative research. *Ethics and Behavior, 10*(4), 311–336.

Spindler, G., and Spindler, L. (1992). *Cultural process and ethnography: An anthropological perspective: The handbook of qualitative research in education.* London: Academic Press.

Spradley, J. (1979). *The ethnographic interview.* New York: Holt, Rinehart, and Winston.

Spradley, J. (1980). *Participant observation.* Orlando, FL: Harcourt Brace Jovanovich.

Stake, R. (2000). Case Studies. In N. Denzin and Y. Lincoln (Eds.), *Handbook of qualitative research,* 2nd ed. (pp. 236–247). Thousand Oaks, CA: Sage.

Steinberg, E. F. and Prost, J. H. (2008). A menu and a mystery: The case of the 1834 Delmonico bill of fare. *Gastronomica, 8*(2), 40–50.

Stephens, C. (2000). *All about readability.* Retrieved November 29, 2008, from http://plainlanguage.com/newreadability.html.

Stewart, A. (1998). *The ethnographer's method.* Newbury Park, CA: Sage.

Stocking, G. (1985). *Objects and others: Essays on museums and material culture.* Madison: University of Wisconsin Press.

Storey, W. (2004). *Writing history: A guide for students* (2nd ed.). Oxford: Oxford University Press.

Strauss, A., and Corbin, J. (1998). *Basics of qualitative research: Techniques and procedures for developing grounded theory.* Thousand Oaks, CA: Sage.

Student Learning Support, University of Waikato. *Literature Review.* Retrieved from http://www.waikato.ac.nz/pathways/student-learning/learning-support/resources/graduate/litreviewdocument.pdf.

Svejenova, S., Mazza, C., and Planellas, M. (2007). Cooking up change in haute cuisine: Ferran Adrià as an institutional entrepreneur. *Journal of Organizational Behavior, 28* (5), 539–561.

Teacher's Guide: What Is Material Culture? (March 3, 2008). retrieved from http://www.pbs.org/wgbh/roadshow/teachers_materialculture.html.

Tedlock, B. (2000). Ethnography and ethnographic representation. In N. Denzin and Y. Lincoln (Eds.), *Handbook of qualitative research,* 2nd ed. (pp. 455–484). Thousand Oaks, CA: Sage.

Trochim, W. (2006). *The research methods knowledge base, 2nd edition.* Retrieved October 20, 2007, from: http://www.socialresearchmethods.net/kb/.

van den Hoonaard, D. K. and van den Hoonaard, W. C. (2008). Data analysis. In Lisa M. Given, (Ed.), *The SAGE Encyclopedia of Qualitative Research Methods* (pp. 186–188). Thousand Oaks, CA: Sage.

van Maanen, J. (1988). *Tales of the field: On writing ethnography.* Chicago: University of Chicago Press.

Waugh, D. (2004). *Material culture/objects.* Retrieved February 22, 2008, from http://chnm.gmu.edu/worldhistorysources/unpacking/objectsmain.html.

Weatherell, C., Tregear, A., and Allinson, J. (2003). In search of the concerned consumer: UK public perceptions of food, farming and buying local. *Journal of Rural Studies, 19*(2), 233–244.

Webster's third new international dictionary of the English language, unabridged. (1993). Springfield, MA: Merriam-Webster, 1993.

Winn, F., Miller, J., Sutherland, B., Most, D., Rogers, K. and Baker, S. (2008). *Effect of Education and Availability of Food Thermometers on Food Thermometer Use among Expanded Food and Nutrition Education Program (EFNEP) Participants.* Presented at Society for Nutrition Education Annual Meeting. Atlanta, GA, July 2008.

Wogan, P. (2004). Deep hanging out: Reflections on fieldwork and multisited Andean ethnography. *Identities: Global Studies in Culture and Power, 11,* 129–39.

Wolcott, H. (1999). *Ethnography: A way of seeing.* Lanham, MD: Alta Mira Press.

Woodward, I. (2007). *Understanding material culture.* London: Sage.

Young, K. (1987). *Taleworlds and storyrealms: The phenomenology of narrative.* Boston, MA: Martinus Nijhoff.

Yow, V. (1994). *Recording oral history: A practical guide for social scientists.* Thousand Oaks, CA: Sage.

NOTES

Chapter 2: What Is Research

1. For an excellent overview of this philosophical debate and some intriguing thoughts about the similarity of qualitative and quantitative data, go to the Web Center for Social Research Methods home page at www.socialresearchmethods.net and read the article entitled "The Qualitative Debate."
2. This dire oversimplification of the spectrum of beliefs about research and does not take into account those who believe in both methods and those who use mixed-methods approaches, but rather is intended to move our descriptions and discussions forward, not to presume that these are the only two worldviews in the research arena.

Chapter 6: Quantitative Methods in Food Studies Research

1. There are numerous statistical tests that can be performed on survey instruments to test their reliability. A full list of them and the various ways they are used are beyond the scope of this text, but many quantitative research texts devote copious amounts of space to this topic and should be consulted if you decide to create your own instrument.

Chapter 7: Using Observational Research Methods in Food Studies

1. When we use the term *field* in ethnography and other forms of research, we are referring to places outside the controlled laboratory-type environment where we conduct research. The field could be around the corner or across the world; it depends on where the phenomenon of interest is taking place.
2. Some voice recorders can be used in conjunction with voice-to-text software. This allows the voice file to "transcribe itself" to a word processing program. Most of these types of software only recognize a few voices and do not transcribe interviews but can be used to transcribe field notes, saving the researcher time.
3. For an excellent detailed description of the ethnographic field note process, see *Writing Ethnographic Fieldnotes* by Emerson, Fretz, and Shaw (1995).
4. Ken Plummer's classic, *Documents of Life*, was one of the early calls for the use of life stories in social sciences research. For those interested in narrative approaches and life story research, the new edition (2001) provides many examples and practical advice on the process and analysis of narrative methods.
5. For a detailed criticism of veracity in narrative, consult the works of D. C. Phillips, a researcher in the field of education who has written extensively about the need for "epistemic respectability" in qualitative research, especially narrative.

Chapter 8: Using Material Objects in Food Studies

1. Ian Hodder, a renowned scholar in material culture, is not denying that stories are told by material objects, but is referring to the idea that objects cannot tell us that story directly; that we must work the story out of the object through our research.

2. The term *artifact* (sometimes rendered *artefact* in texts originating in the United Kingdom) is used in numerous discussions of objects as research items. While the first definition in the *New Oxford American Dictionary* clearly states that an artifact is any "object made by a human being" (p. 88), there is often an unstated connotation with a prehistorical period. Therefore we will use the terms *object* or *material object* to ensure that our discussion encompasses all *artifacts* regardless of the historical period in which they were produced.

3. Not all actors will be inarticulate. Many informants will go on at great length about their motivations. Think about Proust and the seven volumes that resulted from associations stemming from the simple madeleine.

INDEX